Developing Windows Applications Using Delphi

Developing Windows Applications Using Delphi

Paul Penrod

John Wiley & Sons, Inc.

New York • Chichester • Brisbane • Toronto • Singapore

Publisher: Katherine Schowalter
Editor: Tim Ryan
Managing Editor: Mark Hayden
Text Design & Composition: Benchmark Productions, Inc.

Designations used by companies to distinguish their products are often claimed as trademarks. In all instances where John Wiley & Sons, Inc. is aware of a claim, the product names appear in initial capital or all capital letters. Readers, however, should contact the appropriate companies for more complete information regarding trademarks and registration.

This text is printed on acid-free paper.

Published by John Wiley & Sons, Inc.

This publication is designed to provide accurate and authoritative information in regard to the subject matter covered. It is sold with the understanding that the publisher is not engaged in rendering legal, accounting, or other professional service. If legal advice or other expert assistance is required, the services of a competent professional person should be sought.

Library of Congress Cataloging-in-Publication Data:

Penrod, Paul, 1962–
    Developing Windows applications using Delphi / Paul Penrod
        p.   cm.
    Includes index.
    ISBN 0-471-11017-5 (paper : acid-free paper)
    1. Windows (Computer programs) 2. Delphi (Computer file)
I. Title.
QA76.76.W56P46   1995
005.265—dc20   95-15112
                                                                    CIP

Printed in the United States of America

10   9   8   7   6   5   4   3   2   1

To my wife Lori:

For her patience and understanding of my giving birth to this book, while she was waiting to give birth to our newest daughter.

. . . .

To my children:

For remembering who I was after all this.

. . . .

To Nan Borreson and Karen Giles at Borland:

For timely help, information, and generally going above and beyond the call of duty.

. . . .

To Tim Ryan:

For introducing me to Delphi and giving me this opportunity.

❧

Contents

Introduction

Developing Windows Applications with Delphi

The scope of this book is to assist people with some programming background to make the transition to Windows programming through the use of Borland's Delphi application. The book will appeal to Windows programmers of all levels of experience, with special emphasis on the beginning to intermediate levels. The book will be divided into (3) three sections: an introductory and usage section, a programming section, and a language section.

The introductory and usage section will discuss the programming and theory background necessary to use the product effectively. This will be done by analogy and in nontechnical terms. The important features of Delphi will be presented and explained.

The programming section will demonstrate the use of many Delphi components by developing a project and then extending the functionality. Of interest will be the demonstrated use of buttons, toolbars, menus, dialogs, timers, fonts, printers, memo items, and MDI (Multiple Document Interface). In each chapter, the use of all components demonstrated is explained in a how-to fashion. Where appropriate, additional discussion on why the use of a certain component makes the program better is included.

One of the major goals of this book is to introduce Object Pascal and object orientation in a practical manner; especially to C programmers and novices in object orientation. The language section focuses on Object Pascal elements such as reserved words, blocks, loops, variables, constants, units, and strings. Coupled with these Object Pascal elements are examples of demonstrating the similarities and differences between Object Pascal and C. This provides familiar ground upon which to work.

CHAPTER 1

An Introduction to Object Orientation

"Object-oriented." You hear this phrase and all its variants used constantly by marketeers hawking their wares. "Object-oriented!" shouts one. "Objectware!" hollers another. Yet a third can be overhead: "Our software is better because it's based on object design!" Programmers, users, and businesses all shake their heads in confusion and disgust at the amount of noise generated by this one simple phrase.

But just what is *object orientation*, and why should you consider using it? If you should use it, then with what? These are the questions hopefully you will find some practical answers and applications for in this book.

Before diving into the wonderful world of Delphi and the many pleasant surprises that await us there, we must stop and look at where programming has been first to understand where we are going.

A Quick History Lesson

Since computers first existed, the quest for the holy grail has been to make it easier for man to communicate with the machine. In the early days of electronic computers, programmers threw switches on a front panel to enter their instructions in binary. A binary pattern, such as 10011011, would represent an operation directing the computer to load a number into memory. Needless to say, it was very cryptic communication and understood only by a select few.

Later, assembly language was created to make it easier to enter those instructions. Binary patterns were replaced with an alphanumeric shorthand. A binary instruction to load a number into memory would be represented by a pneumonic, such as MOV [ES:DI],AX (in Intel parlance). This was better but still required programmers to learn the assembly language instruction set of the machine they were programming for.

Just as with the binary coding mentioned previously, programs written this way were specific to the CPU upon which they ran. Programs had to be rewritten in their entirety for different manufacturer's machines, and sometimes for machines in the same product line for that manufacturer. Portability still eluded the programming masses.

In 1957, Dartmouth College introduced BASIC (Beginner's All-Purpose Symbolic Instruction Code). Originally, this interpretive language was designed to teach programming concepts without regard for computer hardware details. Programmers could write programs on one manufacturer's machine, such as IBM, and run them on another computer, such as UNIVAC. Portability was born.

The problem with BASIC was several fold. First, it was interpretive, which made it slow. It also made it difficult, if not impossible to create an application that a user could not break out of and tinker with. Second, because of its hardware abstracted nature, the presentation interface was abysmal. The best BASIC could manage was a line-by-line teletype interface. Later versions of BASIC have addressed this problem quite adequately. Third, early BASIC was designed as a teaching tool, not as a full-fledged commercial product-development tool. Projects requiring a lot of code became unmanageable the larger they grew. Fourth, early BASIC also lacked completeness of functionality. This made many problems difficult if not impossible to solve.

In the years to follow, such languages as FORTRAN, COBOL, SNOBOL, ALGOL, and BCPL appeared. These languages sported two advantages to BASIC. First, they were compiled. Compiled languages run faster than interpretive languages, because they are translated one time into the computer's native machine code and stored for later use. This means each time the program is run, the computer does not have to translate it; just execute the instructions it sees.

The second advantage these languages had over BASIC was their slant toward problem solving. FORTRAN and SNOBOL excel at mathematical and scientific calculations. COBOL was readily adopted by business to handle accounting, payroll, and general ledger. ALGOL solved problems using algorithmic constructs. Each language has a particular slant that allows it to excel at solving a particular set of problems.

As languages continued to appear and mature, more abstract concepts of communication incorporated themselves as features. In 1970, Dennis Ritchie and Brian Kernihan, both of Bell Labs, introduced the C programming language, which changed the programming landscape. Previous generation languages relied on procedural methods to accomplish stated goals. C relies on functions to create structure. It is this one attribute of C that started the ball rolling in the direction of development tools.

C, and languages like C that allow functions to be grouped in libraries, popularized the notion of reusability. Programmers found that they could develop generic routines from calculating amortized interest to graphical interfaces. These libraries of functions extended the language and allowed applications to become even more portable than before. A library, properly constructed, provided functionality to an application that did not need to be completely rewritten or reinvented every time the application was moved to a new platform.

As the execution of the concepts of portability and reusability became more refined, languages like C++ arose to address the concept of object orientation in development.

What Is Object Orientation?

Object orientation can be thought of as a method of problem solving that asks the programmer and designer to organize their thoughts around creating a self-contained piece of code and data that can stand on its own within the environment created for it. The basic program structure that does this is called an *object* naturally enough. Before exploring how to create an object programmatically, let's explore the concept that makes an object. In the real world, people think in terms of objects by name or purpose. Let's use the example of a car.

A car is an *object*. People look at and refer to it that way. They don't normally say, "Let's go for a ride in my transporation device that rolls on wheels, is powered by a gasoline engine, and contains seats for humans and dogs to sit in." When they say "car," you identify in your mind an image of a vehicle that does all these things. This single picture contains all the information you need to know to understand the meaning of "car."

Once that image is presented to your mind, the next thing that happens once you've identified the car is defining what kind of car you have. You focus on the *attributes* of the car in question. This car can be distinguished from other cars by such items as:

- Engine
- Color
- Interior
- Body Style
- Wheel Style
- Make
- Model

The next item up for consideration is *function*. Cars take people from point A to point B. How you get there is another story. Some cars can take you there offroad. Some get you there fast, some let you tow things to your intended destination, and some get you there slowly but cheaply.

Now that we have defined our car objects mentally in terms of *attributes* and *functions*, let's take the next step and deal with groupings. Cars come in many different shapes, sizes, makes, and models. The interesting thing about cars is that there are many that are identical and many more that are similar. How does a person work with this? Well, we group similar or like things together.

For instance, we might group cars by their manufacturer, such as Ford, General Motors, or Chrysler. We might think of them in terms of compact, midsize, or full size. We might distinguish them in terms of sports models, utility vehicles, or economy models.

In essence, a distinguishing feature or features of objects allow us to group them together for ease of reference. You could say that we have identified a *class* of cars. If you understand everything so far, you already realize that object orientation is something we do naturally, even automatically. It's when we have to think about it that life gets tough sometimes.

We pretty much defined many of the most important concepts of object orientation, with the exception of *inheritance*. Inheritance means just that—you get something from your ancestors, whether it's your eye color, hair, shape, freckles, and so on. More specifically, with respect to objects, inheritance refers to an object that is a copy of another object, but it also has other additions, or attributes, to make it different.

Going back to our car example, in 1964 Ford introduced the Mustang. Even though it was such a different looking car than anything Ford had introduced at that point in time, it had a parent—the Ford Falcon. The body style and interior were dissimilar, but the mechanical parts, engine, and frame were identical in many respects. So you could honestly say that the Mustang inherited many of its attributes from the Ford Falcon.

Now, let's put all the object-oriented terms together in describing a means of identifying our cars, while keeping it simple to track our information. Remember that the object is the basis from which we work from. Think back over the many different kinds of cars there are. What attributes do they all have in common? Let's list a few:

- Engine
- Interior
- Body Style
- Color
- Wheels
- Size

From this list, we create a parent object called *CAR*. Now think of the differences among all the different kinds of cars there are. The number is staggering; too much for us to work with reasonably. Now find some similarity that allows grouping these vehicles into more manageable numbers. For this example, we use manufacturers:

- Ford
- GM
- Chrysler
- Toyota
- Nissan
- Honda
- BMW
- Mercedes
- Alpha

For the moment, we'll ignore the differences in models under these manufacturers. Now let's create a class of cars called FORD. In order to do this we inherit the attributes of the parent object CAR. Class FORD now has all the attributes of parent object CAR. But wait! What's the difference?

Right now there is no difference, but with the addition of new attributes that don't exist in the parent object CAR, class FORD takes on new meaning. Let's add the following attributes:

- Insurance
- Acceleration
- Maintenance
- Model

Now we can view our list of attributes in Table 1.1.

As you can see, class FORD now has all the attributes of the parent object CAR, plus the new attributes that extend the defintion of CAR to suit our purposes in defining FORD. We can extend this exercise even further by defining classes for other manufacturers based on the parent object CAR. When you look at all of these classes, you will see they share the same basic attributes from CAR, but differ from each other with respect to other new attributes added.

Table 1.1 A List of Attributes	
CAR	**FORD**
Engine	Engine
Interior	Interior
Body Style	Body Style
Color	Color
Wheels	Wheels
Size	Size
	Insurance
	Acceleration
	Maintenance
	Model

This brings up some new terms. Because CAR was defined to be generic to all cars, we can say it was the base *class* from which all other classes of cars are defined. We can also point to it and call it an *abstract object*. In other words, there is nothing unique about CAR that would exclude any class we have defined from using it as a template or parent object.

Now, as an introductory reference, let's take a look at how this might be represented in Borland's Pascal, the language Delphi is based upon. First, we must identify CAR as being an object. Simplistically it would look like this:

```
CAR = object
  Engine:   Integer;
  Interior:   String;
  BodyStyle:   String;
  Color:   String;
  Wheels:   Integer;
  Size:   Integer;
end;
```

Now let's define FORD in terms of CAR and add the additional attributes:

```
FORD = object(CAR)
  Insurance:   Integer;
  Model:  String;
  Acceleration:  Real;
  Maintenance:  Real;
end;
```

Let's take it one step further here. Let's define MUSTANG in terms of FORD:

```
MUSTANG = object(FORD)
   Intrumentation:   String;
   Convertible:      Boolean;
   Pony Package:  Boolean;
   Saleen:      Boolean;
   Suspension:      Integer;
   Special Pricing:  String;
end;
```

Now, we have all the goodies we need to do neat things with our object MUSTANG. Confused? Stay with me for a moment.

Now, let's take a look at what we have.

1. We defined a parent (abstract) object name CAR. It has the following components:

   ```
   Engine:    Integer;
   Interior:    String;
   BodyStyle:    String;
   Color:    String;
   Wheels:    Integer;
   Size:      Integer;
   ```

2. Next, we defined another object FORD, which inherits its base attributes from the object CAR. We also added four more attirbutes unique to FORD, which now has the following components:

   ```
   Inherited from CAR:
      Engine:    Integer;
      Interior:    String;
      BodyStyle:    String;
      Color:    String;
      Wheels:    Integer;
      Size:      Integer;
   New attributes to this object:
      Insurance:    Integer;
   ```

```
Model:  String;
Acceleration:  Real;
Maintenance:  Real;
```

3. Finally, we created a third object MUSTANG, which inherits its base attributes from FORD. We also added six more attributes unique to MUSTANG, which now has the following components:

```
Inherited from CAR:
    Engine:    Integer;
    Interior:    String;
    BodyStyle:    String;
    Color:    String;
    Wheels:    Integer;
    Size:      Integer;
Inherited from FORD:
    Insurance:    Integer;
    Model:  String;
    Acceleration:  Real;
    Maintenance:  Real;
New attributes to this object:
    Instrumentation:  String;
    Convertible:    Boolean;
    Pony Package:  Boolean;
    Saleen:    Boolean;
    Suspension:    Integer;
    Special Pricing:  String;
```

There it all is. Think about the concepts presented here in this brief discussion on object orientation, as it will help you understand and construct your projects more fully as you use and explore the Delphi environment.

CHAPTER 2

Exploring the Delphi Environment

Delphi is a Rapid Application Development (RAD) environment. What makes Delphi unique in many respects to other Graphical User Interface (GUI)-based tools is the dependence upon and integration of components. Each component is an object that exists in the Delphi environment and can be extended to create new components.

With that in mind, let's take Delphi out for a spin and look at some of the main features that you will run across in your development cycle. We'll touch upon the project concept that Delphi employs and even builds a quick little application to show how easy it is to compose a Windows program under Delphi.

Let's get started—we're burning daylight.

Figure 2.1
The Delphi integrated environment.

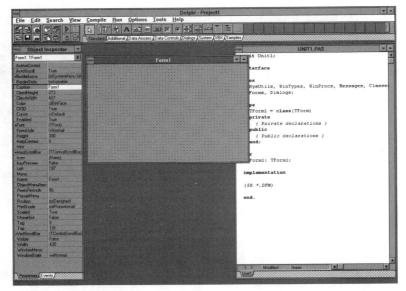

The Nickel Tour

When you start Delphi, you get several different windows that show up on the screen at one time. This has to do with Delphi being an integrated environment. Figure 2.1 shows a default component display. Here we see the Component Palette, Speedbar, Object Inspector, Code Editor, and a default Form. As you become more familiar with Delphi's environment, displays such as this become less frequent as you discover some of the hidden treasures that allow you to customize how your desktop looks and acts. We'll cover that in more detail later. For now, let's explore what we do see.

The Speedbar

Located on the bottom left of Delphi's Component Palette window (Figure 2.2), the Speedbar provides a cache of commonly used functions. These functions are duplicated from the main menu of the Component Palette window, but remain available at all times so that you don't have to go hunting for them inside the menu hierarchy.

Figure 2.3 and Table 2.1 give a closer look at what the Speedbar has to offer (Figure 2.3).

Figure 2.2
The Component Palette window.

![Component Palette window showing Delphi - Project1 with File, Edit, Search, View, Compile, Run, Options, Tools, Help menus and toolbar with Standard, Additional, Data Access, Data Controls, Dialogs, System, VBX, Samples tabs]

Figure 2.3
The Speedbar.

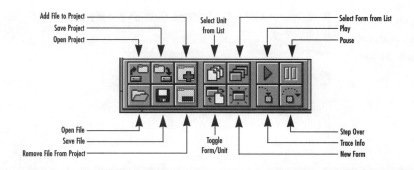

Table 2.1 The Speedbar	
Speedbar Button	**What It's Used For**
Open Project	Calls the Open dialog that lets you pick which existing project you wish to open and work on.
Save Project	Saves your existing project to disk.
Add File to Project	Allows the automatic addition of another Object Pascal source file to the project. This is convenient when you have numbers of units that are not tied directly to a form.
Select Unit from List	Allows you to select from the existing active list of source code Units the one you wish to have brought to the front of the Code Editor.
Select Form from List	Allows you to select from the existing active list of forms.
Run	Runs your project.
Pause	Temporarily halts your running project.
Open File	Calls the Open dialog to allow you to open a file for use (Unit source file by default).
Save File	Saves open Unit source file to disk.
Remove File from Project	Extracts a Unit source file from the project.
Toggle Form/Unit	Toggles front display between Forms and Units.
New Form	Adds a new form to the project.
Trace Into	A debug command that is used only during debug sessions when the project is running and debug information has been turned on. This function allows Delphi to step into function and procedure calls.
Step Over	Another debug command under the same restrictions as Trace Into. This function allows Delphi to skip over tracing into functions and procedures. Instead, it runs the function or procedure and moves to the next source line within the active Unit.

Figure 2.4
The Component
Palette window.

Component Palettes

Delphi provides eight default Component Pages that contain the various objects used by Delphi to help you build your application (Figure 2.4). Selecting a Component Page is easy. Just click on the tab that represents the page you want to look at, and Delphi automatically brings it to the front of the Component Palette for ease of viewing and use.

We'll take a quick look at each Component Page and identify components on that page to get an idea of just what is available for us to use. The following figures and tables each describe one of the Component Pages. All entries in the table will start with the first item on the left of the Component Page and work to the right.

Table 2.2 describes the Standard Component Page (Figure 2.5).

Table 2.2 Standard Component Page	
Component	What It Does
MainMenu	Calls up Delphi's Menu Designer feature with which you create the main menu bar for your application. This feature includes drop-down submenus and accelerator letters (underlined letters used in conjunction with the Alt key to execute functions, or speed keys).
PopupMenu	Calls up Delphi's Menu Designer feature so that you can create a local pop-up menu, or the kind of menu brought up on-screen in an application by pressing the right mouse button.
Label	Allows you to place text on a form for display. You can use this component for displaying titles, comments, and helpful instructions for your application users on-screen.
Edit	Provides a single line box for editing a single string of text. This is useful for small pieces of data, such as dates, names, filenames, numbers, and so on.

Continued

Table 2.2 *Continued*

Component	What It Does
Memo	Provides a multiple-line text editing box for your application users to edit large text strings or lists of text. The Memo component itself is robust enough to create a simple text editor without much additional support.
Button	Provides a general purpose command button that can be used to signal operations, such as starting, stopping, or canceling a process. It can also be used to invoke functions, other forms, Boolean operations, and any other type of operation that can be tied to an event in Delphi.
CheckBox	This component presents Boolean conditions to the user (ON/OFF, YES/NO, TRUE/FALSE). Multiple check boxes operate independently of each other.
RadioButton	Behaves like a CheckBox, but operates in concert with other RadioButtons to create exclusive operations and selections from a group of choices.
ListBox	Displays a list of items from which the user can pick one or more items.
ComboBox	Operates like a ListBox, but has a resident Edit box. This gives the user the ability to type in a selection, bypassing the ListBox part of the component.
ScrollBar	Allows the user to scroll from one end to another of a list, window, memo, or any component whose virtual display space is larger than the displayed region on the screen.
GroupBox	Allows grouping of components on a form.
RadioGroup	Groups RadioButtons together on a form.
Panel	Groups components together on a form. Unlike a GroupBox, the Panel can be used to create status bars, toolbars, speedbars, and so on.

Table 2.3 describes the Additional Component Page (Figure 2.6).

Figure 2.5
The Standard
Component
Page.

Figure 2.6
The Additional
Component
Page.

Table 2.3 The Additional Component Page	
Component	**What It Does**
BitBtn	These buttons allow for the display of a bitmap on their face.
SpeedButton	These buttons are designed so that they can create a tool bar by grouping them on a Panel object. These buttons can also display bitmaps on their face.
TabSet	This object creates tabs for a form to give the appearance of having depth (multiple pages).
Notebook	Provides a multipage object that can be used to stack multiple display menus and operations into a single display region. Each *page,* when selected, activates the components on it and displays them.
TabbedNotebook	Same idea as a Notebook, but with tabs at the top.
MaskEdit	This is an Edit component that allows for formatted input to filter user interaction.
Outline	This component displays data in an outline format.
StringGrid	This component presents and retrieves strings in spreadsheet fashion.
DrawGrid	This components lets you display nontext data in spreadsheet fashion.
Image	This component displays bitmaps, icons, and so on.
Shape	Allows for simple geometric shapes to be created on the form (ellipse, rectangle, rectangle with rounded edges).
Bevel	A 3D border.
Header	This component allows for controlling a section of the form to display text and be resized with the mouse.
ScrollBox	Display area with ScrollBars.

Table 2.4 describes the Data Access Component Page (Figure 2.7).

Figure 2.7
The Data Access
Component
Page.

Figure 2.8
The Data
Controls
Component
Page.

Table 2.4 The Data Access Component Page	
Component	**What It Does**
DataSource	Acts as the pipeline between data-aware components on the form and the Query or Table to which it is attached.
Table	Links a Database table with the Delphi application.
Query	Handles the construction and execution of a database query.
StoredProc	Lets SQL procedures to remote databases be stored locally.
Database	Provides the connection between a database (local or remote) and a Delphi application.
BatchMove	Batch processing for remote SQL.
Report	Lets Delphi applications generate reports using ReportSmith.

Table 2.5 describes the Data Controls Component Page (Figure 2.8).

Table 2.5 The Data Controls Component Page	
Component	**What It Does**
DBGrid	Provides a spreadsheet grid to display database data.
DBNavigator	Toolbar component that allows the display, editing, and navigation of records in a database.
DBText	Data-aware version of Label.
DBEdit	Data-aware version of Edit.
DBMemo	Data-aware version of Memo.
DBImage	Data-aware version of Image.
DBListBox	Data-aware version of ListBox.
DBComboBox	Data-aware version of ComboBox.
DBCheckBox	Data-aware version of CheckBox.
DBRadioGroup	Data-aware version of RadioGroup.
DBLookupList	Provides data from a secondary data table to a ListBox lookup interface.
DBLookupCombo	Provides data from a secondary data table to a ComboBox lookup interface.

Table 2.6 explains the Dialogs Component Page (Figure 2.9).

Figure 2.9
The Dialogs
Component
Page.

Table 2.6 The Dialogs Component Page

Component	What It Does
OpenDialog	Uses Windows Open common dialog box.
SaveDialog	Uses Windows Save common dialog box.
FontDialog	Uses Windows Font common dialog box.
ColorDialog	Uses Windows Color common dialog box.
PrintDialog	Uses Windows Print common dialog box.
PrinterSetupDialog	Uses Windows Printer Setup common dialog box.
FindDialog	Uses Windows Find common dialog box.
ReplaceDialog	Uses Windows Replace common dialog box.

Table 2.7 describes the System Component Page (Figure 2.10).

Table 2.7 The System Component Page

Component	What It Does
Timer	Invisible component that generates events on timed intervals as small as 1 ms.
PaintBox	Provides a rectangular area of the form to be painted.
FileListBox	Provides a ready-made ListBox that tracks the files in the current directory. The ability to scroll though files is only available at runtime.
DirectoryListBox	Provides a ready-made ListBox that tracks the directory tree for the active disk drive. Scrolling and switching directories can be done only at runtime.
DriveComboBox	Provides a ready-made ComboBox for all available drives on the system, with the currently active one as the default. The ability to switch drives is limited to runtime only.
FilterComboBox	Provides a ready-made ComboBox that filters for filenames. The ability to use all the specified filters is good only at runtime.
MediaPlayer	Provides a VCR-type panel to interact with multimedia files.
OLEContainer	Creates an OLE client area on the form.
DDEClientConv	Creates a connection to a DDE Server application.
DDEClientItem	Specifies DDE client data to be exchanged.
DDEServerConv	Creates a connection to a DDE Client application.
DDEServerItem	Specifies DDE server data to be exchanged.

Figure 2.10
The System
Component
Page.

Table 2.8 describes the VBX Component Page (Figure 2.11).

Table 2.8 The VBX Component Page	
Component	**What It Does**
BiSwitch	Cute toggle switch that works similar to a CheckBox.
BiGauge	Progress (%) indicator.
BiPict	Displays bitmaps, icons.
Chart	Provides ready-made charting capability.

Table 2.9 describes the Samples Component Page (Figure 2.12).

Table 2.9 The Samples Component Page	
Component	**What It Does**
Gauge	More flexible display gauge to show (%) progress.
ColorGrid	Allows the user to select colors for elements in the Delphi application.
SpinButton	Allows a user to increment/decrement a number that is located inside an Edit box.
SpinEdit	Same concept as SpinButton, except this time the Edit box is attached to the SpinButton.
DirectoryOutline	Allows the user to see the active drive's directory structure in a hierarchical fashion.
Calendar	Simple calendar component.

The Form

The blank form unit on the screen is your canvas (Figure 2.13). Like other components, you can move the form around on the screen and resize it. You can minimize it, for example, while you work in the Code Editor. Or, you can maximize it to the limits of the screen to take full advantage of the space available.

Figure 2.11
The VBX
Component
Page.

Figure 2.12
The Samples
Component
Page.

Delphi doesn't limit you on the number of forms you can have in your ongoing application project. The only limits you might run into would be indirect limits, such as running out of Windows System Resources or disk space.

To create a new form, click on the New Form SpeedButton, or select File>New Form from the pull-down menus. To view a form, click on the form's title bar. To switch between forms (or get to the View Form pop-up menu, press Shift-F12, or select View>Form from the pull-down menus.

Form Designer

The *Form Designer* detail box is found on the Preferences page under the Options>Environment pull-down menu selections (Figure 2.14).

Display Grid   The *Display Grid* option allows you to turn the dot grid on and off. The grid is turned on when the box is checked, and turned off when the check is absent. The grid is very useful for aligning and sizing the components you place on the form. You can establish a more uniform appearance on your screens with the help of the grid. With the grid turned off, you have the capability of free-forming your screens to fit whatever artistic flair you may desire to demonstrate.

Figure 2.13
A blank form.

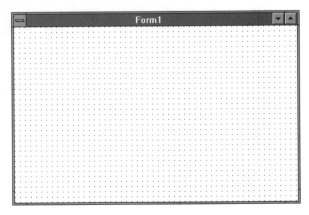

Figure 2.14
The Form
Designer
Environment
Options.

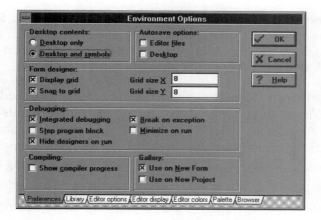

Snap to Grid   The *Snap to Grid* option, when turned on, forces the components you place on the form to adhere to the grid coordinates, thus assisting you in organizing your screen. With Snap to Grid turned off, the grid may still be present but it acts only as a guide for you. The components you place on the form will stay exactly where you put them. Snap to Grid is turned on when the box is checked, and turned off when the check is absent.

Grid Size X and Grid Size Y   These options allow you to set the granularity, or the proportional distance, between the grid dots. *Grid Size X* sets the horizontal (side-to-side) spacing of the dots. *Grid Size Y* sets the vertical (top-to-bottom) spacing of the dots. The number represents the distance between dots as measured in pixels. The larger the number, the greater the distance between the grid dots.

Component Alignment

There are three ways to align components on a form. You can use the Grid and Snap to Grid options (already turned on for you when you enter Delphi) to *eyeball* your component alignment. This is the simplest method for aligning components. Simply click and drag components around the form until they appear to your eye to be aligned properly.

The other two ways to align components are through the use of the Alignment Palette and the Alignment dialog box. To select which components are to be aligned through the use of either of these two methods, place the mouse on the first component to be aligned, press and hold down the Shift key and click on each component to be included in the alignment process; then let up on the Shift key. Each selected component should be clearly marked.

Alignment Palette   The *Alignment Palette* is called up by selecting *Views>Alignment Palette* on the pull-down menus (Figure 2.15). The Alignment Palette can be left on-screen for future alignment needs. From left to right on the first row, the buttons will:

- Align the left edges of the selected components with the left edge of the first selected component.
- Horizontally align the centers of the selected components with the center of the first selected component.
- Horizontally align the centers of the selected components to the center of the form.
- Align the right edges of the selected components with the right edge of the first selected component.

From left to right on the second row, the buttons will:

- Align the top edges of the selected components with the top edge of the first selected component.
- Vertically center the centers of the selected components with the center of the first component selected.
- Vertically align the centers of the selected components with the center of the form.
- Align the bottom edges of the selected components with the bottom edge of the first selected component.

Alignment Dialog Box   The *Alignment dialog box* is called up by selecting *Edit>Align* on the pull-down menus (Figure 2.16). This alignment method, unlike the Alignment Palette, must be called up

Figure 2.15
The Alignment Palette.

each time an alignment is to be made. However, simultaneous horizontal and vertical realignments may be made with this method.

On the Horizontal list:

- **No Change** causes no horizontal changes to the selected components.
- **Left Sides** aligns the left sides of the selected components with the left side of the first selected component.
- **Centers** aligns the centers of the selected components horizontally with the center of the first selected component.
- **Right Sides** aligns the right sides of the selected components with the right side of the first selected component.
- **Space Equally** sets the selected components horizontally equidistant from each other.
- **Center in Window** centers the selected components horizontally with the center of the window.

On the Vertical list:

- **No Change** causes no vertical changes to the selected components.
- **Tops** aligns the tops of the selected components with the top of the first selected component.
- **Centers** aligns the centers of the selected components vertically with the center of the first selected component.
- **Bottoms** aligns the bottoms of the selected components with the bottom of the first selected component.
- **Space Equally** sets the selected components vertically equidistant from each other.

Figure 2.16
Alignment
Dialog Box.

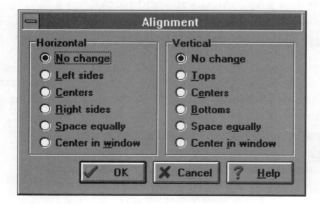

Figure 2.17
The Object
Inspector.

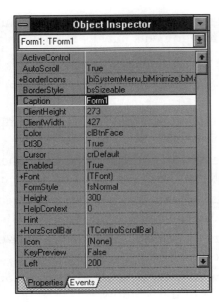

- **Center in Window** centers the selected components vertically with the center of the window.

Object Inspector

The *Object Inspector* (Figure 2.17) is like a speedy middleman between the graphical appearance of your application and your source code. First, you modify your application's visual image by creating, placing, moving, sizing, or deleting components and forms, using the Component Palettes. Then, you use the Object Inspector to fine-tune the properties and create the events associated with these components and forms.

Pull-Down Menu Bar

The pull-down menus, as in most other Windows programs, are the backbone of Delphi. To get help on a particular menu item, highlight it and press F1. Table 2.10 lists each main menu item with its submenu items.

Figure 2.18
The Pull-Down
Menu.

Table 2.10 Delphi's Pull-Down Menus

File Menu

Menu Item	What It Does
New Project	Creates a new project, consisting of a form (.DFM file), a unit (.PAS file), and a project file (.DPR file).
Open Project	Loads an existing project with its accompanying files.
Save Project	Saves the current project with its already given name.
Save Project As	Saves the current project with a new name of your choice.
Close Project	Closes the current project with its accompanying unit and form files.
New Form	Creates a new form to add to the project. This can be accomplished by way of the Speedbar, too.
New Unit	Creates a new unit to add to the project. This also can be accomplished through a SpeedButton.
New Component	Lets you add a new component to Delphi.
Open File	Loads an existing .PAS, or unit, file.
Save File	Saves a text file with its existing name.
Save File As	Saves the active text file with a different name.
Close File	Closes a text file.
Add File	Adds a source file to the active project.
Remove File	Removes a source file from the active project.
Print	Prints a file.
Exit	Closes open files and projects, and exits Delphi.

Edit Menu

Menu Item	What It Does
Undelete	Cancels or expunges the last action.
Redo	Reverses the last undo.
Cut	Removes or deletes a selected item and places it on the Clipboard.
Copy	Makes a duplicate of a selected item and places it on the Clipboard, leaving the original untouched.
Paste	Copies the contents of the Clipboard into a Code Editor window or a form.
Delete	Removes a selected item.
Select All	Selects all items.
Align to Grid	Adjusts or justifies selected components to the closest grid point.
Bring to Front	Moves a selected component to the front.

Continued

Table 2.10 Delphi's Pull-Down Menus *Continued*

Edit Menu *Continued*

Send to Back	Moves a selected component to the back.
Align	Calls up the Alignment dialog box, which allows you to align selected components horizontally and/or vertically.
Size	Calls up the Size dialog box, which allows you to make selected components grow to the size of the largest selected component, or shrink to the size of the smallest selected component.
Scale	Resizes all the components on a form by allowing you to enter a percentage. Any percentage over 100 percent causes the components to grow in size, whereas any percentage under 100 percent causes the components to shrink accordingly.
Tab Order	Lets you set the Tab order of components on a form, or components contained within a component.
Creation Order	Lets you change the order in which your application will create nonvisual components at runtime.
Lock Controls	Secures components in their current position on the active form.
Object	Lets you edit or convert an OLE object on the form.

Search Menu

Menu Item	*What It Does*
Find	Searches for specific text.
Replace	Searches for specific text and replaces it with new text.
Search Again	Repeats the last search.
Incremental Search	Searches for text as you type.
Goto Line Number	Moves the cursor to the line number you specify.
Show Last Compile Error	Places the cursor on the line of code that caused the last compiler error.
Find Error	Searches for the most recent runtime error.
Browse Symbol	Searches for a symbol you specify.

View Menu

Menu Item	*What It Does*
Project Manager	Calls up a window in which you can add, delete, save, and copy files to your current project. It also lists all the units in your current project.

Table 2.10 *Continued*

View Menu *Continued*

Project Source	Lets you make the selected source file the active page in the Code Editor.
Object Inspector	Makes the Object Inspector the active window.
Alignment Palette	Brings up the Alignment Palette window so that you can set the alignment of your objects.
Browser	Invokes the Object Browser so that you can visually explore objects and units in your application.
Breakpoints	Opens the Breakpoints window, which lists all the breakpoints in your current project. Each breakpoint is listed with the file and line number where it can be found, and any conditions or pass count associated with it.
Call Stack	Opens a window that lists the sequence of routines called by your application, along with their procedure names and any parameter values passed to them.
Watches	Opens a window that displays all the set watch expressions for your project. When you use this option during debugging, it will display the current values of your variables and update them as the program runs.
Component List	Brings up a dialog window that lets you add components to your form using the keyboard.
Window List	Brings up a dialog to let you activate a window from the list of available inactive windows.
Toggle Form/Unit	Lets you display the inactive form/unit that is associated with the currently active form/unit.
Units	Opens the View Unit dialog box to allow you to select the active unit window. The shortcut for this option is the View Unit SpeedButton on the Speedbar.
Forms	Opens the View Form dialog box to let you select the active form window. The shortcut for this option is the View Form SpeedButton on the Speedbar.
New Edit Window	Opens the Code Editor again with a copy of the active page from the original Code Editor window. Changes made in one window are also made in the other window.
Speedbar	Toggles the Speedbar display (ON/OFF).
Component Palette	Toggles the Component Palette display (ON/OFF).

Compile Menu

Menu Item	What It Does
Compile	Searches for changes in project source code and recompiles those changes.

Continued

Table 2.10 Delphi's Pull-Down Menus

Compile Menu *Continued*

Build All	Forces a complete compile and link of the whole project.
Syntax Check	Like Link, this forces a syntax check of source code without a compile.
Information	View compile information and status on the active project.

Run Menu

Menu Item	What It Does
Run	Compiles and executes the project. If there is an error, the Code Editor will point to the first occurrence of an error.
Parameters	Allows you to pass command-line arguments to your application under test, when running it from Delphi.
Step Over	**Note: This option works only in Debug Mode.** Executes the highlighted statement in the Code Editor. Step Over will skip any subroutines in your application. You can use this option to debug your program without having to run subroutines you know are already bug-free. The Step Over SpeedButton on the Speedbar executes this same function.
Trace Into	**Note: This option works only in Debug Mode.** Executes the highlighted statement in the Code Editor. Trace Into will execute your subroutines as well. It will skip any subroutines created by Delphi, since they need no debugging. The Trace Into SpeedButton on the Speedbar does the same thing as this menu option.
Run to Cursor	**Note: This option works only in Debug Mode.** Executes your application at full speed from a marked execution point to the current marked cursor point. This option is used to execute blocks of code at one time, as opposed to Step Over and Trace Into, which execute code one line at a time. This option is different than the Run to Cursor option on the Code Editor SpeedMenu, which runs the entire program from the beginning to the cursor position.
Show Execution Point	**Note: This option works only in Debug Mode.** Delphi positions the Code Editor to display the line of source code at the current execution point.
Program Pause	**Note: This option works only in Debug Mode.** Temporarily pauses current application execution.

Table 2.10	
Run Menu *Continued*	
Program Reset	**Note: This option works only in Debug Mode.** Stops the current debugging session. It resets your application by releasing any memory allocated for variables, and so on, and closes any open files your application may have been using.
Add Watch	**Note: This option works only in Debug Mode.** Opens the Watch Properties dialog box, which allows you to add a watch expression to your application during debugging. A watch expression lets you to track the values of variables or expressions in your code during Step Over or Trace Into processes. This function can also be found on the Code Editor SpeedMenu.
Add Breakpoint	**Note: This option works only in Debug Mode.** Opens the Edit Breakpoint dialog box so that you can create new breakpoints for your application.
Evaluate/Modify	**Note: This option works only in Debug Mode.** Opens the Evaluate/Modify dialog box. This option lets you assess Object Pascal expressions as well as change variable values and data-structure element values. This option can also be found on the Code Editor SpeedMenu.
Options Menu	
Menu Item	*What It Does*
Project	Lets you designate compiler and linker options, and lets you indicate the locations of files needed to compile and link your application.
Environment	Brings up a multipage dialog that lets you change global settings for such things as component placement on forms, debugging, compiling, libraries, editor operation and presentation, and object browsing.
Tools	Lets you add or delete tools from your Tools menu.
Gallery	Brings up the Gallery dialog, where you can specify templates and experts for forms and projects.
Open Library	Lets you install Dynamic Component Library (DCL files).
Install Components	Lets you install components, such as VBX controls, into the Component Palette.
Rebuild Library	Recompile the component library without leaving Delphi.

Continued

Table 2.10 Delphi's Pull-Down Menus

Tools menu *Continued*

Menu Item	What It does
Report Smith	Invokes Report Smith.
Image Editor	Invokes the Image Editor Tool.
Database Desktop	Invokes the Database Desktop.
BDE Config	Invokes the Borland Database Engine Configuration utility.

Help Menu

Menu Item	What It Does
Contents	Brings up the main Help Topical Index.
Topic Search	Searches for Help on a specific topic.
How to Use Help	Provides a tutorial on the Help Facility.
Interactive Tutors	Opens the list of interactive tutors to be selected and run.
Windows API	Lets you display online information on the Windows API.
Database Form Expert	Tells you to invoke the DFE to get help on it.
About	Quick information about Delphi.

The Code Editor

The *Code Editor* (Figure 2.19) is a feature-rich programmer's editor. It contains the code created and inserted by the Object Inspector and the Component Palettes from your visual manipulation of forms and components, and the code you insert to respond to the actions of those forms and components.

Each form is assigned its own *unit.* A unit in the Code Editor contains all the source code for the form itself, the components on the form, and the event handlers containing the code you install to respond to the actions of the components on the form.

Code Editor SpeedMenu

By clicking the right mouse button in the Code Editor, you can call up the SpeedMenu (Figure 2.20). The SpeedMenu gives you several editor keystroke shortcuts. Table 2.11 identifies the function of each menu item.

Customizing the Code Editor

Under the pull-down menu selection *Options>Environment,* there are three pages of options you can use to customize the Code Editor to your liking (Figure 2.21).

The *Editor Options* page allows you to control text handling. You can modify specific settings set by the automatic keyboard mapping scheme. You can also specify the number of spaces to indent a marked block, set the number of keystrokes to be allowed under undo, set tab stops, and set the extensions of files that will display syntax highlighting information.

Figure 2.19
The Code Editor.

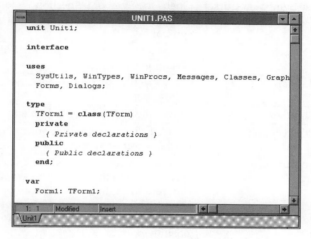

Figure 2.20
The Code Editor SpeedMenu.

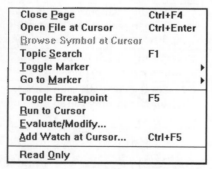

Figure 2.21
The Code Editor Environment Options.

Table 2.11 SpeedMenu Menu

Menu Item	What It Does
Close Page	Closes the current Code Editor page.
Open File at Cursor	Opens a file whose filename the cursor is positioned on.
Browse Symbol at Cursor	Opens the Symbol Inspection window for the highlighted, predefined object, unit, or variable symbol.
Topic Search	Opens a Help window for the word the cursor is positioned on.
Toggle Marker	Allows you to set/unset markers for use in debugging.
Goto Marker	Moves the cursor to a predefined marker.
Toggle Breakpoint	Toggles a breakpoint off if on, and on if off, at the current position of the cursor.
Run to Cursor	Compiles your source code and executes the entire program up to the current cursor position. This is different from the Run to Cursor option on the Debug pull-down menu, which executes your program from a marked position to the cursor position only.
Evaluate/Modify	Opens the Evaluate/Modify dialog box so that you can either evaluate an expression in your code, or modify a variable as you run your application.
Add Watch at Cursor	Opens the Watch Properties dialog box so that you can set a watch expression.
Read Only	Makes the currently active source file in the Code Editor a read-only file so that changes cannot be made.

The *Editor Display* (Figure 2.22) page lets you choose whether to use BRIEF cursor shapes, create a backup file during file saves, preserve the end-of-line position, display a line at the right margin, set the right margin, select a font type and size, or switch key bindings. Switching key bindings on this page is similar to resetting the keyboard mapping scheme on the Editor Summary page, except that it does not automatically adjust any options on the Editor Options page. You are left to customize them yourself. The four key bindings to choose from are: Default, which uses CUA mapping; Classic, which uses DOS editor mapping; BRIEF, which emulates BRIEF editor mappings; and Epsilon, which emulates Epsilon mapping.

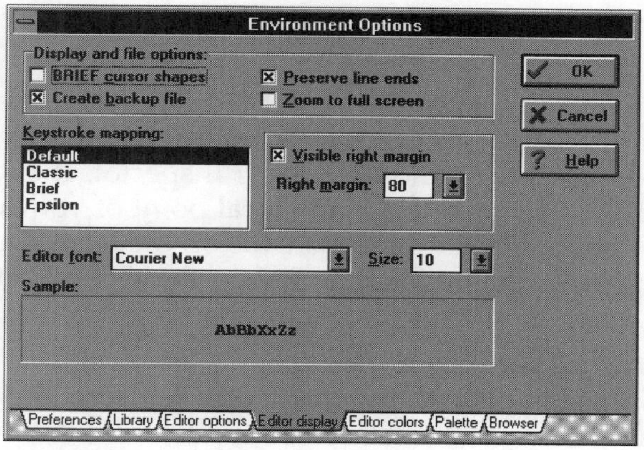

Figure 2.22
Setting the Code Editor's keyboard options.

The *Editor Colors* page (Figure 2.23) allows you to set foreground and background colors and attributes for specific text elements. You can also choose to display elements using the default Windows system colors.

How Delphi Defines a Project

In the past, a simple DOS application consisted of one executable file. Now, in a GUI environment of today, such as Windows, a single application can require dozens of files for data and information in order to function properly.

In Delphi, all the files that make up a single application are known as a *project*. There are three main types of files that make up a Delphi project. They are the *Project file*, the *Form file*, and the *Unit file*.

There is only one Project file per project. You can think of it as the main program file. Its extension is always *.DPR*. The Project file acts as the conductor of the orchestra, calling into play when

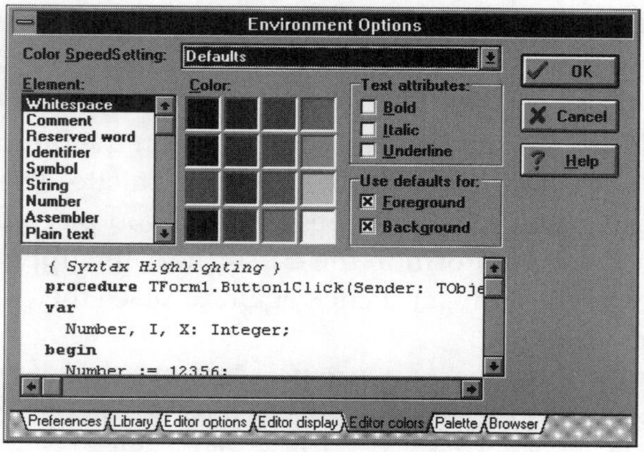

Figure 2.23
Setting the Code Editor's color options.

needed all the other form and code modules you create in Delphi to run your application.

A Form file is a binary file, and it is the graphical representation of your application, which you create with the assistance of the Component Palette and the Object Inspector. It ends in the extension *.DFM.* The form file is the focal point of your work in Delphi. While you manipulate components on the form, Delphi makes the code changes in the background in the Code Editor, both in the form's associated Unit file and in the Project file.

A *Unit file* is the source code module associated with the Form file. As you manipulate components on the form, and change their attributes in the Object Inspector, Delphi writes the source code in the Unit file to reflect the form. Then, after you have prepared the form to your liking, you add the final touches to the source code to be executed in response to the actions of the components on the form.

A Quickie: "HELLO WORLD"

Okay, now that you've toured the place and learned a little about Delphi organization, let's create your first Delphi application. This will give you a feel for what we've discussed in this chapter.

Fresh Start: If you haven't already, go ahead and launch Delphi. If you are already in Delphi and you experimented with some of the features and components as you went through the chapter, select File>New Project to clear out the current project. You want to start off fresh, with a *clear screen.*

1. **Rename the Form:** Click on the Caption field text in the Object Inspector, delete the text **Form1** from the field, and type the text **Hello World!** Notice the text is displayed across the top of the form as you type it in. Then, scroll down the Object Inspector to the Name item. Click on the Name field text, delete the text **Form1** from the field, type the text **Hello1**, and press Enter. This becomes the filename of the form.

2. **Place a Button on the Form:** Click on the Button component, found on the Standard component palette. The component button will remain depressed until you place the component on the form. Position the cursor near the upper left-hand corner of the form, and click again to place the component on the form.

3. **Modify the Button's attributes:** Click on the Caption field text in the Object Inspector, delete the text **Button1** from the field, and type the word **Run**. Then, click on the Name field

text, delete the text **Button1**, type in the text **Hello2**, and press Enter.

Click on the Button component to make it the active component again. The little black sizing blocks will show up again. Place the mouse pointer on the middle block at one end of the Button (it doesn't matter which end). The pointer will become a bidirectional arrow, letting you know it's in position for resizing the Button. Click and drag the Button edge inward so that the Button takes up less space on the screen. Notice the white line indicating the new edge of the button. You want the Button size to be a little bit larger than the word *Run* on its face.

4. **Place a Label on the Form:** Click on the Label component, also on the Standard component palette. Position the cursor to the side of the Run Button. Click again to place the Label component on the Form.

5. **Modify the Label's Attributes:** Click on the Caption field text in the Object Inspector, delete the text **Label1** from the field, and type the text **Execute Program**. Click on the Name field text, delete the text **Label1**, type in the text **Hello3**, and press Enter.

6. **Switch Active Components:** Click on the drop-down list button at the top of the Object Inspector. Position the pointer on **Hello2** and click to make the Run Button the active component once again.

7. **Create an Event Handler:** Click on the Events tab at the bottom of the Object Inspector. Double-click on the blank field of the **OnClick** event. This creates an OnClick event handler in the Code Editor. The text **Hello2Click** appears in the field, and the Code Editor becomes active.

8. **Insert Include File:** Use the Code Editor's scroll bar to move to the top of the Unit. Position the cursor right after the reserved word *uses* and type in **WinCrt**. This tells your application to use the WinCrt unit, which is a text file driver that redirects your application's output to a scrollable window.

9. **Insert Variables:** Scroll down in the Unit to the **var** section. Position the cursor at the end of the line **Form1: Tform1;** and press Enter. Type **Text1, Text2: string[30];** and press Enter. The reserved word *var* is short for variable. This section sets up the variables for the application. Text1 and Text2 are

string variables, each with a defined maximum limit of 30 characters.

10. **Insert Program Code:** Use the Code Editor scroll bar to move back down to the **begin...end** portion of the OnClick event handler (where the cursor was first positioned when the Code Editor became active). Position your cursor on the line below **begin**, and press Tab once. Then type the following code, including the punctuation:

```
Writeln('Please enter your first name: ');
Readln(Text1);
Writeln('Please enter your last name: ');
Readln(Text2);
Writeln('Hello World! My name is');
Writeln(Text1, ' ', Text2, ',');
Writeln('and this is my first Delphi program!');
```

11. **Compile and Execute:** Click on the Run SpeedButton located on the Speedbar. The application is compiled and executed. Your Hello World! form is displayed. Click on the Run button you created to select the Execute Program option. A scrollable window pops up, labeled with the path and filename of the project, which is PROJECT1.EXE. You are prompted for your first name. Type it in and press Enter. At the next prompt, type in your last name and press Enter. And there's your message!

12. **Close Out:** Double-click on the Control Menu box in the upper left-hand corner of your application's scrollable window. This returns you to the Delphi working environment, where your application project is still on the screen.

13. **Save:** Select **File>Save Project** on the pull-down menus. The SaveAs dialog box pops up. Delete the proposed filename of **unit1.pas**, type in the filename **hello4.pas**, and press Enter or click on the OK button. Next, the **SaveAs** dialog box for the project pops up. Delete the proposed filename of **project1.DPR**, type in the filename **hello.DPR**, and press Enter or click on the OK button.

Congratulations! You just successfully wrote, compiled, executed, and saved your first Delphi application. Good work! Now it's time to move on to planning a Delphi project, which you'll do in the next chapter.

CHAPTER 3

Planning a Software Project

Software is designed for one reason and one reason only: to solve a problem. The Holy Grail has been to design software that solves a problem without becoming one itself. Over the years many people have advanced theories and methodologies to address this one issue; some with good success, some without. Each time we take this trip around the block, the process seems to get more complicated as people rush to build the ivory tower of software quality and design.

Some Basic Rules

All management metrics and methods aside, software design is an art form that is simple in concept, but very detailed and exacting in its execution. As with any art form, there are some simple, basic rules that should be followed if one is to achieve a measure of success. Remember, a software project is really just a work in progress. Realistically you achieve only a level of *done*, but you never quite finish.

Following are the five basic rules for good software and project planning.

1. Understand the Problem

This is the most crucial piece of the whole puzzle. It also happens to be where you need to start. There are three areas of focus to understanding the problem you are trying to solve:

- Describing the problem
- Describing the data
- Establishing limits

But before you can address these three, you must have at least a good if not thorough comprehension of what the problem really is. Several years ago, I was invited to look at a problem that involved a paper-making machine. If you have never seen one, they are quite something to look at. They are not very tall, but they can stretch out for several hundred feet in length; brimming with chemicals, water, steam, and pulp, all the while making the devil's own noise.

At the meeting, the chief engineer told us that they were losing too much paper to mechanical defects in the rollers and felts that were used to make the paper. The rollers on a paper machine are big cast-metal cylinders weighing from several to many tons, and come in several sizes. Felts on a paper machine are really belts of metal screening that paper pulp clings to during part of the paper-making process.

They wanted a method to detect a potentially bad roller or felt based upon the number and frequency of defects they saw reported by the computer. They figured it would save them quite a bit of money in good product to find the flawed part before the defects became too numerous and visible to the eye.

It took some time. First, we had to understand in a general fashion how the machine operated to make the paper. Then we had to learn how the machine measured and reported data to the machine operators and the engineers doing quality control. Next we had to learn about what kinds of defects exist in the paper making process, which ones were reported and important, and which ones were caused by mechanical defects in the roller or felt. We had to look at how the paper machine changed its tolerances over periods of time. A brand-new felt that might be 137 feet in length when it is first put on the machine might expand to as long as 145 feet as it got hot. Last, we had to look at the kinds of data reported, and look at samples from good rolls of paper and bad rolls of paper.

The end result from all of this was a small program that evaluated the data from each reel of paper. If it detected a defect that consistently repeated itself at a relatively fixed distance on the sheet of paper, then the engineer could inspect the machine to see which roller or felt could be the culprit.

The point to this little story is simple. While some problems may be very obvious, make sure you understand what the real problem is; otherwise, what you think is the problem may just be a symptom of the real issue.

Describe the Problem

Many times I have asked a client or an engineer "Do you understand the problem?" Usually I get a response in the affirmative. Then I ask them to describe the problem to me in detail, and all I get back are stares. Why is this? Well, in our day-to-day lives we do many things, such as walking, talking, writing, and eating, without having to think about it. It's just intuitive.

When we are put in the position of having to describe something or some action that comes naturally to us or we have learned to do by practice, it becomes frustrating as our conscious mind attempts to contemplate all the minute details associated with the action or object. The more we actively think about it, the more detail we uncover and the more frustrated we can become.

Years ago I was asked by an instructor to describe how to sharpen a pencil. When it was all said and done, 2+ hours later, I had managed to come up with at least 153 individual actions that were required to perform this simple task. Many of these actions were aggregates of simpler actions yet to be described. Needless to say, it was very nerve-wracking but enlightening.

When describing an understood problem, it is necessary to ascertain what the goal is. Without a goal there is no direction. For instance, if I were to describe on paper the problem of designing a graphical window-based presentation interface, I have done only half the job. I need to have a stated goal. A more complete picture would arise if I stated that the goal of this windowed interface was to provide generic symbols to an application that was to be sent to several different countries where they all spoke different languages.

Now that changes things. Instead of postulating about some generic graphical windowing interface, I have now stated that the goal in the interface is to ease understanding of the application across international boundaries. With this constraint placed on the table, the design and implementation should reflect this goal, and the chances for a product being more successful at solving the real problem have just increased.

Describe the Data

Part of understanding the problem is also describing the types of data that are involved. This not only goes to describing the problem you are trying to solve, but also works toward the solution. A good exercise for this is describing the data kept in a phone book. Up until recently, it was customary to keep a list of items that might look like this:

- First Name
- Middle Initial
- Last Name
- Address
- City
- State/Province
- Zip
- Phone
- Work
- Fax
- Comments

With the recent popularity of electronic gadgetry, such as phones, pagers, and e-mail, the above list may not cover all your bases. Today, you might have a list of relevant data that looks like this:

- First Name
- Middle Initial

- Last Name
- Address
- City
- State/Province
- Zip
- Phone
- Work
- Fax
- Second Fax
- Cellular
- Pager
- Data/Modem
- Internet Account
- CompuServe Account
- Delphi Account
- America Online Account
- MCI Mail Account
- Genie Account
- Other E-mail Account
- Comments

Always check to make sure you have every necessary corner covered. It is much easier to remove superfluous data than add it in later.

Establish Limits

One of the biggest sins committed by consultants, designers, engineers, managers, marketers, and programmers is that of *feature-itis*. During design and even way into the production phase of a software project, invariably somebody will pipe up and say "Wouldn't it be nice if the product did <insert new feature here>?" Resist this. Unless there is a critical need to place it in the existing product, there is always the next revision of the software. Good design will allow for additions later.

Another variation on the same theme shows up in design review meetings or during a *fix-it* session. One of the most amazing examples of this lack of limits I have ever witnessed occurred at a fix-it session with five engineers, the original software author and three other programmers.

One of the items I had been tasked with was to provide a data path between two separate applications within a major miniframe software system. The applications did not communicate with each other and their databases were incompatible. I was also instructed to do this with as little impact as possible to the integrity of both sets of software.

As a simple but effective solution, I proposed that the one side of the software write out the data it wished to exchange to a temporary file. This file would then be converted and read by the other side of the system, and incorporated into its database using the existing code. The temporary file was supposed to exist only for about five minutes, tops.

As fate would have it, one of the engineers saw the temporary file. He asked me what it was doing there, so I told him. Thirty minutes later, two of the programmers and three of the engineers had taken this little temporary file and defined a complex structure for it; added additional programming support so that it could talk to several other areas of the system; defined it to be an extension of the master database; and wanted five new programs written to use this new feature. One engineer suggested we build a whole new data structure around this file for a new software system that would be in place in the next release.

The moral of the story is: Time and resources are not infinite. Set realistic expectations on what the software will do and stick to them.

2. Design a General Method Solution

Now that you understand the problem, the fun part is working out a manual solution. This is where creativity and ingenuity come into play.

Do It by Hand—On Paper

Computers are very dumb creatures. They do only exactly what they are told to do. When their instructions are good, the feats of fancy they will perform may seem magical. When the instructions are flawed, the results are, as a friend of mine put it: "It would take

1,000 people working around the clock for two years to produce the amount of garbage generated by a computer in two seconds."

It comes down to algorithms, both small and large. Once you understand the true nature of the problem you are trying to solve, the solution seems to pop out at you just as plainly. The key here is to develop an algorithm or series of algorithms that can be done by a person, given a specific set of instructions.

This manual solution can be as simple as how a bookkeeper is to balance a set of books, or can be as complex as controlling traffic flow by synchronizing the traffic lights over a large area. Either way, you have to be able to demonstrate a workable solution manually if you ever hope to have a working software solution. Some of the most successful software systems are directly translated from well-understood working manual systems from the past.

Will the Computer Do It Better than Manually?

This is a crucial decision point. The whole purpose of a computer in business, or other pursuit is efficiency. If the computer cannot do a job faster and/or more accurately than a person or group of people, then one of two things must happen. One, you either need to find a better method that will work, or two, drop the idea altogether.

Sometimes, there are problems that we don't realistically have the required computing power cheap enough to deal with yet. And other times, no matter how you look at it, a manual system is faster or cheaper.

3. Design a Computer Solution Based on the General Method

At this point in the process, you can now make the transition from paper to computer. In order to do this, there are some issues that must be considered.

Identify the Processes Involved

The processes themselves are nothing more than the tasks necessary to solve the problem. This should be fairly evident from the manual system or general method developed earlier. Identifying separate tasks does two things for you:

1. It makes it easier to tackle the overall problem by breaking them up into a series of manageable smaller problems and solutions.
2. It makes it easier to manage a large project and delegate work out in manageable chunks.

Identify the Data Involved

Here again, this is just translating the types of data required to implement the general method.

Identify the Relationships between Processes and Data

The relationship between tasks and data can be a strong or weak one. The general method developed previously will identify which data relates to which task, but may only hint as to how important that data is to the operation of that task. The actual decision as to that relationship occurs here in the software design phase. Using the general method as a model, you decide how much emphasis needs to be placed upon the relationship between data and a related task.

Identify the Relationships between Processes

This is an interface boundary. Processes that relate to each other have to communicate by data, direct call, or via the operating system. When identifying these relationships, look very carefully at how you can generalize or standardize how all the processes can realistically talk to each other. By doing this, you allow for future additions and changes with a minimum of hassle.

Identify the Relationships between Data

This is where you consider the use of a database manager if you have lots of data that is related to each other. This will also be identified by the general method you developed earlier.

4. Build It!

This is where Delphi comes into the picture. Delphi is the magic that makes it happen. As one of many available software construction tools, such as compilers, database managers, editors, debuggers, profilers, and so on, Delphi's job is to take your already organized thoughts, solutions, and designs, and to help you make them real.

If you start the problem-solving process with Delphi, or any compiler or design tool for that matter, before even getting through Rule #1 (Understand the Problem), then you won't get the results you want. Remember, before using Delphi, you must already have solved the problem the new software you want to create will address.

5. Quality Assurance

Quality assurance is left many times to the very end of the project. Realistically, quality should be a part of every step of the process, not just coding and testing. In the following paragraphs, I want to pass along some suggestions that have worked for me and still do.

Designing Quality into Your Software

Even though everyone who writes code does so in their own style, there are some common sense things you can do that help to reduce the number of errors and extraneous code that creeps into every project.

Remember, somebody has to maintain your project. Chances are it will be you. If you do a sloppy job, then you will be kicking yourself six months or even two years from then, when you try to figure out just what you did and why.

Comments   Many programmers dislike comments. A good friend of mine firmly believes that the code is the only documentation he ever needs. He also stays up all night with it, too.

Comments, when used properly, can enhance and explain at a glance just what is going on in the program at that point. Comments are useful, especially when you have special circumstances to deal with. For instance, the following comments actually appear in some communications software that talks to paging terminals:

```
:(*******************************************************************************
July 18, 1991

Right here we have deviation from the standard. According to the Glennaire
manual, published 1989, MOTOROLA specifications for response says that the
responding paging central can give only three types of responses after the
```

```
banner string, if any, is printed out from the terminal. They are:
<CR><ACK><CR>
<CR><NAK><CR>
<CR><ESC><EOT><CR>
They are defined as follows:
<CR><ACK><CR> - defines the acknowledgment of a successful login and to
                 proceed with the message transmission.
<CR><NAK><CR> - defines an invalid login and requests a retransmission
                 to kick paging central into automated dump or TAP mode.
<CR><ESC><EOT><CR> - defines an end of transmission sequence. Paging
                       Central is bored and wants to play with someone
                       else for a change. This is the drop dead notice.
On testing with <company deleted> NEW Glennaire system, as of January
1991, the first <CR> attached to these responses has been removed so
the response now comes on the end of the banner message. The software
will now test only for the characters that are present behind the first
<CR> had it been there. There will be more entries to follow this one
I am sure. Film at 11.
December 4, 1991
On testing with <company deleted> system, I have discovered that character
drops are a regular occurrence, so now we strip it to the actual control
character that is tested for. Neat huh?
*************************************************************************** )
```

I usually come back to this file about once every 6 to 12 months to tweak things. As the software in the paging central terminals changes, so must this software. Without comments in the files, I would be spending many, many hours trying to remember what I did.

Even though Borland's Delphi does much of the code generation for you. Well-placed comments will always enhance the clean code generated by Delphi.

Exit Points   To keep functions simpler if possible, try and limit the number of times and points in the code where a routine can be exited from. This makes your testing easier and the code more readable.

Headers   Headers are comments, but they deserve special consideration. I consider them mandatory in any coding that I do.

Headers provide a quick description as to what the file, function, or procedure does. Here is an example of a (modified from C) file header:

```
(*
*  TITLE:     JOURNAL
*
*  PURPOSE:  Routines for use with the JOURNAL
*
*  AUTHOR:    Paul S. Penrod
*
*  REVISION:
*
*  #1.04     April 7, 1991
*         1. Added zap function to clear out entire journal.
*
*  #1.03     March 9, 1991
*         1. Added flags to function save_changes()
*
*_____
*  RELEASE 1.00 January 31, 1991. All enhancements stop here for this rev.
*_____
*
*  #1.02     November 5, 1990
*         1. Removed bell() per request.
*
*  #1.01     September 13, 1990
*         1. Upgraded to VV 2.00.
*         2. Converted backdrops to shadows.
*         3. Windows now explode onto screen.
*
*  #1.00     August 1, 1990
*         1. Original Draft
*
*)
```

Every time you open a file with a header like this, you can immediately see the last change that was made and the history of modifications to the source file. For functions and procedures, you might try a header such as:

```
(*
*
*   FUNCTION:
*
*   PURPOSE:
*
*   ARGUMENTS:
*
*   CALLS:
*
*   RETURNS:
*
*   NOTES:
*
*)
```

This is useful for separating functions and procedures from each other. You will also find this header helpful when you use a program like UNIX's grep or other text scanning program, or when you use the search feature of your text editor to locate code.

Magic Numbers   *Magic numbers* are constants that show up in code. Their meaning may be obvious. Many times these numbers leave people scratching their heads. Let's look at a quick example:

```
PROCEDURE vid_write(VAR str : String)
BEGIN
  gotoXY(5,15);
  WRITELN(str);
END;
```

From the context, you can tell that 5 means column 5, and that 15 means row 15. However, in this example:

```
    tax_rate := 0.00345 * 1457.45;
```

these two numbers could be anybody's guess. However, if these numbers were defined as constants, we might see this same statement rewritten as:

```
tax_rate := IncomeTaxScale * MinimumMonthlyIncome;
```

Now we can see instantly what is happening here. Declared constants have one more advantage. If you have fixed values that are used in more than one spot, by using the constant instead, you needn't worry about whether the number was mistyped. Also, if the value changes, just change the declared constant and recompile. No need to edit numbers of files for one value.

Reusability   After constructing a few software projects, you might begin to notice that even though the applications are not related at all, the kinds of functions needed to build them are. This leaves you with the idea of *reusability*. Even if there are just a few functions that can be reused, that still saves the time to create them and debug them all over again.

In order to be reusable, functions must be generic in what they do. One of the keys to writing a good reusable function is to keep it simple, and dependencies on external factors to a minimum. The following **vid_write()** function shows an example of a generic function with no external dependencies:

```
PROCEDURE vid_write(VAR str : String row : Integer col : Integer)
BEGIN
  gotoXY(row,col);
  WRITELN(str);
END;
```

Notice that all the data necessary for **vid_write()** comes in from the outside. This means that I can call **vid_write()** from anywhere in my program and display strings of any kind of data anywhere on the screen. Here is a more dependent **vid_write()**:

```
PROCEDURE vid_write(VAR str : String)
BEGIN
  gotoXY(5,15);
```

```
      WRITELN(str);
  END;
```

Notice the statement **gotoXY(5,15)**. Now I have limited the operation of **vid_write()** to displaying any string at location 5,15 on the screen. By doing this, I have limited the use of **vid_write()** in my program to only those times I need to display a string at that screen location.

Going one step further, we have:

```
PROCEDURE vid_write()
BEGIN
  gotoXY(5,15);
  WRITELN('Video output string');
END;
```

Now **vid_write()** is specifically set to print the string '**Video output string**' at location 5,15 on the screen. This is the least reusable of the three functions, but at least they are portable.

Portability   *Portability* means just that; you can carry your code from project to project and/or from platform to platform. Designing proper functions that are not OS or machine-dependent is the ideal. The more portable a function is, generally the more reusable it can be. The least portable functions are those that are tied directly to a piece of hardware, such as a video card.

For example, to write directly to the screen in the PC environment under MS/PC-DOS, you can do the following:

```
_vid_write  proc
   push  bp      ;save the base pointer
   push  di      ;save the destination index
   push  es      ;save the extra segment register
   mov   bp,sp    ;look at the stack for arguments to the function
   mov   ax,B800h
   mov   es,ax    ;set es equal to the video memory
   mov   ax,bp+4  ;get the offset from the start of video memory
   mov   di,ax    ;save it in the destination index
   mov   ax,bp+6  ;get the character to write
```

```
 mov  es:[di],ax  ;write the character to video memory so it will display
 pop  es
 pop  di
 pop  bp     ;clean up the stack
_vid_write    endp
```

It is not important to fully understand the function; rather, the point being that it is constructed entirely in Intel 86 assembly language. This means that the function will work on PCs that use Intel 86-based CPUs and have video cards that support the B800h address in memory. Now, if we want to move this function to another type of PC, such as a Power PC or Macintosh, we would be required to rewrite the entire function to suit the needs of the new platform. A rewrite would also be required if we were to take our DOS function and move it to a new operating system, such as OS/2, UNIX, or Apple System 7.

A much more portable function written in PASCAL to send output to the screen would be:

```
PROCEDURE vid_write(VAR str : String row : Integer col : Integer)
BEGIN
    gotoXY(row,col);
    WRITELN(str);
END;
```

Notice that there are no hardware dependencies mentioned. The dependencies are handled by the library function calls **gotoXY()** and **WRITELN()**. These function calls will work for every platform (OS and/or hardware) that Borland has a PASCAL compiler for and has these functions as part of the standard library.

Testing at the Function Level

Function-level testing is the most flexible and the most critical component in development and in quality assurance. Here's why.

When you develop a function or procedure, you have in front of you a code snippet that contains, for the most part, a reasonable number of pathways through the code that need to be tested. By testing the pathways through the code now, while you can isolate it, you can eliminate many of the simple errors that become very difficult to find when you have that same function buried six calls deep, with several thousand lines of code between you and the problem.

To demonstrate how quickly you can get buried by trying to test several functions or modules at once, consider this:

Let's say we have six functions; each with three distinct pathways through the code. If you test each one separately, you have to test only 18 path combinations. However, let's say we get adventurous and want to start testing multiple functions simultaneously. Table 3.1 shows how it breaks down. As you can see, the number of combinations explodes rather quickly. To test effectively, you must develop test code for each and every procedure and function that does at least the following:

1. Test every pathway through the function/procedure.
2. Test arguments by using a range of valid values (every valid value if reasonable).
3. Test arguments by using boundary values (maximums, minimums, 0, etc.).
4. Test arguments by using a range of invalid values (error conditions).
5. Test error conditions based upon hardware, OS, or software states.

If your function/procedure passes these tests, then you can be reasonably sure that it will survive pretty much anything that any calling function may throw at it.

Table 3.1 Testing Multiple Functions

Number of Functions	Pathways	Combinations to Test
1	3	3
2	6	9
3	9	27
4	12	81
5	15	243
6	18	729

Testing at the Unit Level

Unit-level, or module, testing is the next step up in detail from function testing. Here, the function/procedure under test may be called by other functions also being tested. This provides opportunity to stress the function's/procedure's interaction in a larger environment. At this level, you do not have to test every single pathway the CPU can take through the code. The combinations can be so enormously large as to be impractical.

When designing the code for this kind of testing, try and use multiple calls to functions/procedures under test. Use return values of functions, when realistic to do so, as arguments to other functions under test. Get creative and recursively call a function with a return value as the next set of arguments if it is reasonable to do so. If these functions/procedures rely on hardware or the OS being in a certain state, create error conditions to see if they still respond the same way they did at the function level of testing.

Testing at the Environment Level

This is the more formalized testing that many people see. Essentially, the environmental test is a complete compile and run of the software product as a whole, with formalized scripts of operations to be performed. The testing can consist of one person or many, but the goal is to try every feature as a new user to see what works and what doesn't. This is a fun test to run, because the object is not only to validate all the functionality of the system, but also to break it.

Some things to try during testing are:

1. Type all sorts of random nonsense at the keyboard.
2. Try to press as many keys as your hand can cover at once.
3. Enter invalid values or data in fields that validate such data.
4. Unplug the keyboard and plug it back in.
5. Fiddle with the mouse to see if anything happens that shouldn't.
6. Unplug the mouse and plug it back in.
7. Open the floppy drive door and perform a user function that will cause a write to the disk.
8. Disconnect the printer cable during printing.

9. Disconnect the printer cable during printing and plug it back in.

10. If the operating system allows more than one task to run, switch your program into the background for a while, then switch it back.

11. Try running the application on an improperly configured machine.

The list goes on and on. Get creative in your testing. You'll have to. User's are just too darn smart. Murphy's Law says that if you test everything you can think of, a new user will find another way you had not counted on to break your software.

CHAPTER 4

Our First Project— The WIM Editor

I could spend all day discussing the ins and outs of Graphical User Interfaces (GUI), and present the various objects and components that you have at your disposal. Frankly, I would fall asleep at the keyboard trying to make a dry and detailed subject interesting and exciting. There are some things better left alone. This may be one of them. However, past experience has shown that doing things and seeing results is much more fun than sifting through mounds of paperwork trying to understand the material. So, with that in mind, let me state what we should accomplish here before we're done.

First, we will learn by doing. In this chapter we will construct an honest-to-goodness text editor that you can use to do real work. There will be features you will want to add to it, and changes you might want to make. That's good. We want to be interested in our work. It always makes for better results.

Second, we will learn by observation. As we go through the process of building our first project, the most important thing to watch for is relationships. How do all the pieces interact with each other? Why does the code look the way it does? What does the project look like as it is being constructed? Why are we doing things this way?

Third, when we are done, we will evaluate our work. Did the program we design do the task properly? Did we address all the issues surrounding the problem? Does the presentation make sense? Is there a better way to present the program to the user? I'll provide some personal observations along the way, but more importantly, you as the reader should be thinking about what we just did and how you can adapt this more closely to your own needs and use.

This may sound like a lot of work; you're right, it is. However, keep in mind that the majority of this work is done in your head or on paper before you even apply mouse to screen and hand to keyboard.

The last thing I want to say before we get started is that you don't need to worry about many of these questions here to actually build this editor. What is presented is an example that has many of these questions answered for you in the hope that it will provide a guide to help you become familiar and productive with Delphi.

Forms, Buttons, Panels, and Dialogs

Building our editor in Delphi is simple. We will be using components and objects that are already constructed for us. What does this buy us? Time, and lots of it. Let me explain.

Windows has a standardized interface of buttons, toolbars, windows, borders, dialogs, and other components that look the same from program to program. This consistency of presentation is what makes Windows programs easier to navigate for the user, and in some ways simpler to design for the programmer. However, many of these objects are not provided *ready built* by the operating system. This means that somebody has to put them together so that your program can use them. Many times this means you. Even though Windows provides the functionality to build all these wonderful presentation objects, it is not a trivial task.

To give you an idea about how much time and effort goes into building a GUI component, let's look at the issues surrounding building one of the simplest objects—a button.

What It Takes to Make a Button

In Windows, OS/2 Presentation Manager, Motif, X Windows, or any GUI for that matter, there are considerations and functionality that are generic to a display item such as a button. Here is a list of some of these items:

Display Considerations

- Are we in a toolbar or panel?
- Are we in a menu?
- Are we in the title bar?
- Are we floating in a window?
- Are we on the desktop?
- What is our top left coordinate?
- What is our width?
- What is our height?
- What is our text color?
- What is our button color?
- Are we 3D?
- IF we are 3D:
    - What is our shadow color?
    - What is our highlight color?
    - What direction do we *move* when *pushed*?
- Do we display text?
- What are the text margins for the button face?
- What kind of font do we display?
- What size of font do we display?
- What is the text we display?
- Do we display graphics (glyphs)?

- Do we display as inactive?
- Do we display as default?
- Do we display as active?
- Do we display as visible?
- Do we automatically size the button to the parent object (such as a toolbar)?
- How big is our active area on the button (*hotspot*) to recognize a mouse event?

Type Considerations

Are we a:

- SpeedButton?
- Standard button (OK, YES, NO, CANCEL, etc.)?
- Graphics button?

Function Consideration

Do we perform a function on an event, such as:

- Clicking on our active area?
- Double-clicking on our active area?
- Dragging an object over and dropping it onto our hotspot?
- Dragging an object over our hotspot?
- Ceasing to drag our button from one point on the display to another?
- Getting the *focus* (becoming the active object) in a window?
- Losing the focus in a window?
- Responding to a specified key on the keyboard being pressed and released?
- Responding to a specified key being pressed down?
- Responding to a specified key being released from a pressed condition?
- Responding to a mouse down click on our hotspot?
- Responding to a mouse up click on our hotspot?
- Responding to a mouse moving over our hotspot?

As you can see, there are a lot of questions to be answered. You may think of even more. The point is, a button is a simple object but contains a large amount of detail describing what it is and what it does. Objects that are more complicated will have many more questions and details to be dealt with. Hence, with components and objects already provided by Delphi, the time spent to figure out how to build all of these visual components can be better utilized solving the problem you were given in the first place, instead of fighting with the GUI and/or operating system.

Now, on to the fun part—creating the WIM (Wrote It Myself) Editor.

Creating the WIM Editor Interface

The first thing we must do is start Delphi (Figure 4.1). For creating the interface, we will be working primarily with the form itself and the Object Inspector. If necessary, review the chapter on Exploring the Delphi Environment to make sure you are familiar with how to get around in Delphi.

Looking at the Object Inspector (Figure 4.2), you will notice that it contains data arranged in a 3D table. The top page (by default) lists the properties of the selected object, while the back page displays the events that the object will support.

To make things simpler where appropriate, the properties and events that will be changed for each component of the form will be listed in a table. When you look at the Object Inspector for an object and you don't see a corresponding property or event entry listed in the table here or specifically mentioned, then leave the entry in the Object Inspector alone for now.

Step 1: Create a New Project

By default, if you have not been working on a project, a new one comes up. If you need to, close out an existing project and start a new one. For our WIM Editor, change the form properties as shown in Table 4.1.

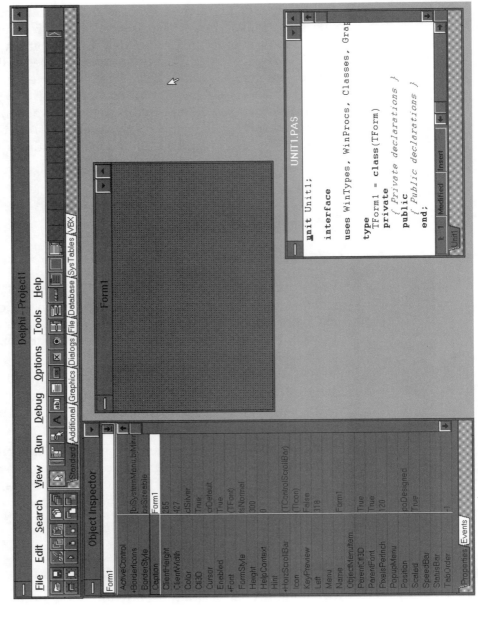

Figure 4.1
Beginning a
new project.

Figure 4.2
The Object
Inspector.

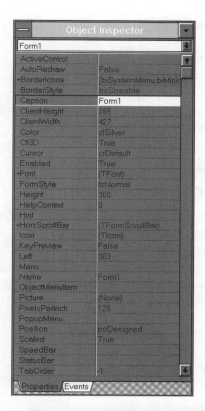

Object Inspector	
Form1	
ActiveControl	
AutoRedraw	False
+BorderIcons	[biSystemMenu,biMinir
BorderStyle	bsSizeable
Caption	Form1
ClientHeight	265
ClientWidth	427
Color	clSilver
Ctl3D	True
Cursor	crDefault
Enabled	True
+Font	(TFont)
FormStyle	fsNormal
Height	300
HelpContext	0
Hint	
+HorzScrollBar	(TFormScrollBar)
Icon	(TIcon)
KeyPreview	False
Left	303
Menu	
Name	Form1
ObjectMenuItem	
Picture	(None)
PixelsPerInch	120
PopupMenu	
Position	poDesigned
Scaled	True
SpeedBar	
StatusBar	
TabOrder	-1
Properties / Events	

Table 4.1 Properties List for Form WIMform	
Property	**Setting**
Caption	WIM Editor
ClientHeight	262
ClientWidth	418
Height	324
Left	260
Name	WIMform
Width	426

We are not quite done here yet; we still have to create a memo field.
Once we have done that, we can go back and identify it to the form
WIMform and then call it good.

Step 2: Create and Save Your Project Files

From the main menu, select **File**. From the menu selection displays, select **Save Project As** and save this project as **WIMEDIT.PRJ**. Then select **File** from the main menu, select **Save File As**, and save the source code as **EDIT.PAS**.

Step 3: Create the Main Menu for Form WIMform

On the Standard palette, double-click on the **MainMenu** button to insert a **MainMenu** component on the form.

NOTE: Double-clicking on a palette button places an iteration of the component in the center of the form. To place a component in a position other than in the center of the form, you can click once on the Component Palette, then click once again on the form in the position where you want the component to show up. Note the sizing handles (little black boxes) around the sides of the component. You can always tell which component is active on a screen by the fact that it has sizing handles. The Object Inspector displays the attributes and name of the active component as well.

In the Object Inspector, change the name of the menu to **WIMmenu**. Double-click on the **Items** property where it says **(Menu)**. This will bring up the Menu Designer (Figure 4.3).

Figure 4.3
The Menu
Designer.

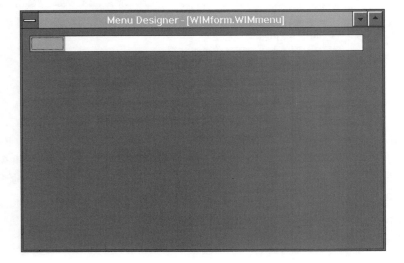

Note

You can also bring up the Menu Designer by double-clicking on the menu icon located in the WIMform.

On the Object Inspector, click on the Caption field and enter the text **&File**. Placing an ampersand (&) in front of a letter in the caption of a main menu option causes the letter to become the accelerator key for that option, meaning that when an application is running, users can press the Alt key and the accelerator key to execute the main menu item, rather than having to click on it with the mouse. Notice that the first menu item has been renamed **File**, and that a second blank menu option has been added. Another blank menu or submenu option is created whenever the current menu item is named or captioned for the first time.

Click on the Menu Designer **File** option to create a blank submenu option. Click on the blank submenu option box to activate it.

Note

You can also open a submenu option box by pressing the Enter key after entering the main menu Caption.

Click on the Caption field, enter the text **New**. The submenu item is renamed **New**.

Create four more submenu options in the same manner as you did in the previous step. Caption them, in order, **Open**, **Save**, **Delete**, and **Exit**. Your menu should now look like Figure 4.4.

Press the right arrow key, or click the mouse on the outlined area next to **File**. This is our next main menu item. Click on the Caption field and enter the text **&Edit**. Create submenu items for **Cut**, **Copy**, and **Paste**.

Press the right arrow key, or click the mouse on the outlined area next to **Edit** to create our next main menu item, **Print**. Create submenu items **Print** and **Printer Setup** beneath it.

Figure 4.4
Adding the File
Menu.

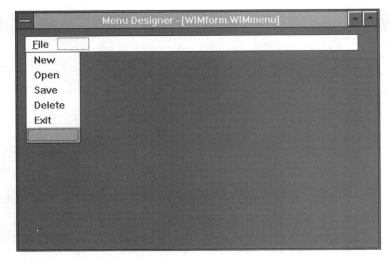

Press the right arrow key, or click the mouse on the outlined area next to **Print** to create our last main menu item, **Utility**. Create submenu items **Change Font**, **Paper Color**, **Text Color**, and **Default Colors** beneath it.

When you are done, the Menu Designer should look like Figure 4.5.

Close out the Menu Designer, and view the WIMform. The menu bar should be displayed on the form just below the title bar (Figure 4.6).

Figure 4.5
The completed
menus.

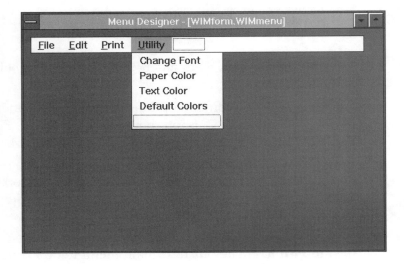

Figure 4.6
The menu is reduced to an icon.

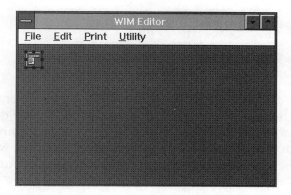

Step 4: Create a Toolbar

We want to place SpeedButtons on the form, and we're going to place them all on a panel component. Why? Well, panel components are good for organization on a form. Let's say we want to move a whole row of SpeedButtons from one side of the form to another. If they were all placed on a panel component we would have to move only the panel component, not each of the individual buttons.

So, double-click the Panel button on the Standard palette to place a panel component on the form (Figure 4.7).

Delete the text **Panel1** from the Caption field in the Object Inspector, leaving the field blank. In the Name field, rename the component **WIMbar**. In the Alignment field, select **alTop** so that the Panel will resize to the width of the Window and place itself at the top of the client workspace automatically.

Figure 4.7
Placing a new panel on a form.

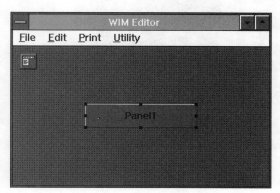

Figure 4.8
Select the
Additional tab on
the Palette menu
for a secondary
set of standard
controls.

Now we can add SpeedButtons to the panel. From the Palette menu at the top, select the Additional tab to expose the secondary set of standard controls (Figure 4.8). The object we are looking for is the button with the Lightning Bolt on it. Since we want to create nine of these on the panel, let's do this using the multiple placement mode of Delphi.

Hold down the Shift key and click on the SpeedButton. A dotted blue border will appear around the SpeedButton. Now place the mouse inside the panel component and click the left mouse button. A button will appear on the panel. Do this eight more times from left to right across the panel. When you have completed this task, click on the SpeedButton in the Component Palette to turn off multiple placement mode, then click on one of the Component Palette tabs to default back to using the mouse as a selector.

We are now ready to clean up the toolbar and make it presentable. From the Object Inspector, select each of the SpeedButtons in turn. Make the changes listed for the fields that appear in the tables for each SpeedButton (Table 4.2). This will reflect on the form and in the Object Inspector automatically. When you have completed the changes, the form should look like Figure 4.9.

Figure 4.9
The form with
SpeedButtons
added.

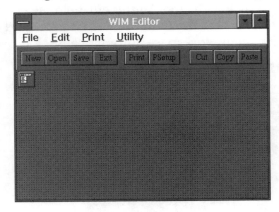

Table 4.2 Properties for the SpeedButtons

SpeedButton1

Properties	Values
Caption	New
+Font	8pt MS Serif
Left	8
Name	NewButton
Width	41

SpeedButton2

Properties	Values
Caption	Open
+Font	8pt MS Serif
Left	48
Name	OpenButton
Width	41

SpeedButton3

Properties	Values
Caption	Save
+Font	8pt MS Serif
Left	88
Name	SaveButton
Width	41

SpeedButton4

Properties	Values
Caption	Exit
+Font	8pt MS Serif
Left	128
Name	ExitButton
Width	41

SpeedButton5

Properties	Values
Caption	Print
+Font	8pt MS Serif
Left	180
Name	PrintButton
Width	41

Continued

Table 4.2 *Continued*

SpeedButton6

Properties	Values
Caption	PSetup
+Font	8pt MS Serif
Left	220
Name	PrinterSetupButton
Width	53

SpeedButton7

Properties	Values
Caption	Cut
+Font	8pt MS Serif
Left	288
Name	CutButton
Width	41

SpeedButton8

Properties	Values
Caption	Copy
+Font	8pt MS Serif
Left	328
Name	CopyButton
Width	41

SpeedButton9

Properties	Values
Caption	Paste
+Font	8pt MS Serif
Left	368
Name	PasteButton
Width	41

Step 5: Add File Dialogs

To open files for editing and save them afterward, we'll use the Open File Dialog and the Save File Dialog. Go to the Component Palette and select the Dialogs tab to expose the Dialogs toolbar. Place OpenFile and SaveFile dialog components onto the form and make the changes to each one's properties, as shown in Table 4.3.

Table 4.3 Properties for Dialogs

OpenDialog1	
Properties	*Values*
FileName	*.*
Filter All Files	(*.*) | *.*
InitialDir	C:\
Name	OpenDialog1

SaveDialog1	
Properties	*Values*
Name	SaveDialog1

Step 6: Add Printer Dialogs

Just as we open and save files with dialog components, we'll set up and use our printer the same way. From the Dialogs toolbar, place PrinterSetup and Printer dialog components on the form and make the changes to their default property values, as shown in Table 4.4.

Step 7: Add Font and Color Dialogs

Font and Color adjustments to our editor can also be run from dialog boxes. From the Dialogs toolbar on the Component Palette, place Font and Color dialogs on the form and make the changes shown in Table 4.5.

Table 4.4 Properties for a Printer

PrinterSetupDialog1	
Properties	*Values*
Name	PrinterSetupDialog1

PrintDialog1	
Properties	*Values*
Name	PrintDialog1

Table 4.5 Properties for Fonts and Colors

FontDialog1	
Properties	*Values*
Name	FontDialog1
ColorDialog1	
Properties	*Values*
Name	ColorDialog1

Step 8: Add the Memo Component

This is the last component we need before we stitch everything together. From the Standard toolbar of the Component Palette, select a Memo component, place it on the form, and make the changes to its properties listed in Table 4.6.

Step 9: Save Your Work

Now that we have everything in place (Figure 4.10), it's time to save what we have before we add code to our project. Remember to save the source file *and* the project file.

Making Everything Work

You've decorated the place, laid out the banquet, and all the guests have arrived. However, the party is pretty dead at the moment. Everyone is just standing around waiting for something to do or someone to take the lead.

Table 4.6 Properties for Memo1

Properties	*Values*
Align	alClient
BorderStyle	bsNone
ScrollBars	ssBoth
Text	(delete "Memo1")

Figure 4.10
The final
WIM Editor.

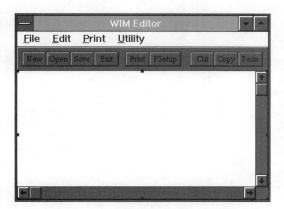

Essentially, this is what happens at this point if you try to run the editor. The menus and buttons all come up and introduce themselves, but nothing gets done. You won't see the dialog boxes at all, since they cannot be invoked directly with a mouse. The reason for this is simple. No event handling has been added to the project outside of the operating system *built-ins* that are part of Windows. Let's look at the source code that has been generated to this point and you will see why:

```
unit Edit;
interface
uses WinTypes, WinProcs, Classes, Graphics, Forms, Controls, Menus,
  StdCtrls, Buttons, CDialogs;
type
    TWIMForm = class(TForm)
    WIMmenu: TMainMenu;
    File1: TMenuItem;
    Open1: TMenuItem;
    Save1: TMenuItem;
    Delete1: TMenuItem;
    Exit1: TMenuItem;
    Edit1: TMenuItem;
    Cut1: TMenuItem;
    Copy1: TMenuItem;
    Paste1: TMenuItem;
    Print1: TMenuItem;
```

```
        Print2: TMenuItem;
        PrinterSetup1: TMenuItem;
        Utility1: TMenuItem;
        ChangeFont1: TMenuItem;
        PaperColor1: TMenuItem;
        TextColor1: TMenuItem;
        DefaultColors1: TMenuItem;
        Panel1: TPanel;
        NewButton: TSpeedButton;
        OpenButton: TSpeedButton;
        SaveButton: TSpeedButton;
        ExitButton: TSpeedButton;
        PrintButton: TSpeedButton;
        PrinterSetupButton: TSpeedButton;
        CutButton: TSpeedButton;
        CopyButton: TSpeedButton;
        PasteButton: TSpeedButton;
        OpenDialog1: TOpenDialog;
        SaveDialog1: TSaveDialog;
        PrinterSetupDialog1: TPrinterSetupDialog;
        PrintDialog1: TPrintDialog;
        FontDialog1: TFontDialog;
        ColorDialog1: TColorDialog;
        Memo1: TMemo;
private
  { Private declarations }
public
  { Public declarations }
  end;
var
  WIMForm: TWIMForm;
implementation
{$R *.FRM}
begin
  RegisterClasses([TWIMForm, TMainMenu, TMenuItem, TPanel, TSpeedButton,
 TOpenDialog, TSaveDialog, TPrinterSetupDialog, TPrintDialog,
 TFontDialog, TColorDialog, TMemo]);
  WIMForm := TWIMForm.Create(Application);
end.
```

You will notice that the vast majority of the code is nothing but declarations. Way down at the bottom, you will see that Delphi registers the various classes of components (the invitation to the party), and then creates the application space in memory to run everything (the party itself).

Let's put some life into this shindig!

Handling Events

Each of the components we are using in the WIM Editor responds to events. Events are actions that are usually generated by the user with some kind of a device, such as a keyboard or mouse. Other kinds of events can also be recognized, such as ticks of the system clock, and cause a component to take action.

Messages are the way Delphi notifies components that some action they should respond to has occurred. For example, if I place the mouse over the Open button on the toolbar, Windows keeps track of where the mouse is and sends a message to the Delphi application saying "The mouse is now located here on the screen." Delphi then takes that message and looks to see which active component owns that section of the screen. Seeing that the Open SpeedButton has control over the screen in that region, Delphi sends a message to the button saying "The mouse just got dragged over the top of you."

At this point, the Open SpeedButton decides whether it wants to do anything about it. This is where we come in. If we don't write some code for the Open SpeedButton that does something when the mouse gets dragged over the button, then nothing will happen. The same is true when we click the mouse over the button. Internally to the SpeedButton component, it will respond to the mouse click by visually pressing itself down, then back up. Even so, nothing useful beyond that really happens, since we have to provide for some kind of action to take place.

The moral of the story is that Delphi provides events for each component that lets us attach some kind of useful action (in the form of code) to the component in question. Let's continue on by using the Copy SpeedButton to demonstrate how we'll write an event handler.

Writing Our First Event Handler

From the Object Inspector, select the CopyButton component. At the bottom of the Properties List you will see a tab that says **Events**; select that.

The new events list for CopyButton now displays all the different types of events to which you can attach code (Figure 4.11). From this list, double-click the mouse on the **On Click** event. Delphi will immediately create an empty procedure for you, as shown in the following:

```
procedure TWIMForm.CopyButtonClick(Sender: TObject);
begin
end;
```

Delphi also places the declaration:

```
procedure CopyButtonClick(Sender: TObject);
```

in the **Type** section of the source code, and establishes a link to this procedure in the Object Inspector (Figure 4.12).

Now all you do is add the following code inside the procedure:

```
WIMmemo.CopyToClipboard;
```

That's all there is to it. You now have a fully functioning event handler. Here is how it looks all together:

```
procedure TWIMForm.CopyButtonClick(Sender: TObject);
begin
  Memo1.CopyToClipboard;
end;
```

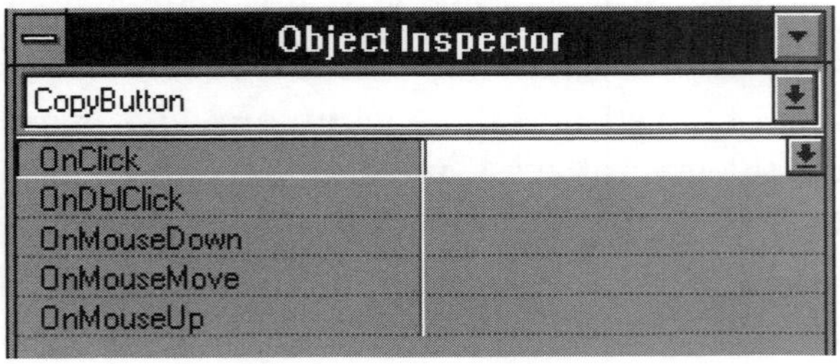

Figure 4.11
Using the Object Inspector to view the events list for CopyButton.

Figure 4.12
Linking a procedure to the CopyButton's OnClick command.

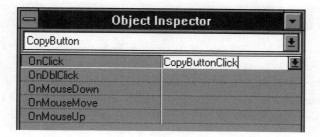

Before we can test it to see if it works right, we need to create one more event handler to paste our data that we have copied to the DDE Clipboard. To do this, select the PasteButton and double-click on the On Click event to create a procedure. Then add the following code to it:

```
Memo1.PasteFromClipboard;
```

Here is the event handler in its entirety:

```
procedure TWIMForm.PasteButtonClick(Sender: TObject);
begin
  Memo1.PasteFromClipboard;
end;
```

Now, Press the **F9** key, or select **Run** from the main menu to run the WIM Editor.

Sharing Event Handlers

As demonstrated previously, in order for an object to do something useful in Delphi, it must have an event handler attached to it. This implies that every button, menu item, or other widget should have its own event handler. While this is a reasonable method, there are many times when objects are intended to duplicate another object's functionality (as is the case here with our buttons and menu items), or the functionality of a group of objects is similar enough that you may want to share some of the code between them.

In the following section we will explore how to share a single function with two objects.

Different Events, Same Code

This is the simplest way of sharing. We'll create a single event handler and then let two objects share this one handler. Much of our code will be done this way. Let's use the Cut button and the Cut option from the Edit item on the main menu.

First we must create the handler. We do this by first selecting the CutButton from the Object Inspector, then selecting the Events tab at the bottom of the Inspector, and finally double-clicking the mouse on the On Click event line. Delphi responds by inserting a blank procedure in the source code, like so:

```
procedure TWIMForm.CutButtonClick(Sender: TObject);
begin
end;
```

Next we add the line:

```
Memo1.CutToClipboard;
```

and save the file. Our event handler looks like this:

```
procedure TWIMForm.CutButtonClick(Sender: TObject);
begin
Memo1.CutToClipboard;
end;
```

Now, we will point a second object to this handler:

1. Select the **Cut1** object from the Object Inspector. This is the **Cut** option from the **Edit** menu item located on the main menu.

2. Select the **Events** tab at the bottom of the Object Inspector to expose that list.

3. Open the drop-down menu attached to the **On Click** event item by clicking on the visible down arrow button (Figure 4.13).

4. From the list of event handlers, select **CutButtonClick**.

Figure 4.13
Accessing the drop-down menu for the OnClick event.

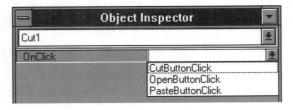

That's all there is to it. You can save your work at this point and run the WIM Editor to test this. Type in some text and mark it with the mouse. Use the **Cut** button to cut the text from the Memo object to the DDE Clipboard. Paste it back onto the memo object using the **Paste** button. Now type in some more text, mark it, and cut it to the Clipboard using the **Cut** menu item from **Edit**. Repaste it back to the memo object to verify that **Cut** did its job.

We can run through many of our event handlers this way and save ourselves time and duplicated code. Below are event handlers for the **New**, **Open**, **Save**, **Exit**, **Print**, and **PSetup** buttons. Create these event handlers and attach the corresponding menu items to them. Remember to attach the **Copy** and **Paste** menu items to the **Copy** and **Paste** buttons, since we have already created those handlers.

Before you enter these handlers, there are three new items that must be placed in the source file to make the procedures run:

1. In the *private* section of the source code, enter the following declaration:

   ```
   FileName:  string;
   ```

2. In the *implementation* section of the source code (just before the first procedure), enter the following constant declaration:

   ```
   const
     DefaultFile = 'NONAME.TXT'
   ```

3. Add **Printers** to the *uses* clause at the top of the source file.

Here are the event handlers:

For the **New** Button:

```
procedure TWIMForm.NewButtonClick(Sender: TObject);
begin
  if Memo1.Modified then SaveButtonClick(Sender);
  Memo1.SelectAll;
  Memo1.ClearSelection;
  Filename := DefaultFile;
  Caption := Filename;
  Memo1.SelStart := 0;
end;
```

For the **Open** Button:

```
procedure TWIMForm.OpenButtonClick(Sender: TObject);
begin
  if Memo1.Modified then SaveButtonClick(Sender);
  if OpenDialog1.Execute then
  begin
    FileName := OpenDialog1.FileName;
    Memo1.Lines.LoadFromFile(FileName);
    Memo1.SelStart := 0;
    Caption := ExtractFileName(FileName);
    Memo1.Modified := False;
  end;
end;
```

For the **Save** Button:

```
procedure TWIMForm.SaveButtonClick(Sender: TObject);
begin
  SaveDialog1.Filename := FileName;
  if SaveDialog1.Execute = True then
  begin
    FileName := SaveDialog1.FileName;
    Caption := ExtractFileName(FileName);
    Memo1.Lines.SaveToFile(FileName);
    Memo1.Modified := False;
  end;
end;
```

For the **Exit** Button:

```
procedure TWIMForm.ExitButtonClick(Sender: TObject);
begin
  if Memo1.Modified then SaveButtonClick(Sender);
  Close;
end;
```

For the **Print** Button:

```
procedure TWIMForm.PrintButtonClick(Sender: TObject);
var
  LineNumber:  Integer;
  PrintText:   System.Text;
begin
  if PrintDialog1.Execute then
  begin
    AssignPrn(PrintText);
    Rewrite(PrintText);
    Printer.Canvas.Font := Memo1.Font;
    for LineNumber := 0 to Memo1.Lines.Count -1 do
      Writeln(PrintText, Memo1.Lines[LineNumber]);
    System.Close(PrintText);
  end;
end;
```

For the **PSetup** Button:

```
procedure TWIMForm.PrinterSetupButtonClick(Sender: TObject);
begin
  PrinterSetupDialog1.Execute;
end;
```

Picking Up the Loose Ends

We are almost done with the WIM Editor but there are still a few loose ends to deal with, especially in the **Utility** section of the main menu and the **Delete** function locate under **File**. Here are the rest of the event handlers:

For the **Delete1** menu item:

```
procedure TWIMForm.Delete1Click(Sender: TObject);
begin
  Memo1.ClearSelection;
end;
```

For the **ChangeFont1** menu item:

```
procedure TWIMForm.ChangeFont1Click(Sender: TObject);
```

```
begin
  FontDialog1.Font := Memo1.Font;
  if FOntDialog1.Execute then Memo1.Font := FontDialog1.Font;
end;
```

For the **PaperColor1** menu item:

```
procedure TWIMForm.PaperColor1Click(Sender: TObject);
begin
  if ColorDialog1.Execute then
    Memo1.Color := ColorDialog1.Color;
end;
```

For the **TextColor1** menu item:

```
procedure TWIMForm.TextColor1Click(Sender: TObject);
begin
  If ColorDialog1.Execute then
    Memo1.Font.Color := ColorDialog1.Color;
end;
```

For the **DefaultColors1** menu item:

```
procedure TWIMForm.DefaultColors1Click(Sender: TObject);
begin
  Memo1.Color := clWindow;
  Memo1.Font.Color := clWindowText;
end;
```

Now that you have all the event handlers in place, save the project and source files, then run WIM Editor to see how everything works.

All Together Now

Once you are satisfied that all the buttons and menu items work, it is always a good idea to clean up the source code with notations and comments about things so that you can come back later and remember what you did, especially if you want to make changes or additions later on. Here is a sample commented listing of the WIM

Editor source file:

```
{
*
*   Program:  EDIT.PAS
*
*   Purpose:  Main Program file.
*
*   Author:  Paul S. Penrod
*
*   Revision:
*
*   #1.00  Original Draft
*
}
{
*
*   Dependancies…
*
}
unit Edit;
interface
uses WinTypes, WinProcs, Classes, Graphics, Forms, Controls,
Menus,StdCtrls, Buttons, CDialogs, Clipbrd;
{
*
*   Types…
*
}
type
    TWIMForm = class(TForm)
    WIMmenu: TMainMenu;
    File1: TMenuItem;
    Open1: TMenuItem;
    Save1: TMenuItem;
    Delete1: TMenuItem;
    Exit1: TMenuItem;
    Edit1: TMenuItem;
```

```
Cut1: TMenuItem;
Copy1: TMenuItem;
Paste1: TMenuItem;
Print1: TMenuItem;
Print2: TMenuItem;
PrinterSetup1: TMenuItem;
Utility1: TMenuItem;
ChangeFont1: TMenuItem;
PaperColor1: TMenuItem;
TextColor1: TMenuItem;
DefaultColors1: TMenuItem;
Panel1: TPanel;
NewButton: TSpeedButton;
OpenButton: TSpeedButton;
SaveButton: TSpeedButton;
ExitButton: TSpeedButton;
PrintButton: TSpeedButton;
PrinterSetupButton: TSpeedButton;
CutButton: TSpeedButton;
CopyButton: TSpeedButton;
PasteButton: TSpeedButton;
OpenDialog1: TOpenDialog;
SaveDialog1: TSaveDialog;
PrinterSetupDialog1: TPrinterSetupDialog;
PrintDialog1: TPrintDialog;
FontDialog1: TFontDialog;
ColorDialog1: TColorDialog;
Memo1: TMemo;
procedure OpenButtonClick(Sender: TObject);
procedure PasteButtonClick(Sender: TObject);
procedure CutButtonClick(Sender: TObject);
procedure NewButtonClick(Sender: TObject);
procedure SaveButtonClick(Sender: TObject);
procedure CopyButtonClick(Sender: TObject);
procedure ExitButtonClick(Sender: TObject);
procedure PrintButtonClick(Sender: TObject);
procedure PrinterSetupButtonClick(Sender: TObject);
```

```pascal
    procedure Delete1Click(Sender: TObject);
    procedure ChangeFont1Click(Sender: TObject);
    procedure PaperColor1Click(Sender: TObject);
    procedure TextColor1Click(Sender: TObject);
    procedure DefaultColors1Click(Sender: TObject);
  private
    { Private declarations }
    FileName:  string;
  public
    { Public declarations }
  end;
var
  WIMForm: TWIMForm;
implementation
{$R *.FRM}
const
    DefaultFile = 'NONAME.TXT';
{
*   Procedure:  CopyButtonClick
*
*   Purpose:    Copy Selected Memo data to clipboard.
*
*   Arguments:  Sender: TObject
*
*   Calls:      none.
*
*   Returns:    none.
*
*   Notes:      none.
*
}
procedure TWIMForm.CopyButtonClick(Sender: TObject);
begin
    Memo1.CopyToClipboard;
end;

{
```

```
*   Procedure:   PasteButtonClick
*
*   Purpose:     Paste data from clipboard to Memo.
*
*   Arguments:   Sender: TObject
*
*   Calls:       none.
*
*   Returns:     none.
*
*   Notes:       none.
*
}
procedure TWIMForm.PasteButtonClick(Sender: TObject);
begin
  Memo1.PasteFromClipboard;
end;
{
*   Procedure:   CutButtonClick
*
*   Purpose:     Cut Selected Memo data to clipboard.
*
*   Arguments:   Sender: TObject
*
*   Calls:       none.
*
*   Returns:     none.
*
*   Notes:       none.
*
}
procedure TWIMForm.CutButtonClick(Sender: TObject);
begin
  Memo1.CutToClipboard;
end;
{
*   Procedure:   NewButtonClick
```

```
*
*  Purpose:    Create a new blank data file to edit.
*
*  Arguments:  Sender: TObject
*
*  Calls:      none.
*
*  Returns:    none.
*
*  Notes:
*
```

This procedure does the following:

1. Check to see if the text in our memo object has been modified. This condition accounts for an existing edit that is currently in WIM Editor.
2. If it has, then call SaveButtonClick and give the user a chance to save his or her work.

Now to the fun stuff...

3. Select all the text in the memo.
4. Blow it away.
5. Set our internal filename to the default filename.
6. Set our caption to the internal filename.
7. And finally, put the cursor to the top of the memo object.

```
}
procedure TWIMForm.NewButtonClick(Sender: TObject);
begin
  if Memo1.Modified then SaveButtonClick(Sender);
  Memo1.SelectAll;
  Memo1.ClearSelection;
  Filename := DefaultFile;
  Caption := Filename;
  Memo1.SelStart := 0;
end;
{
*  Procedure:  OpenButtonClick
```

```
 *
 *  Purpose:     Open an existing data file.
 *
 *  Arguments:   Sender: TObject
 *
 *  Calls:      none.
 *
 *  Returns:     none.
 *
 *  Notes:
 *
```

This procedure does the following:

1. Check to see if the text in our memo object has been modified. This condition accounts for an existing edit that is currently in WIM Editor.
2. If it has, then call SaveButtonClick and give the user a chance
to save his work.
3. Run the open dialog box and let the user play with it for a
while.
4. When the user is done, check the return value to see if the
user was really serious about loading a file.
5. If the return value is TRUE, then:
a. Go get the selected filename and store it internally.
b. Load the file from disk into the memo object.
c. Set the cursor to the top of the memo object.
d. Change our caption to show the new filename.
e. Set the memo modified flag to FALSE.

```
}
procedure TWIMForm.OpenButtonClick(Sender: TObject);
begin
  if Memo1.Modified then SaveButtonClick(Sender);
  if OpenDialog1.Execute then
  begin
    FileName := OpenDialog1.FileName;
    Memo1.Lines.LoadFromFile(FileName);
```

```
      Memo1.SelStart := 0;
      Caption := ExtractFileName(FileName);
      Memo1.Modified := False;
    end;
end;
{
*  Procedure:  SaveButtonClick
*
*  Purpose:    Run Save Dialog to save edits to disk.
*
*  Arguments:  Sender: TObject
*
*  Calls:      none.
*
*  Returns:    none.
*
*  Notes:      none.
*
```

This procedure does the following:

1. Sets the SaveDialog to the name of the file being edited.
2. Let the user save the file if he wants to.

    User decides to save file:

    a. Set our internal file name variable to the name selected by the user through the Save dialog.

    b. Set the Window Caption to the selected file name.

    c. Save the file to disk.

    d. Reset the memo object to indicate that no changes have been made, since we have already saved what changes we did make.

User decides not to save file:

3. Do nothing.

```
    }
    procedure TWIMForm.SaveButtonClick(Sender: TObject);
    begin
      SaveDialog1.Filename := FileName;
      if SaveDialog1.Execute = True then
```

```
       begin
         FileName := SaveDialog1.FileName;
         Caption := ExtractFileName(FileName);
         Memo1.Lines.SaveToFile(FileName);
         Memo1.Modified := False;
       end;
    end;


    {
    *   Procedure:   ExitButtonClick
    *
    *   Purpose:     Close out program execution.
    *
    *   Arguments:   Sender: TObject
    *
    *   Calls:       none.
    *
    *   Returns:     none.
    *
    *   Notes:
    *
```

This procedure does the following:

If we have made any unsaved changes to the data in the memo object, then call the SaveButtonClick procedure to give the user an opportunity to save his work. Otherwise, just exit.

```
}
procedure TWIMForm.ExitButtonClick(Sender: TObject);
begin
  if Memo1.Modified then SaveButtonClick(Sender);
  Close;
end;
{
*   Procedure:   PrintButtonClick
*
*   Purpose:     Print data in memo object to printer.
*
```

```
*    Arguments:  Sender: TObject
*
*    Calls:      AssignPrn, Rewrite, Writeln
*
*    Returns:    none.
*
*    Notes:
*
```

This procedure does the following:

1. Run the Print dialog so the user can select a printer.
2. Setup the printer variable.
3. Hand off the memo display font to the printer so the output looks like what's displayed in the memo object.
4. Print the data line by line to the printer.
5. Close the printer variable.

```
}
procedure TWIMForm.PrintButtonClick(Sender: TObject);
var
  LineNumber:  Integer;
  PrintText:  Text;
begin
  if PrintDialog1.Execute then
  begin
    AssignPrn(PrintText);
    Rewrite(PrintText);
    Printer.Canvas.Font := Memo1.Font;
    for LineNumber := 0 to Memo1.Lines.Count -1 do
      Writeln(PrintText, Memo1.Lines[LineNumber]);
    System.Close(PrintText);
  end;
end;
{
*  Procedure:  PrinterSetupButtonClick
*
*  Purpose:    Uses PrinterSetup dialog to select printer.
```

```
*
*   Arguments:   Sender: TObject
*
*   Calls:      none.
*
*   Returns:     none.
*
*   Notes:      none.
*
}
procedure TWIMForm.PrinterSetupButtonClick(Sender: TObject);
begin
   PrinterSetupDialog1.Execute;
end;
{
*   Procedure:   Delete1Click
*
*   Purpose:    Clear section of text in memo that is marked.
*
*   Arguments:   Sender: TObject
*
*   Calls:      none.
*
*   Returns:     none.
*
*   Notes:      none.
*
}
procedure TWIMForm.Delete1Click(Sender: TObject);
begin
   Memo1.ClearSelection;
end;
{
*   Procedure:   ChangeFont1Click
*
*   Purpose:    Use Font dialog to change memo display font.
*
```

```
*   Arguments:  Sender: TObject
*
*   Calls:      none.
*
*   Returns:    none.
*
*   Notes:      none.
*
}
procedure TWIMForm.ChangeFont1Click(Sender: TObject);
begin
  FontDialog1.Font := Memo1.Font;
  if FontDialog1.Execute then Memo1.Font := FontDialog1.Font;
end;
{
*   Procedure:  PaperColor1Click
*
*   Purpose:    Use Color dialog to change memo background.
*
*   Arguments:  Sender: TObject
*
*   Calls:      none.
*
*   Returns:    none.
*
*   Notes:      none.
*
}
procedure TWIMForm.PaperColor1Click(Sender: TObject);
begin
  if ColorDialog1.Execute then
    Memo1.Color := ColorDialog1.Color;
end;
{
*   Procedure:  TextColor1Click
*
*   Purpose:    Use Color dialog to change memo font color.
```

```
*
*   Arguments:   Sender: TObject
*
*   Calls:      none.
*
*   Returns:     none.
*
*   Notes:      none.
*
}
procedure TWIMForm.TextColor1Click(Sender: TObject);
begin
  If ColorDialog1.Execute then
    Memo1.Font.Color := ColorDialog1.Color;
end;
{
*   Procedure:   DefaultColors1Click
*
*   Purpose:     Restore original color settings.
*
*   Arguments:   Sender: TObject
*
*   Calls:      none.
*
*   Returns:     none.
*
*   Notes:      none.
*
}
procedure TWIMForm.DefaultColors1Click(Sender: TObject);
begin
  Memo1.Color := clWindow;
  Memo1.Font.Color := clWindowText;
end;
{
*   Procedure:  N/A
*
*   Purpose:     We start here…
*
```

```
*   Arguments:   none.
*
*   Calls:       none.
*
*   Returns:     none.
*
*   Notes:       none.
*
}
begin
  RegisterClasses([TWIMForm, TMainMenu, TMenuItem, TPanel, TSpeedButton,
  TOpenDialog, TSaveDialog, TPrinterSetupDialog, TPrintDialog,
  TFontDialog, TColorDialog, TMemo]);
  WIMForm := TWIMForm.Create(Application);
end.
```

Additions and Improvements

While we have a functioning editor that lets us open files, create new ones, save files, print files, and change our presentation, there are a couple of changes that would make things easier.

Passing Arguments to the WIM Editor

One of the nice features in Windows is the use of icons to represent executable files and data. With the ability to pass a data file to the WIM Editor on the command line, you could create a copy of the WIM Editor icon and modify the Properties list so that it would launch and open a specific file each time for that icon.

To do that you must add the code to let WIM Editor see the command line. It looks something like this:

```
procedure StartUp;
begin
  if ParamCount = 0 then
  begin
    WIMform.FileName := DefaultFile;
    WIMform.Memo1.SelStart := 0;
  end
```

```
  else
  begin
    WIMform.FileName := ParamStr(1);
    WIMform.Memo1.Lines.LoadFromFile(WIMform.FileName);
    WIMform.Caption := ExtractFileName(WIMform.FileName);
    WIMform.Memo1.Modified := False;
    WIMform.Memo1.SelStart := 0;
  end;
end;
```

Once you have created this procedure, be sure to declare it in the types section. You can then call it from the main procedure block, like so:

```
begin
  RegisterClasses([TWIMForm, TMainMenu, TMenuItem, TPanel,
TSpeedButton,
    TOpenDialog, TSaveDialog, TPrinterSetupDialog, TPrintDialog,
    TFontDialog, TColorDialog, TMemo]);
  WIMForm := TWIMForm.Create(Application);
{
    Place the call right after the Create method, otherwise there
will be nothing for StartUp to work with.
}
    StartUp;
end.
```

Preserving Current Position and Display Settings

While not necessary to use WIM Editor, it is a real convenience to be able to have the editor appear in the same manner and place as the last time you used it. Delphi allows you to modify many object settings at runtime. Creating a configuration file allows you to save your current settings on exit so that you can reconfigure the editor automatically on startup. Some sample code to show how to change properties at runtime would look like this:

```
  WIMform.Height := FormHeight;
```

```
WIMform.Width := FormWidth;

WIMform.Left := FormLeft;

WIMform.Top := FormTop;

WIMform.ClientHeight := FormCHeight;

WIMform.ClientWidth := FormCWidth;

WIMform.PixelsPerInch := FormPPI;

WIMform.JAFEmemo.Color := FormColor;

WIMform.JAFEmemo.Font.Color := FontColor;
```

You can find these settings in the Properties section of the Object Inspector for the object in question (in this case, the Form and Memo objects). You can also locate properties in the sections of Delphi where these objects are declared.

Conclusion

There are many different ways in which WIM Editor could be modified to be more robust in error handling, or providing more features. The point of this first project was to get your feet wet and do something useful at the same time. The program was kept simple so that you could see how things fit together. For our next project, we will take what we have learned here and build a more powerful editor that makes up for some of what WIM Editor lacks, through the use of Multiple Document Interface (MDI) windows.

Project 2: Improving the WIM Editor with MDI

In the previous chapter, we built the WIM Editor, and now have a working program. In retrospect, there are some shortcomings that should be addressed. For the purposes of this chapter, in particular, there are three that stand out:

- Program size relative to screen resolution
- Only one document can be open at a time
- Printing should be formatted

We'll address the size problem up front when we build our new editor, but first we need to deal with handling multiple files.

What Is MDI?

MDI (Multiple Document Interface) is a means whereby you can use a single Window to contain other windows to display more

Figure 5.1
The WIM MDI
Editor.

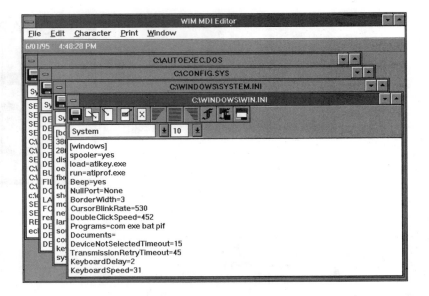

than one file. Think of it as your program's own personal Program Manager, with each Window inside being an active program. One of the side benefits of this way of presenting documents is that you can group child documents (displayed in a cascade or tiled in the parent window) and/or quickly maneuver between all of them with the touch of the mouse. Close down a window and it reduces to an icon with the filename attached, tucked away at the bottom of the parent window. You can then reopen it at any time by double-clicking on the icon (Figure 5.1).

Besides the visual grouping, an MDI-based application provides a convenient way to exchange data between open documents that share its common workspace. This becomes very important when you have many open files and you want to cut and paste between them. MDI just makes it easier. Here is a look at what we are going to build. Let's get to work.

Creating the WIM MDI Interface

Unlike the WIM Editor, we will work not only with the Object Inspector, but also with the BitMap Editor to create glyphs and icons for this project.

To make things simpler in creating objects for our editor, where appropriate, the properties and events that will be changed for each component of the form will be listed in a table. When you look at the Object Inspector for an object and you don't see a corresponding property or event entry listed in the table here or specifically mentioned, then leave the entry in the Object Inspector alone for now. In the case of glyphs for the SpeedButtons, we will come back and add them later in the chapter.

Each section is presented fairly self-contained, but there is a certain amount of skipping around that you can do as you become more familiar with how Delphi works. There are only a few of the components that must have other components exist on the form first before they can be made to work together, so there is some latitude as to how you can approach building this version of the WIM Editor. Another reason I chose to do this chapter differently is to present some of the components in such a way that demonstrating their use will help foster ideas on how to make them work in your own projects, or let you use them as mini-lessons on one particular aspect of Delphi. This chapter is by no means comprehensive but should give you a good grounding that can be extended to those components not covered here.

Now, on to the foundation of the program.

Forms

In the previous chapter, we embarked by starting a new project and working with the new form that was displayed. We'll do the same thing here but with a twist—using two forms: one for the parent window, and the second as a template for child documents that will be opened at runtime.

To start the WIM MDI project:

1. Start a New Project.
2. Change the **Caption** property from **Form1** to **WIM MDI Editor**.
3. Change the **FormStyle** property from **fsNormal** to **fsMDIform**.
4. Change the Name property from **Form1** to **Frame**.
5. Save the project as **WIMMDI**, and the **UNIT1** Pascal source file as **MAIN.PAS** (See Figure 5.2).

Figure 5.2
The saved
project.

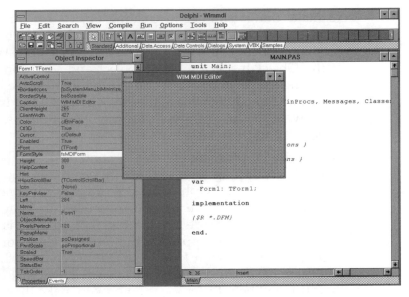

6. Add a new form to the project by selecting **New Form** from Delphi's **File** menu.

7. Select **Blank Form** from the Browse Gallery window (Figure 5.3), as we want to work with just a raw form.

8. If you look at the source code window, you will notice a new page has been added to it titled **UNIT1**. Save this new source file as **MDICHILD.PAS** by selecting **Save File As** from Delphi's File menu. The tab in the source window will update to show the new filename.

Figure 5.3
Selecting a form
from the
Browse Gallery.

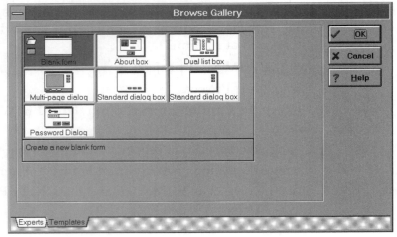

9. Select the new **Form1** form displayed on the screen and change the **FormStyle** property from **fsNormal** to **fsMDIChild**. Change the Name property from **Form1** to **Child**. Also delete **Child** from the **Caption** property.

Note

In creating an MDI application, you must have one form specified as **fsMDIform** to signify it as the parent MDI frame. This should be the form you will designate as your main program form. If you experiment, you will discover that you can set any of the forms you have assigned to a project to be the parent MDI frame. You will also find that your program may not compile properly or run right either.

10. Save the project at this point. It should look something like Figure 5.4.

Now, for the first zinger of the day. If you look at the source code contained in both **MAIN** and **MDICHILD**, you will see references to themselves, but not each other. By design, each *page* of code (unit) within Delphi is set up to identify and take

Figure 5.4
The saved
project, so far.

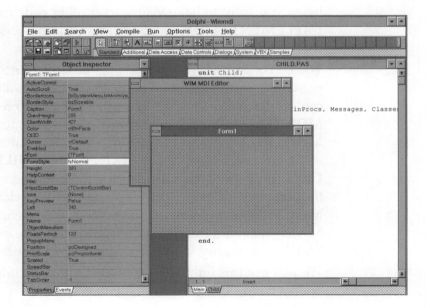

care of the various components that make up the form (object). This creates a self-contained unit of code that addresses the form object and its internal component's display and behavior. The unit code does not know about any other object outside of what it has already identified internally to itself. So, in order to give our form the *vision* to see other objects out in the world, we need to add references so that **MAIN** and **MDICHILD** can get access to each other.

To do this (at least for this MDI application), add **MDICHILD** to the **USES** clause in the **interface section** of **MAIN**. Then add a **USES** clause to **MDICHILD** in the **implementation section**. It should look something like:

```
implementation
uses main;
{$R *.DFM}
end.
```

Here's why we do it this way: Inside the Turbo Pascal unit, there are two sections, **INTERFACE** and **IMPLEMENTATION**. Each one provides a different kind of visibility. The **INTERFACE** section contains public declarations—those items you want to have visible to another code unit. The **IMPLEMENTATION** section is private and is visible only to code within the unit itself.

The **USES** clause is roughly analogous to the **#include** statement in C. It provides the link to another code unit so that we can resolve references. When we include the reference to **MDICHILD** in **MAIN**'s use clause, we are able to *see* into **MDICHILD.PAS** and access functions, procedures, and variables. However, if we added **MAIN** to **MDICHILD**'s interface **USES** clause, we would be creating a circular reference which the compiler will choke on. By placing a **USES** clause in **MDICHILD**'s **implementation section** to reference back to **MAIN**, we avoid the circular reference and give ourselves the back link necessary to call procedures and functions in **MAIN**.

We will use this link later on when we attach code to create or open a child document from the main menu.

11. First of the three problems: We want to automatically size the parent window to account for changing display resolutions (i.e., 640×480, 800×600, 1024×768, etc.). It can be really annoying to have to resize your program windows every time you change display resolutions. What we want to do here is force the initial size of the parent MDI window to scale to the resolution of the screen. From there, we can push it around however we want.

How we are going to do this is rather simple. We will create an event handler that will be called when the parent window form is activated. Then we will look at the screen object and see how many pixels up and down we have to play with, and adjust the size and offset of the parent window, accordingly.

Select the **MAIN** unit in the source window. Create a procedure called **StartUp**, as follows:

In the **INTERFACE** section, enter the following line at the end of the **TYPE** declaration:

```
procedure StartUp(Sender: TOBject);
```

Your code in this section should look something like this:

```
interface
uses
   SysUtils, WinTypes, WinProcs, Messages, Classes, Graphics,
Controls, Forms, Dialogs;
type
  TFrame = class(TForm)
  procedure StartUp(Sender: TOBject);
private
  { Private declarations }
public
  { Public declarations }
end;
```

Normally, a procedure not attached to any object would be declared in the **PUBLIC** or **PRIVATE** sections of **INTERFACE**. By placing the declaration here after **TYPE**, the procedure becomes one of the functional components of the object **TFrame**. It is still visible to the outside because of the public declaration, but in this case it has an owner. So in order to call it from outside the **MAIN** unit, you would address it this way:

```
Frame.StartUp(Sender);
```

Internally from the **IMPLEMENTATION** section, you would call it this way:

```
StartUp(Sender);
```

In the **IMPLEMENTATION** section, enter the following code:

```
procedure TFrame.StartUp(Sender: TOBject);
begin

  Height := Round(Screen.Height * 0.9);
  Width  := Round(Screen.Width * 0.9);
  Left   := Round(Screen.Width * 0.05);
  Top    := Round(Screen.Height * 0.05);
end;
```

Some explanation is in order: Since this procedure is now part of the object **Frame**, it has access to data that is part of **Frame**. The variables, **Height**, **Width**, **Left**, and **Top**, are part of **Frame**'s dataset and correspond to the entries found in the Object Inspector. Changing these values at runtime is the same as changing them during design; the form responds accordingly. We could continue on and extend these modifications at runtime by changing fonts, color, form style, cursors, and so on.

Once you have finished writing this handler, point the Object Inspector to **Frame** and select the **Events** page. Click on **OnCreate** and select **StartUp** (it will be the only menu item there). This now hooks the handler you have just written into

Frame so that each time the WIM Editor is started and **Frame** is activated, **StartUp** will run.

For now, we will leave this procedure alone, but not forgotten. We will need to come back to it later.

Menus

With both forms established, and a link between code modules, we are ready to set up the menus for both parent and child forms. Once we have menus configured for both the parent MDI form and the child template, we'll use some nifty sleight of hand to merge the two menus so that we have only one main menu to deal with in the parent window.

1. From the Component palette, place a Menu component on the **Frame** form, and double-click on the icon to bring up the Menu Editor.

   Create two main menu items, **File** and **Window**, and then add the subitems listed in Table 5.1. Enter the names as you see them into the Tmenuitem **Caption** property in the Object Inspector.

Table 5.1 The File and Window Main Menu Items and Subitems

&File	&Window
&New	&Tile
&Open	&Cascade
E&xit	&Arrange Icons

2. From the Component palette, place a Menu component on the **Child** form, and double-click on the icon to bring up the Menu Editor.

   This time, create four menu items, **File**, **Edit**, **Character**, and **Print**, and then add the subitems listed in Table 5.2. Enter the names as you see them into the Tmenuitem **Caption** property in the Object Inspector.

Figure 5.5
The forms for
your project.

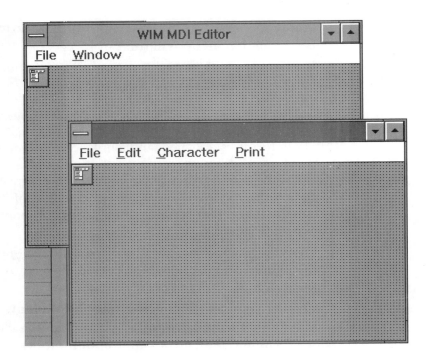

Table 5.2 Four Menu Items and Their Subitems

&File	&Edit	&Character	&Print
&New	Cu&t	Left	&Print
&Open	&Copy	&Right	Print &Setup
&Save	&Paste	&Center	
Save &As	&Delete	&Font	
E&xit	&Select All	&Word Wrap	

3. Save the project at this point. Your forms should look something like Figure 5.5.

The Magic of Merging Menus

For the most part, MDI child windows do not sport their own menus. But, when they do, they often interact with the parent's main menu. The best way to eliminate confusion as to which **File** option to select from the six or so showing on the application is to merge the menus into the parent's main menu, leaving just one showing. This is much easier to cope with.

In our case, once the WIM Editor is started, we will see the menu we created for the **Frame** form. However, once we have a child window active with a new or opened file, the **Frame** menu shifts and we see the other items and options that we created for the form **Child**. Once all child windows are gone, the **Frame** menu reverts back to its original form.

This sleight of hand is accomplished by two very important properties of the **MainMenu1** objects we have created for both forms: **AutoMerge** and **GroupIndex**.

AutoMerge determines the direction that menu items will merge. If a menu's AutoMerge property is set to True, then its menu items will merge into another menu. If the value is **False**, then another menu will have to merge into it.

For our MDI application (and for all MDI and OLE applications, according to Borland), the **AutoMerge** property of the parent form's menu must be set to **False** to force other menus to merge into it. Since the parent menu will be receiving menu items, we also need to set the **Child** form's **AutoMerge** property to **True**, so it will hand off its items to **Frame**'s menu.

To do this, click on the menu object icon within each form, select **AutoMerge**, and set it to the correct value.

Okay, so the menus merge, but that's only half the story. Once we get all these new menu items, we must put them somewhere and resolve what we do when we get multiples of an item. This is where **GroupIndex** comes in.

GroupIndex is just that, an index. This menu property tells Delphi where to place menu items on the shared menu bar, and in what order. Counting starts with zero (0). This places the menu item in the left-most position on the menu bar. If two items have the same index, then the one being shared can overlay the original. This is what will happen in our case. Notice that both **Frame** and **Child** forms have a **File** menu item. This is no accident. We want **Child**'s **File** menu items to overlay **Frame**'s when there is a file being edited. **Frame**'s reappears when there are no **Child** windows present. This still leaves us with the ability to create a new file, open an existing one, or exit the program.

Invoke the Menu Editor for each form and set the indexes as shown in Table 5.3.

Table 5.3 Group Index Settings			
Frame Menu		**Child Menu**	
Menu Title	*Group Index*	*Menu Title*	*Group Index*
&File	0	&File	0
&Window	9	&Edit	1
		&Character	1
		&Print	1

Now that we have the menus ready to go, we are just lacking one thing to make everything play: event handlers!

Event Handlers: The Muscle in Menu Motion

We've spent quite a bit of time moving this, changing that, and plugging everything together. One problem—if we run the program right now, we would get only the **Frame** form with a menu that did nothing but let you select options. Adding event handlers to each of the menu items lets us get productive real fast.

But first, we need to add two things to the **Child** form—a panel for our **SpeedButtons**, **combo boxes**, a **check box** to come later, and a **memo** item. The **panel** is strictly for show, but it needs to be installed before the **memo** item, as we'll see in a minute.

The **memo** is our workhorse component. This one object will be the focus of much poking, prodding, loading, and saving of data from all the other objects that make up the **Child** form. In fact, most of the event handlers depend on it being there, so better to put it in now so that we can test things as we go along, rather than take it on faith that our code will work first time out.

First, grab a panel off the Component palette and place it on the **Child** form. Make the following **Panel** property changes:

Align	alTop
Caption	<none>
Height	73

Once that is completed, place a **memo** component from the palette onto the **Child** form. Delete the text located in the **Text** property and change the **Align** property to **alClient**.

With these components in place, we are ready to finish our work on the **Frame** form. We'll come back to our panel on the **Child** form later to fill it in.

1. Select the **MDICHILD** unit from the source code window and enter the following procedure:

```
procedure TChild.ParseFile(const path: string);
begin

  fullpath := path;
  filename := ExtractFileName(path);
  extension := ExtractFileExt(path);
  directory := ExtractFilePath(path);
  backup := ChangeFileExt(filename,BackupExt);
end;
```

Be sure to register this procedure in the **INTERFACE** section under **TYPE**.

ParseFile is a generic procedure that will get called from several different places. Its main purpose is to stuff these local strings with a filename, file extension, directory path, and a backup filename. Once these strings are made current, other functions will use them to display the filename on the title bar, load the file, save the file, create a back up, and so on. It's small but important.

2. Add the following variables and constants to **MDICHILD**:

In the **PRIVATE** section:

```
fullpath:  string;
Filename:  string;
Extension:  string;
Directory:  string;
backup:  string;
```

Create a **CONST** section for:

```
BackupExt = '.BAK';
CloseText = 'Save Changes to ';
```

3. Now, it's time to return to **MAIN**. Select **MAIN** in the source window. We will go down the list of menu items that must be dealt with, and provide something for them to do.

   In the **INTERFACE** section under **VAR**, make an entry for the global variable **NewDoc** as an Integer. Then create a **CONST** section and create the constant **DefaultTitle**. Assign it the string "**DOCUMENT**". When you are done, it should look something like this:

```
var

  Frame: TFrame;
  NewDoc: Integer;
const
  DefaultTitle = 'DOCUMENT';
```

Select the **New** option from **Frame**'s main menu. Enter the following for **New1Click**:

```
procedure TFrame.New1Click(Sender: TObject);
var
  Child: TChild;
  title: array [0..12] of Char;
  S: array [0..12] of Char;
begin
  if NewDoc<1 then NewDoc := 1;
  Child:=TChild.Create(Self);
  Str((NewDoc/1000):4:3,s);
  StrCopy(title,DefaultTitle);
  StrCat(title,StrPos(S,'.'));
  Child.ParseFile(title);
  Child.Caption := title;
  Child.Height := Round(ClientHeight * 0.7);
  Child.Width := Round(ClientWidth * 0.7);
  Child.Visible := True;
  Child.BringToFront;
  Child.Memo1.SetFocus;
  NewDoc := NewDoc + 1;
end;
```

Figure 5.6
Your four file
windows.

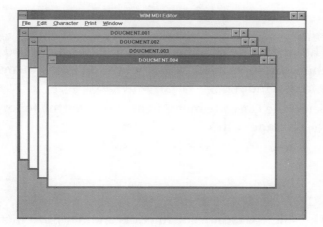

New1Click creates a new blank file by first causing the **Child** form to clone itself into a new process. Once that has occurred, **NewDoc** is used to create a unique default filename with a new extension for the current session, which is then parsed out and the name is set in the **Child**'s title bar. The new **Child** is scaled to fit inside the parent window based upon its current visible client area (work area). This is done for aesthetics.

Run the editor now and open four new file windows. You should see something like Figure 5.6.

4. We will come back to the **Open** menu item in a moment. First we need to take care of the rest of the menu items. Select **Exit** from the Frame menu and enter the following code for **Exit1Click**:

```
procedure TFrame.Exit1Click(Sender: TObject);
begin
   Close;
end;
```

The single **Close** statement invokes the form's method that performs an orderly shutdown of the application.

5. Select the **Tile** menu item and enter the following code for **Tile1Click**:

```
procedure TFrame.Tile1Click(Sender: TObject);
begin
```

```
     Tile;
  end;
```

The single **Tile** statement is another form method that tells all child windows in an MDI application to tile themselves in the parent window.

6. Select the **Cascade** menu item and enter the following code for **Cascade1Click**:

```
procedure TFrame.Cascade1Click(Sender: TObject);
begin
   Cascade;
end;
```

The single **Cascade** statement is another form method that tells all child windows in an MDI application to cascade themselves in the parent window.

7. Select the **Arrange Icons** menu item and enter the following code for **ArrangeIcons1Click**:

```
procedure TFrame.ArrangeIcons1Click(Sender: TObject);
begin
   ArrangeIcons;
end;
```

The single **ArrangeIcons** statement is another form method that tells all child window icons in an MDI application to arrange themselves along the bottom of the parent window.

Run the WIM Editor and open several new file windows. Try tiling, cascading, and arranging closed windoWicons on the parent window to see how everything responds.

8. Now we are ready for **Open**. Because both the **Child** and **Frame** forms can make a call to open a file, we will create a generic **OpenWindow** routine that will be called directly by both form menus. In actuality, **OpenWindow** will bounce the responsibility for opening a file back to the **Child** form. This makes it a bit tough to follow, but just hang in there for a moment.

Add an **OpenDialog** box from the Component palette to the **Frame** form. Change the **DefaultExt** property to *.*. Double-click on the **Filter** property to invoke the **Filter Editor**. Enter

Figure 5.7
The Filter
Editor.

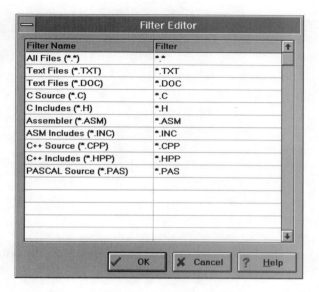

filters as they are listed in Table 5.4. When you have completed entering the filters, the Editor should look something like Figure 5.7.

Table 5.4 Filter Names and Their Filters

Filter Name	Filter
All Files (*.*)	*.*
Text Files (*.TXT)	*.TXT
Text Files (*.DOC)	*.DOC
C Source (*.C)	*.C
C Includes (*.H)	*.H
Assembler (*.ASM)	*.ASM
ASM Includes (*.INC)	*.INC
C++ Source (*.CPP)	*.CPP
C++ Includes (*.HPP)	*.HPP
PASCAL Source (*.PAS)	*.PAS

Create the **OpenWindow** procedure and register it in **MAIN**:

```
procedure TFrame.OpenWindow(Sender: TObject);
var
  Child: TChild;
```

```
        title: array[0..12] of Char;
        S: array[0..12] of Char;
    begin
        if OpenDialog1.Execute then
        begin
            Child := Tchild.Create(Self);
            Child.Open(OpenDialog1.Filename);
            Child.Caption:=OpenDialog1.Filename;
            Child.ParseFile(OpenDialog1.Filename);
            Child.Visible:=True;
            Child.BringToFront;
            Child.Memo1.SetFocus;
        end;
    end;
```

9. Select the **Open** menu item and enter the following code for **Open1Click**:

```
procedure TFrame.Open1Click(Sender: TObject);
begin
    OpenWindow(Sender);
end;
```

Now, let's pause for a moment and take a closer look at the logic. When the WIM editor is first started and the **Open** menu item is selected, the event handler **Open1Click** will handle the event and call **OpenWindow** to get the file. Once a file has been created or opened, the **Child** form's **File** menu options overlay **Frame**'s **File** menu options. Thus, when **Open** is selected, an event is generated from **Child**'s menu, not **Frame**'s. So, to take advantage of the situation, we will write the **Open1Click** event handler for **Child** to call **Frame**'s **OpenWindow** also. That's why **OpenWindow** exists. It keeps code from being unnecessarily duplicated, plus also demonstrates pointing two or more components at one event handler.

Let's do that now.

10. Select the **Child** form to make it active. Select **Child**'s **Open** menu item and enter the following code for **Open1Click**:

```
procedure TChild.Open1Click(Sender: TObject);
begin
    Frame.OpenWindow(Sender);
end;
```

11. We've established all our connections between menu items to open a file, but we have not generated the code to actually do the opening. The **Child**'s **memo** component will do the actual open and read for us. So, we will create a generic **Open** procedure in **MDICHILD** to use the **LoadFromFile** method that is part of **Child**'s **memo** component. Enter the code for **TChild.Open** and register it in **MDICHILD**:

```
procedure TChild.Open(const path: string);
begin
  ParseFile(path);
  Memo1.Cursor := crHourGlass;
  Memo1.Lines.LoadfromFile(Filename);
  Caption := Filename;
  Memo1.SelStart:=0;
  Memo1.Modified := False;
  Memo1.Cursor := crDefault;
end;
```

Basically, **TChild.Open** divvies up the file and pathname, and then loads the file into the memo component. Afterward, the name is displayed on the title bar and some housekeeping is done for the memo to preset the user with the top of the file displayed, and the **Modified** property is reset, so we don't prompt to save the file if we exit without changing anything.

12. Select **Child**'s **New** menu item and enter the code for **New1Click**:

```
procedure TChild.New1Click(Sender: TObject);
begin
  Frame.New1Click(Sender);
end;
```

13. Select **Child**'s **Exit** menu item and enter the code for **Exit1Click**:

```
procedure TChild.Exit1Click(Sender: TObject);
begin
  Frame.Exit1Click(Sender);
end;
```

The **New** and **Exit** event handlers are pretty straightforward. These invoke the event handlers from **Frame**'s menu. However, **Exit** poses an interesting twist. When the **Child** window is about to be terminated, the **Close** method calls the procedure **FormCloseQuery** to check and see if it is okay to proceed and close out the window (in this case, the **Child** form). We are going to write our own version of **FormCloseQuery** and override the default version found in the object **Tform**. This allows us to do some last minute processing before we close up shop.

FormCloseQuery sets the boolean flag **CanClose**. If **CanClose** is **True**, then Delphi proceeds and closes the form and/or application. If **CanClose** is **False**, then Delphi bounces the **Close** request. Inside our version of **FormCloseQuery** we will check our **memo** component to see if the text it holds has been modified. If so, then we present the user with a **message dialog** box giving them the option to save the changes, cancel the close, or toss the changes and close anyway. If the text has not been modified, then the **Close** request zips right through as if nothing happened.

Enter the following code for **FormCloseQuery** and register the procedure in **MDICHILD**:

```
procedure TChild.FormCloseQuery(Sender: TObject; var CanClose:
Boolean);
var
  choice: Integer;
begin
  if Memo1.Modified then
  begin
    choice := MessageDlg(CloseText+filename+'?',
mtConfirmation,
    [mbYes, mbNo, mbCancel],0);
    case choice of
      id_Yes: Save1Click(Self);
      id_Cancel: CanClose := False;
    end;
```

```
      end;
   end;
```

14. Saving a file is the last big piece that needs to be activated for file processing. There is very little difference between **Save** and **Save As**. **Save** presumes you already have a valid name, while **Save As** forces the issue. Since choosing a filename is a process that is done prior to saving, we can use **Save** as the base procedure that **Save As** calls when it is done getting a filename. One other procedure that we should do is create a backup file anytime we save work.

    First, write the procedure **CreateBackup** and register it in **MDICHILD**:

```
procedure TChild.CreateBackup(const path: string);
begin
   DeleteFile(backup);
   RenameFile(filename,backup);
end;
```

15. Select **Child**'s **Save** menu item and enter the code for **Save1Click**:

```
procedure TChild.Save1Click(Sender: TObject);
begin
   if filename ='' then SaveAs1Click(Sender)
   else
   begin
     CreateBackup(filename);
     Memo1.Lines.SaveToFile(fullpath);
     Memo1.Modified := False;
   end;
end;
```

16. Select **Child**'s **Save As** menu item and enter the code for **SaveAs1Click**:

```
procedure TChild.SaveAs1Click(Sender: TObject);
begin
   SaveDialog1.DefaultExt := extension;
```

```
SaveDialog1.FIleName := filename;
SaveDialog1.InitialDir := directory;
if SaveDialog1.Execute then
begin
  ParseFile(SaveDialog1.FileName);
  Caption := filename;
  Save1Click(sender);
end;
end;
```

Before we can execute this code, it is necessary to get a **Save Dialog** component from the Component Palette and place it on the **Child** form. No properties need to be changed, as **SaveAs1Click** sets the values necessary to do this before invoking the dialog.

Menus, Memos, and the Clipboard

Delphi's **memo** component is very powerful all by itself, but it requires the use of other visual components, such as **buttons**, **menu items**, **check boxes**, and the like, to make it work. One of the nifty things about Delphi's **memo** component is that you can access the **Clipboard** from the component—no extra goodies required. This makes perfect sense, as a **memo** would be a logical place to do such things as Cut, Paste, Copy, and so on. At this stage in the WIM Editor's construction, we are going to manipulate the **memo** directly from the menu, and with particular attention to the **DDE Clipboard**.

To hook up the editing features and the Clipboard:

1. Select **Child**'s **Cut** menu item and enter the code for **Cut1Click**:

```
procedure TChild.Cut1Click(Sender: TObject);
begin
  Memo1.CutToClipboard;
end;
```

2. Select **Child**'s **Copy** menu item and enter the code for **Copy1Click**:

```
procedure TChild.Copy1Click(Sender: TObject);
```

```
begin
    Memo1.CopyToClipboard;
end;
```

3. Select **Child**'s **Paste** menu item and enter the code for **Paste1Click**:

```
procedure TChild.Paste1Click(Sender: TObject);
begin
    Memo1.PasteFromClipboard;
end;
```

4. Select **Child**'s **Delete** menu item and enter the code for **Delete1Click**:

```
procedure TChild.Delete1Click(Sender: TObject);
begin
    Memo1.ClearSelection;
end;
```

5. Select **Child**'s **Select All** menu item and enter the code for **SelectAll1Click**:

```
procedure TChild.SelectAll1Click(Sender: TObject);
begin
    Memo1.SelectAll;
end;
```

Now that all the **memo** edit functions are attached to menu items, we need one more thing to make the edit operations more robust. There are times when it would not be practical to Cut text from the Memo if there was nothing selected, or Paste to it if there was no text in the Clipboard. Basically, we want to disable some of the edit functions during those times when there is nothing for them to do, or it would cause a problem for that function to be activated.

One way to do this is remove the menu item from the menu when it was not needed, and replace it when it was valid to be used. Neat trick, but that's too much work. The easier way to do this is to *dim* the function on the menu to show it is disabled. Delphi will do this for us automatically as we switch the **Enabled** property for a menu item from **True** to **False**.

For the purposes of WIM Edit, we will split this into two pieces. The event handler **Edit1Click** is the trigger for the menu items **Cut**, **Copy**, **Paste**, and **Delete**. In order to get at these items, you must always select **Edit** first. This gives us a way to always update the status for each of these menu items before the user ever sees them.

Later on when we add **SpeedButtons**, we will come back to our **EnableEdits** procedure and add the links to enable and disable the function of the **SpeedButtons** as needed. By splitting the actual work off into a procedure not attached to any particular event handler, it makes it more understandable as to what's going on. We could just point everything at **Edit1Click** and be done with it, but that makes for more work when we have to come back to fix or add something.

6. Create the **EnableEdits** procedure and register it in **MDICHILD**:

```
procedure TChild.EnableEdits;
var
  data: Boolean;
begin
  Paste1.Enabled := Clipboard.HasFormat(CF_TEXT);
  data := Memo1.SelLength <> 0;
  Cut1.Enabled := data;
  Copy1.Enabled := data;
  Delete1.Enabled := data;
end;
```

7. Select **Child's Edit** menu item and enter the code for **Edit1Click**:

```
procedure TChild.Edit1Click(Sender: TObject);
begin
  EnableEdits;
end;
```

Now our menu items are secured. Don't forget, we have to come back here in awhile for the SpeedButtons as well.

Menus, Memos, and Text Manipulation

At this stage of the game, we will hook up the memo methods that control fonts, text alignment, and word wrapping. While it is obvious to the casual observer as to whether our text is lined up on the left, the right, or centered, our menu items should reflect which of the three options is currently chosen and in use by placing a check mark next to it on the menu. Not doing this won't affect the alignment of memo text one bit, but it does make the program look more professional if not more friendly.

1. Create the procedure **AlignClick** and register it in **MDICHILD**:

```
procedure TChild.AlignClick(Sender: TOBject);
begin
  Left1.Checked := False;
  Right1.Checked := False;
  Center1.Checked := False;
with Sender as TMenuItem do Checked := True;
  with Memo1 do
    if Left1.Checked then
      Alignment := taLeftJustify
    else if Right1.Checked then
      Alignment := taRightJustify
    else if Center1.Checked then
      Alignment := taCenter;
end;
```

A few words on this procedure are in order here. In the following code snippet, the first thing we do is set our menu items' **Checked** property to **False**. The **with** statement then tells Delphi to focus on the TMenuItem that caused the event handler to be run and force its **Checked** property to **True**. By doing it this way, we don't have to evaluate each and every option to see if that menu item is the one to be checked. This becomes very valuable if you are working with a very long list of menu items.

```
Left1.Checked := False;
Right1.Checked := False;
```

```
Center1.Checked := False;
with Sender as TMenuItem do Checked := True;
```

The next construct we need to look at is:

```
with Memo1 do
  if Left1.Checked then
    Alignment := taLeftJustify
  else if Right1.Checked then
    Alignment := taRightJustify
  else if Center1.Checked then
    Alignment := taCenter;
```

Basically, this is just another way of doing things. Using the **with Memo1 do** statement lets us directly address the methods and properties of **Memo1**. If we chose not to use the **with** statement, the code would look something like this:

```
if Left1.Checked then
  Memo1.Alignment := taLeftJustify
else if Right1.Checked then
  Memo1.Alignment := taRightJustify
else if Center1.Checked then
  Memo1.Alignment := taCenter;
```

2. Select **Child's Left** menu item and enter the code for **Left1Click**:

```
procedure TChild.Left1Click(Sender: Tobject);
begin
  AlignClick(Sender);
end;
```

3. Select **Child's Right** menu item and enter the code for **Right1Click**:

```
procedure TChild.Right1Click(Sender: Tobject);
begin
  AlignClick(Sender);
end;
```

4. Select **Child**'s **Center** menu item and enter the code for **Center1Click**:

```
procedure TChild.Center1Click(Sender: Tobject);
begin
  AlignClick(Sender);
end;
```

As an alternative, you could select each of these objects from the **Object Inspector**, switch to the **Events** page, click on the **OnClick** event, and assign the event to **AlignClick**. Just remember that there are times when it is better to have an event handler for each object for readability's sake.

5. The big display issue with word wrapping and the memo item has to do with scroll bars. By default, scroll bars do not appear on the memo component unless you specify it at design time.

Memo components are either vertical or horizontal. For our purposes, we will always have vertical scroll bars, as most of the time the length of the file loaded into the child window will exceed the memo's screen display area. This is not an unreasonable assumption. On the other hand, it looks a bit silly to have a horizontal scroll bar present, when each line of text is wrapped around, never to reach beyond the left or right edge of the memo display area. Besides that, you get back a line's worth of display by it not being there.

Create the procedure **WrapIt** and register it in **MDICHILD**:

```
procedure TChild.WrapIt(Sender: TObject);
begin

  with Memo1 do
  begin
    WordWrap := not WordWrap;
    if WordWrap then
      ScrollBars := ssVertical else
      ScrollBars := ssBoth;
    WordWrap1.Checked := WordWrap;
  end;
end;
```

Assign **WrapIt** to the **OnClick** event for the **WordWrap1** menu item.

6. The last thing on our list is to handle the fonts for our memo. This is very simple to do, as Delphi provides a **FontDialog** component to work with. To get started, grab a **FontDialog** object from the Component palette and place it on the **Child** form.

7. Select **Child's Font** menu item and enter the code for **Font1Click**:

```
procedure TChild.Font1Click(Sender: TObject);
var
  old_color: TColor;
begin
  old_color := Memo1.Font.Color;
  If FontDialog1.Execute then
    Memo1.Font := FontDialog1.Font;
  Memo1.Font.Color := old_color;
end;
```

The **FontDialog Execute** method activates and runs the **Font Dialog** box (Figure 5.8). Upon exiting the dialog box, a boolean status of **True** (if a font or status of an existing font was changed) is returned, or **False** if nothing happened.

Figure 5.8
Font dialog box.

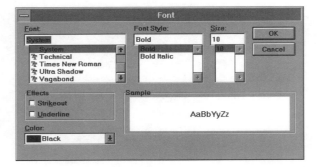

> ## Note
>
> To keep colors from changing while exchanging fonts, it is a good idea to save the existing font color before getting a new font from the FontDialog, and then restore it. This keeps you from being dependent on the FontDialog respecting the current settings of its parent window. If something did change, then all we do is assign the Font property of the Font Dialog to Memo1 and Memo1 takes on the font selected and redisplays its text in the new font.

Menus, Memos, and Printing

After all is said and done, at some point in time while editing a file, you will want to print the results. Creating printing output itself can occupy as much time as creating the rest of the program. In the previous chapter, we sent the output right to the printer in the same manner as just copying a text file to the printer port. In this section, we'll format our output to make it look more readable.

Before you print, it is a wise idea to make sure you have the right printer driver activated, especially if you have multiple Windows printer drivers installed. Delphi provides a Printer Setup dialog to do this (see Figure 5.9).

1. Grab a **PrinterSetup** dialog from the Component palette and place it on the **Child** form.

2. Select **Child**'s **Printer Setup** menu item and enter the code for **PrinterSetup1Click**:

```
procedure TChild.PrintSetup1Click(Sender: TObject);
begin
  PrinterSetupDialog1.Execute;
end;
```

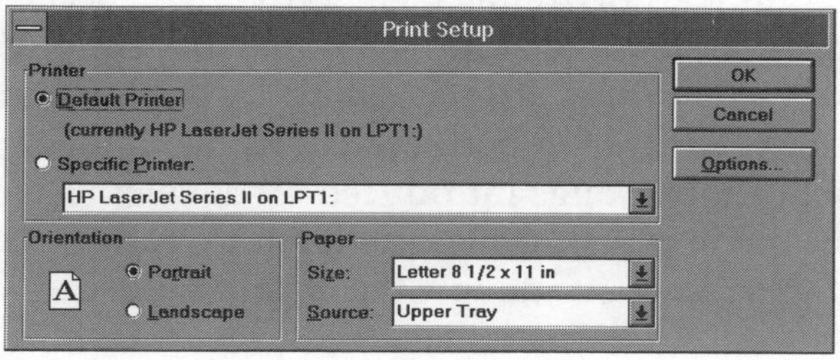

Figure 5.9
The Printer Setup dialog box.

By running the Printer Setup dialog, Windows is properly configured for the printer you select.

Designing the Printed Output Page Sophisticated print software in applications lets the user print in What You See Is What You Get (WYSIWYG). Well, we're not quite that sophisticated—at least not in terms of this project. This topic alone could be the subject of a whole new book. Instead, we will provide some formatting to our printed output to make it more readable and to demonstrate the amount of work required to deal with simple headers, footers, titles, page numbers, print areas, margins, and fonts.

Printer information and output is provided by Delphi's Printer object. The Printer object is composed of a number of different properties and methods to allow for all kinds of printed output.

Today, we will use a subset of them:

Properties	Methods
Canvas	Abort
Fonts	BeginDoc
PageHeight	EndDoc
PageNumber	NewPage
Page Width	

In order to tackle the print page and create a generic template that will work with all types of printers, you need to create a yardstick that can be used over and over again. Our yardstick for this purpose will be the inch. For all intents and purposes, you can choose any basis of measurement you like. The trick is to convert the printer's basic unit of measure to your defined yardstick.

In calculating our yardstick, we need two kinds of inches: a vertical inch and a horizontal inch. Why? Not because the paper is oblong, but because we cannot assume that the physical print measurement the printer uses is going to be the same real distance between two points in both directions. Doing it this way saves us the grief of subtle bugs introduced by developing for a printer that uses the same physical measurement in both directions, versus a printer that may have double the resolution in the vertical direction and thus requires doubling its vertical measurements to compensate. For this project, we will standardize on 8 1/2 by 11-inch paper.

To get a vertical inch, do the following:

```
Vinch := Round(Printer.PageHeight / 11);
```

To get a horizontal inch:

```
Hinch := Round(Printer.PageWidth / 8.5);
```

If you want to use metric, then you can convert from inches to cm:

```
1 cm = 0.3937 in or 2.54 cm = 1 in
```

Thus, if we were calculating our yardstick based on centimeters, the math would look like this:

```
11 in = 27.94 cm
8.5 in = 21.59 cm
Vcm = Round(Printer.PageHeight / 27.94);
Hcm = Round(Printer.PageWidth / 21.59);
```

Now that we have our yardstick, let's look at what other measurements we should create for our page.

Margins   Margins are necessary to keep printed output on the page and sufficient whitespace around it to be aesthetically pleasing and leave room for binder holes, document titles, decorative borders and graphics, and just about anything else you can think of.

For the WIM Editor, we will establish margins for the top, bottom, left, and right sides of the paper. Within these margins, we will also draw a line across the top and bottom of the page to provide some visual separation between the body of the printed output and the titles and page numbers. With this in mind, let's begin.

1. First, we establish a vertical margin:

   ```
   Vmargin := Vinch;
   ```

2. Next, we set our top margin to be the size of our vertical margin. Along with this, we will mark the offset of where to draw a line across the top 1/8 inch on the inside of the top margin,

plus mark the offset for the title of the document 1/4 inch on the inside of the top margin:

```
TopMargin := VMargin;
TopLine := VMargin - Round(VInch/8);
TVOffset := Vmargin - Round(VInch/4);
Tmargin := TopMargin - TVOffset;
```

3. Now we set the bottom margin to be the size of our vertical margin. We will again mark the offset to draw a line 1/8 inch inside the bottom margin, and mark the offset for page numbering to be 1/4 inch on the inside of the bottom margin:

```
BotMargin := Printer.PageHeight - Vmargin;
BotLine := BotMargin + Round(VInch/8);
PVOffset := Round(VInch/4);
Pmargin := BotMargin + PVOffset;
```

4. Set the left and right margins:

```
Lmargin := Hinch;
Rmargin := Printer.Pagewidth - Hinch;
```

5. Now calculate the vertical and horizontal work areas, so we can figure such goodies as how many lines per page:

```
VWorkArea := BotMargin - TopMargin;
HWorkArea := Rmargin - Lmargin;
```

6. Here's the fun part. We now calculate all of the other values we are going to need to help this printer code scale itself according to what font size, paper size, and printer are in use:

```
TitleSize := 10; { Use 10 Point always }
PixelRatio := 4; { For now 4 pixels/Point }
Printer.Canvas.Font := Memo1.Font;
PenWidth := Printer.Canvas.Pen.Width;
DeckHeight := Memo1.Font.Size * PixelRatio;
Indent := LMargin;
LinesPerPage := Round(VWorkArea / (Memo1.Font.Size *
```

```
    PixelRatio));
    PageCount := Round((Memo1.Lines.Count / LinesPerPage)+0.49);
```

The pixel ratio was hand-figured to work with an HP Laserjet Series II and other 300-DPI printers that use the same print measurement scheme as the HP. Calculating a scalable PixelRatio is left as an exercise for the reader. I do this on purpose, so there is some challenge and mystery left.

One other oddity you might notice is the number 0.49. This is a *magic* number that is used to force the Round() function to behave the way I want it to. According to Borland's documentation and observed behavior, Round() will force a rational number to the next highest whole number if the fractional part is at least .5. Since we don't count or print fractional pages (usually), we want to force the final page count to the next highest whole number. By adding 0.49 to the dividend, we can force that to occur, as even one line on a new page will generate a sufficient fractional page value that adding 0.49 to it will push it over 0.5. Better living through simple math.

Printing the Page—Finally It's fish or cut-bait time. We've calculated all the offsets we need. We know how many lines and pages the output will be, so all that is needed is a working printer and a copy count. After we have chosen to print by way of the PrinterDialog, the following code shuttles the data to the printer:

```
if PrintDialog1.Execute then
  begin
    NumCopies := PrintDialog1.Copies;
```

We start here with an outer control loop to force a print of the number of specified copies retrieved from the Printer Dialog. We reset our control flags here to show we are at the start of a document:

```
repeat
Printed := False;
LinePrinted := 0;
LeftOnPage := LinesPerPage;
LeftInDoc := Memo1.Lines.Count;
```

The easiest way to get at the printer is by using the BeginDoc method. It does all the detail work of setting up the connection to the printer so that all you have to do is send it. On the flip side, you can handle all the details yourself by assigning a printer and rewinding the stream, plus any additional setup that is required to initialize your printer.

```
Printer.BeginDoc;
```

Here is the start of inner control loop 1. This controls the entire page, and when headers, footers, and text body for the current page is completed, forces a new page to be started

```
repeat
```

We switch fonts here to print out the title, plus set the pen width in pixels that will draw the line across the top of the screen.

```
{
  Header…
}
Printer.Canvas.Font.Size := TitleSize;
Printer.Canvas.TextOut(Indent,TMargin,'Filename: '+filename);
Printer.Canvas.Pen.Width := PixelRatio * 2;
Printer.Canvas.MoveTo(LMargin,TopLine);
Printer.Canvas.LineTo(RMargin,TopLine);
Printer.Canvas.Pen.Width := PenWidth;
{
  Body of document…
}
LineOffset := TopMargin;
LeftOnPage := LinesPerPage;
Printer.Canvas.Font := Memo1.Font;
```

This is where the dirty work takes place. Inner control loop 2 takes care of printing the body of the text only, and rolls out when the page is filled with the calculated number of permissible lines.

```
repeat
Printer.Canvas.TextOut(Indent,LineOffset,Memo1.Lines[LinePrinted]);
    LineOffset := LineOffset + DeckHeight;
    LinePrinted := LinePrinted+1;
    LeftInDoc := LeftInDoc - 1;
    If LeftInDoc < 1 then
    begin
        LeftOnPage := 0;
        Printed := True;
    end;
    if LeftInDoc > 0 then
        LeftOnPage := LeftOnPage - 1;
    until LeftOnPage < 1;
```

Once we roll out of inner control loop 2, we finish off the page by printing the footer at the bottom and incrementing the page count by one to let inner control loop 1 evaluate whether we've completed printing the document.

```
{
    Footer…
}
Printer.Canvas.Pen.Width := PixelRatio * 2;
Printer.Canvas.MoveTo(LMargin,BotLine);
Printer.Canvas.LineTo(RMargin,BotLine);
Printer.Canvas.Pen.Width := PenWidth;
Printer.Canvas.Font.Size := TitleSize;
Printer.Canvas.TextOut(Indent,PMargin,'Page
'+IntToStr(Printer.PageNumber)+' of '+IntToStr(PageCount));
Printer.NewPage;
until Printed;
```

We will close out the print stream here with the EndDoc method; the counterpart to BeginDoc. At this point, we need to check and make sure we have printed all requested copies of the document. If we have, then we are done. If not, then go back and waltz with the printer some more until we've filled our dance card.

```
    {
        Close the Document Stream...
    }
    Printer.EndDoc;
    NumCopies := NumCopies - 1;
    until NumCopies < 1;
end;
```

Note

Very Important. Make sure that the **Printers** module is referenced in the **interface** section's **USES** clause. Otherwise, Delphi will complain that the object **Printer** is unknown when you try to compile the code.

Select **Child's Print** submenu item under **Print,** and enter the following code for the **OnClick** event:

```
procedure TChild.Print2Click(Sender: TObject);
var
    {
        This group handles the page boundaries.
    }
    VInch: Integer;
    HInch: Integer;
    VMargin: Integer;
    TopLine: Integer;
    TopMargin: Integer;
    BotMargin: Integer;
    HMargin: Integer;
    LMargin: Integer;
    RMargin: Integer;
    TVOffset: Integer;
    TMargin: Integer;
    BotLine: Integer;
    PVOffset: Integer;
    PMargin: Integer;
    {
```

```
    This group handles the Title and Page print.
}
VWorkArea: Integer;
HWorkArea: Integer;
Indent: Integer;
THOffset: Integer;
PHOffset: Integer;
TitleSize: Integer;
PenWidth: Integer;
{
    This group handles the data.
}
DeckHeight: Integer;
PixelRatio: Integer;
LinesPerPage: Integer;
PageCount: Integer;
LineOffset: Integer;
NumCopies: Integer;
Printed: Boolean;
LinePrinted: Integer;
LeftOnPage: Integer;
LeftInDoc: Integer;
begin
{
  First, find the boundaries of the page.
  Everything is calculated based on inches with 8.5 x 11 paper as
default.
}
  VInch := Round(Printer.PageHeight/11);
  HInch := Round(Printer.PageWidth/8.5);
  VMargin := VInch;
  TopMargin := VMargin;
  TopLine := VMargin - Round(VInch/8);
  TVOffset := VMargin - Round(VInch/4);
  TMargin := TopMargin - TVOffset;
  BotMargin := Printer.PageHeight - VInch;
  BotLine := BotMargin + Round(VInch/8);
```

```
PVOffset := (BotMargin + Round(VInch/4)) - BotMargin;
PMargin := BotMargin + PVOffset;
LMargin := HInch;
RMargin := Printer.PageWidth - HInch;
VWorkArea := BotMargin - TopMargin;
HWorkArea := RMargin - LMargin;
TitleSize := 10; { Use 10 Point always }
PixelRatio := 4; { For now 4 pixels/Point }
Printer.Canvas.Font := Memo1.Font;
PenWidth := Printer.Canvas.Pen.Width;
DeckHeight := Memo1.Font.Size * PixelRatio;
Indent := LMargin;
LinesPerPage := Round(VWorkArea / (Memo1.Font.Size *
PixelRatio));
PageCount := Round((Memo1.Lines.Count / LinesPerPage)+0.49);
NumCopies := PrintDialog1.Copies;
if PrintDialog1.Execute then
begin
  repeat
  Printed := False;
  LinePrinted := 0;
  LeftOnPage := LinesPerPage;
  LeftInDoc := Memo1.Lines.Count;
  Printer.BeginDoc;
  repeat
  {
    Header…
  }
  Printer.Canvas.Font.Size := TitleSize;
  Printer.Canvas.TextOut(Indent,TMargin,'Filename: '+filename);
  Printer.Canvas.Pen.Width := PixelRatio * 2;
  Printer.Canvas.MoveTo(LMargin,TopLine);
  Printer.Canvas.LineTo(RMargin,TopLine);
  Printer.Canvas.Pen.Width := PenWidth;
  {
    Body of document…
  }
```

```
    LineOffset := TopMargin;
      LeftOnPage := LinesPerPage;
      Printer.Canvas.Font := Memo1.Font;
    repeat
Printer.Canvas.TextOut(Indent,LineOffset,Memo1.Lines[LinePrinted]);
    LineOffset := LineOffset + DeckHeight;
    LinePrinted := LinePrinted+1;
    LeftInDoc := LeftInDoc - 1;
    If LeftInDoc < 1 then
    begin
      LeftOnPage := 0;
      Printed := True;
    end;
    if LeftInDoc > 0 then
      LeftOnPage := LeftOnPage - 1;
    until LeftOnPage < 1;
    {
      Footer...
    }
    Printer.Canvas.Pen.Width := PixelRatio * 2;
    Printer.Canvas.MoveTo(LMargin,BotLine);
    Printer.Canvas.LineTo(RMargin,BotLine);
    Printer.Canvas.Pen.Width := PenWidth;
    Printer.Canvas.Font.Size := TitleSize;
    Printer.Canvas.TextOut(Indent,PMargin,'Page
'+IntToStr(Printer.PageNumber)+' of '+IntToStr(PageCount));
    Printer.NewPage;
    until Printed;
    {
      Close the Document Stream...
    }
    Printer.EndDoc;
    NumCopies := NumCopies - 1;
    until NumCopies < 1;
  end;
end;
```

SpeedButtons...with Graphics!

In the previous version of the WIM Editor, we had a series of **SpeedButtons** on a panel to facilitate editing, printing, and display functions. On those buttons, we imprinted text, so their use was known. This time, we will create icons that hopefully will be just as clear as to the button's purpose, and place those on the **SpeedButtons,** instead of text. Besides the aesthetic value, it looks neat to whack on colorful buttons with a mouse.

1. From the Component palette, place 11 **SpeedButtons** on the **Child** form's **panel**.

2. Change the properties for each of the buttons, as shown in Table 5.5.

Table 5.5 SpeedButtons and Their Properties

Object	Height	Hint	Left	Width
SpeedButton1	37	Save File	0	37
SpeedButton2	37	Copy Text	36	37
SpeedButton3	37	Paste Text	72	37
SpeedButton4	37	Cut Text	108	37
SpeedButton5	37	Delete Text	144	37
SpeedButton6	37	Left Justify	180	37
SpeedButton7	37	Center Text	216	37
SpeedButton8	37	Right Justify	252	37
SpeedButton9	37	Select Font	288	37
SpeedButton10	37	Foreground Color	324	37
SpeedButton11	37	Background Color	380	37

When you are done, the **child** form should look like Figure 5.10. Now, to recall that little reminder we made to ourselves about the panel.

3. Select the **Panel1** object from the Object Inspector and set the **ShowHints** Property to **True**. By doing this, every time we put the mouse over one of the **SpeedButtons** that has a hint, the callout box displaying the hint will automatically display it.

If you want to display the hints faster or slower, change the **HintPause** property value. The delay is measured in milliseconds, so you can adjust the delay quite precisely. Usually, I

Figure 5.10
Your form
should now look
like this.

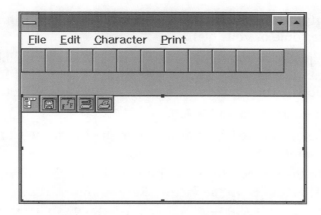

have found that the default value (800 ms) is quite sufficient for most uses.

Now to experiment, you can run the WIM Editor and drag the mouse over each of the buttons to see the hints and select buttons at will. They won't do anything yet, as we have not assigned them to any event handlers, but that is about to change.

Making and Attaching Glyphs

In order to create small bitmaps (glyphs) for each of the buttons, you must use the **Image Editor** (Figure 5.11). This editor will automatically generate the proper size (32 pixels by 32 pixels) glyph that will fit on the SpeedButtons. Figures 5.12 through 5.23 show

Figure 5.11
Delphi's Image
Editor.

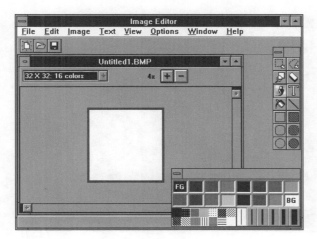

the glyphs I created for each SpeedButton. You can use these, or create some of your own.

And, just to round things out, Figure 5.24 shows a sample icon that we can use later for each MDI child window, and for the parent window's icon.

To put a glyph on a button:

1. Select the first **SpeedButton** on the left of the **Child** form's **panel**.

2. In the **Object Browser**, double-click on the **Glyph** property. This brings up the Picture Editor (Figure 5.25).

3. Press the **Load** button and select the **SAVE.BMP** file from the dialog box. This loads the image you created a short time ago into the Picture Editor so that you can see what you are attaching (Figure 5.26).

4. Press **OK** and the image is immediately transferred onto the SpeedButton (Figure 5.27).

5. Repeat the process for the rest of the SpeedButtons, matching each glyph you created with the button that will handle the function the glyph represents.

Figure 5.12
The Save glyph.

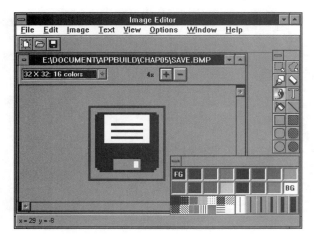

Figure 5.13
The Cut glyph.

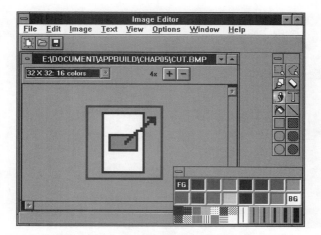

Figure 5.14
The Background
Color glyph.

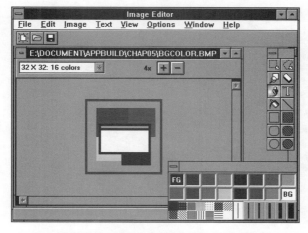

Figure 5.15
The Center
glyph.

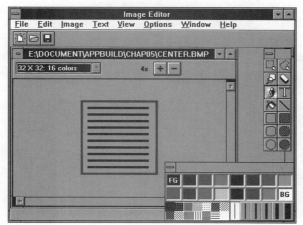

Figure 5.16
The Color glyph.

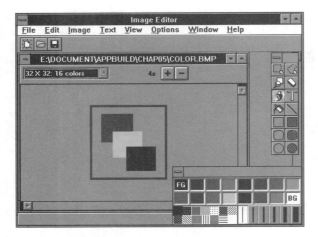

Figure 5.17
The Copy glyph.

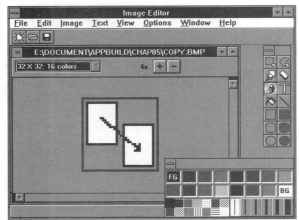

Figure. 5.18
The Delete
glyph.

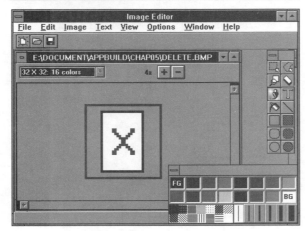

Figure 5.19
The Foreground glyph.

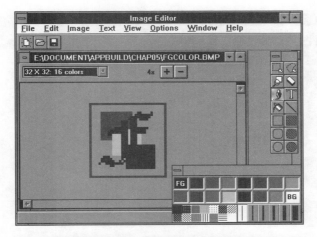

Figure 5.20
The Font glyph.

Figure 5.21
The Left glyph.

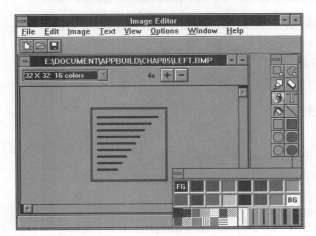

Figure 5.22
The Paste
glyph.

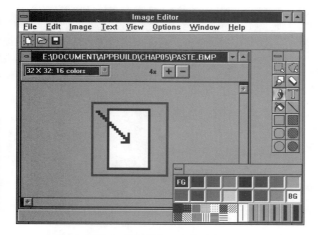

Figure 5.23
The Right glyph.

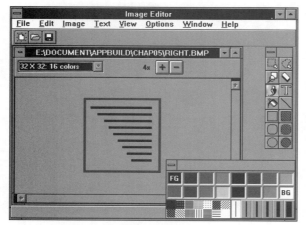

Figure 5.24
The
WIMMDI.ICO
icon.

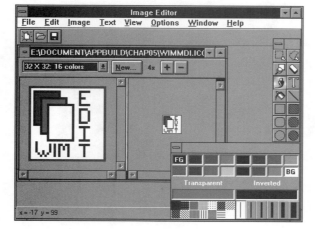

Figure 5.25
The Picture
Editor.

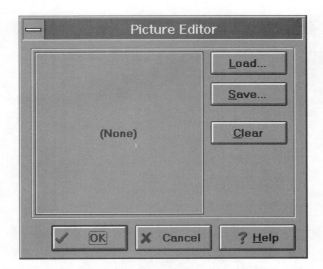

Figure 5.26
An image
loaded into the
Picture Editor.

Figure 5.27
The image is transferred onto a SpeedButton.

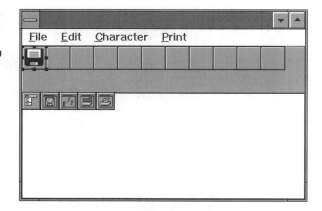

Making the SpeedButtons Play

We've placed the **SpeedButton**s on the form's panel, sized them, added hints, and prettied them up with pictures, now the only thing left is to make them do something useful. Since these **SpeedButton**s will replicate functionality that already exists, we will write only a few new handlers for text alignment and colors, while the rest will share existing event handlers.

1. Assign the following buttons to event handlers by selecting the **Events** page of the Object Inspector and, after locating the correct **SpeedButton**, highlight the triggering event and press the **down arrow** to select the event handler you need from the list shown in Table 5.6.

Table 5.6 The WIM Edit's SpeedButtons and Event Handlers

Object	Event Handler	Triggering Event
SpeedButton1	Save1Click	OnClick
SpeedButton2	Copy1Click	OnClick
SpeedButton3	Paste1Click	OnClick
SpeedButton4	Cut1Click	OnClick
SpeedButton5	Delete1Click	OnClick
SpeedButton9	Font1Click	OnClick

2. Select the **Left Justify SpeedButton** (SpeedButton6) from the panel. Move to the **Events** page of the Object Browser and double-click on the **OnClick** event. Enter the following code:

```
procedure TChild.SpeedButton6Click(Sender: TObject);
begin
  with MainMenu1 do
  begin
    Left1.Checked := True;
    Right1.Checked := False;
    Center1.Checked := False;
  end;
  with Memo1 do Alignment := taLeftJustify;
end;
```

3. Select the **Center SpeedButton** (SpeedButton7) from the panel. Move to the **Events** page of the Object Browser and double-click on the **OnClick** event. Enter the following code:

```
procedure TChild.SpeedButton7Click(Sender: TObject);
begin
  with MainMenu1 do
  begin
    Left1.Checked := False;
    Right1.Checked := False;
    Center1.Checked := True;
  end;
  with Memo1 do Alignment := taCenter;
end;
```

4. Select the **Right Justify SpeedButton** (SpeedButton8) from the panel. Move to the **Events** page of the Object Browser and double-click on the **OnClick** event. Enter the following code:

```
procedure TChild.SpeedButton8Click(Sender: TObject);
begin
  with MainMenu1 do
  begin
    Left1.Checked := False;
    Right1.Checked := True;
    Center1.Checked := False;
  end;
  with Memo1 do Alignment := taRightJustify;
end;
```

5. From the Component palette, grab a **ColorDialog** and place it on the **Child** form.

6. Select the **Foreground Color SpeedButton** (SpeedButton10) from the panel. Move to the **Events** page of the Object Browser and double-click on the **OnClick** event. Enter the following code:

```
procedure TChild.SpeedButton10Click(Sender: TObject);
begin
   if ColorDialog1.Execute then
      Memo1.Font.Color := ColorDialog1.Color;
end;
```

7. Select the **Background Color Justify SpeedButton** (SpeedButton11) from the panel. Move to the **Events** page of the Object Browser and double-click on the **OnClick** event. Enter the following code:

```
procedure TChild.SpeedButton11Click(Sender: TObject);
begin
   If ColorDialog1.Execute then
      Memo1.Color := ColorDialog1.Color;
end;
```

Combo Boxes as Active Lists

Combo Boxes are aggregate objects themselves. They are composed of an edit box and a list box that drop down to show their contents when invoked. We are going to provide a quick means to adjust fonts and font sizes, just like many word processors do.

To quickly adjust fonts and font sizes:

1. From the Component palette, grab a **ComboBox** and place it on the **Child** form's panel.

2. Change the **Left** property to 4, the **Width** to 217, and delete the **ComboBox1** in the **Text** property.

3. From the Component palette, grab another **ComboBox** and place it on the **Child** form's panel.

4. Change the **Left** property to 224, the **Width** to 69, and delete the **ComboBox2** in the **Text** property.

When you are done, the **Child** form should look like Figure 5.28.

While many types of lists are static in the respect that they never change much (which will be the case with **ComboBox2**), the font

Figure 5.28
All the glyphs
are transferred
onto the
SpeedButtons.

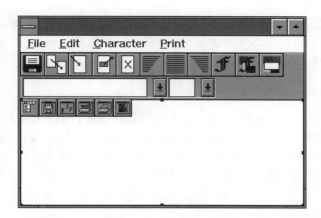

name list attached to **ComboBox1** is dynamic. We don't know ahead of time how many different types of fonts will be in Windows at any point in time or on any system. For this reason, we will need to poke at another Delphi goody, the **Screen** object.

Just like the **Printer** object, the **Screen** object maintains information about Windows with respect to certain subsystems. In this case, we are talking about the display. The **Screen** object maintains a list of currently active fonts, and we will be able to get at that list fairly quickly. In fact, we could update this list anytime if we chose just to validate our font selection.

To make use of both combo boxes requires two steps of processing: The first step initializes the string list that the combo boxes maintain and operate on. The second step generates a list of font sizes from 6- to 72-point, and adds them to **ComboBox2**'s string list so that we have some font sizes to choose from.

To initialize the string list that the combo boxes maintain and operate on:

1. Create the procedure **StartUp** and register it in **MDICHILD**:

```
procedure TChild.Startup(Sender: TObject);
var
  count: Integer;
  i: Integer;
  j: array[0..12] of char;
begin
```

2. By default, we are going to set the current **Memo** font as the selected choice in **ComboBox1** so that we are in sync with the **memo** object.

```
ComboBox1.Text := Memo1.Font.Name;
```

3. The string list attached to **ComboBox1** is empty at this point. We need to query the **screen** object and get the number of active fonts in Windows, then run through that list and add the names to our own list.

```
count := Screen.Fonts.Count;
for i:=0 to count-1 do
begin
  ComboBox1.Items.Add(Screen.Fonts.Strings[i]);
end;
```

4. For **ComboBox2**, we need to set the selected font size to the current font size that is in use by the **memo** object. This keeps **ComboBox2** in sync with the **memo** object.

```
Str(Memo1.Font.Size,j);
ComboBox2.Text := j;
```

5. Now we generate a list of font sizes from 6- to 72-point, and add them to **ComboBox2**'s string list so that we have some font sizes to choose from.

```
  for i:=6 to 72 do
  begin
    Str(i,j);
    ComboBox2.Items.Add(j);
  end;
end;
```

6. Select **Child** from the Object Browser, and switch to the **Events** page.

7. Select the **OnCreate** event and select **StartUp** from the drop-down list of functions. This attaches the procedure to the **Child** form so that each time a **Child** form is created, **StartUp** will be run to initialize the combo boxes.

To activate the combo boxes that do the actual work of resetting Memo1's font to the new selection:

1. For **ComboBox1**, create the procedure **ComboBox1FontName** and register it in **MDICHILD**:

```
procedure TChild.ComboBox1FontName(Sender: Tobject);
var
   old_color:  TColor;
begin
   old_color := Memo1.Font.Color;
   Memo1.Font.Name := ComboBox1.Text;
   Memo1.Font.Color := old_color;
   Memo1.SetFocus;
end;
```

2. Select **ComboBox1** from the Object Browser and switch to the **Events** page.

3. Select the **OnChange** event and point it at **ComboBox1FontName**. Each time **ComboBox1** is exited from processing, then this procedure runs automatically to update **Memo1** with the selected font.

4. For **ComboBox2**, create the procedure **ComboBox2FontSize** and register it in **MDICHILD**:

```
procedure TChild.ComboBox2FontSize(Sender: TObject);
var
   size: Integer;
   ptr: Integer;
begin
   Val(ComboBox2.Text,size,ptr);
   Memo1.Font.Size := size;
   Memo1.Font.Name := ComboBox1.Text;
   Memo1.SetFocus;
end;
```

5. Select **ComboBox2** from the Object Browser and switch to the **Events** page.

6. Select the **OnChange** event and point it at **ComboBox2FontSize**. Each time **ComboBox2** is exited from processing, then this procedure runs automatically to update **Memo1** with the selected font size.

The Hidden Goody

As a last act to finish the WIM Editor for the moment, we will add a running clock to the parent window so that the date and current time can be displayed. The object that will drive the display and keep the display in sync with the PC's clock is the Timer object.

The Timer object falls into the invisible object category. That is, there is no component that you can directly attach to it to make it visible. However, you can witness the operation of it through the response of other visual objects controlled by it.

The Timer, by default, samples over 1 ms, or 1000 times per second. This gives this object a very high degree of timing resolution that can be used for many different kinds of problems. For our purposes, we don't want the Timer sampling any faster than once a second, as the displayed time string can flicker with annoying regularity.

To make our clock reality:

1. Select the **Frame** form and place a **panel** component on it from the Component palette.
2. Set the **Alignment** property for the panel to **alTop**.
3. Set the **Height** to 30 and delete the **Panel1** from the caption.
4. Place a **timer** object on the form from the Component palette.
5. Place a **Label** on the panel and change the properties as follows:
6. Change **Left** to **4**, **Width** to **69**, **Name** to **DateLabel**, and **Autosize** to **False**.
7. Select the fonts and change the color to **white**.
8. Place another **Label** on the panel and change the properties as follows:
9. Change **Left** to **76**, **Width** to **89**, **Name** to **TimeLabel**, and **Autosize** to **False**.
10. Select the fonts and change the color to white.

11. Select the **MAIN** code page from the source window and add
the following lines to the **CONST** section under
INTERFACE:

```
DateFullYear = True;
DateLeadZero = True;
Time24Hour = True;
TimeLeadZero = True;
```

Here's what they mean in a nutshell:

DateFullYear—when set to **True**, the entire four-digit year is
displayed. When **False**, only the last two digits of the year are
displayed.

DateLeadZero—when **True**, a leading zero is displayed when
appropriate.

Time24Hour—when **True**, time is displayed in 24-hour format; otherwise, time is displayed in 12-hour A.M./P.M. format.

TimeLeadZero—when **True**, a leading zero is displayed when
appropriate.

12. Add the global variable **OldDate** in the **interface** section as:

```
OldDate   :   TDateTime;
```

13. Modify the **StartUp** procedure to look like:

```
procedure TFrame.StartUp(Sender: TObject);
begin
   DateLabel.Caption := DateToStr(Date);
   TimeLabel.Caption := TImeToStr(TIme);
   OldDate := Date;
   Height := Round(Screen.Height * 0.9);
   Width := Round(Screen.Width * 0.9);
   Left := Round(Screen.Width * 0.05);
   Top := Round(Screen.Height * 0.05);
end;
```

14. Select the **Timer1** timer object from the Object Browser, and
enter the following procedure for the **OnTimer** event:

```
procedure TFrame.Timer1Timer(Sender: TObject);
```

```
begin
  If OldDate <> Date then
  begin
    OldDate := Date;
    DateLabel.Caption := DateToStr(Date);
  end;
  TimeLabel.Caption := TimeToStr(Time);
end;
```

When an **OnTimer** event occurs and the **Timer1Timer** handler is called, the old stored data is checked against the current date. If there is a difference, then the new date is stored away and the display is updated to reflect the new date. On the other hand, every time the **Timer1Timer** handler is called, the time is automatically updated to the display. Doing things this way keeps display updates to a minimum.

Now, compile and run the WIM Editor and see how the panel updates with the new date and time.

Code, Code, and More Code

Stepping back and looking at the WIM Editor, it is quite obvious that things have changed a great deal. No longer is it just a simple program. This puppy scoots along and does much more than the original version. But, as with all good things, this program is really just a work in progress. It is done only when you step back and say it's done.

As you review the chapter and the complete source code following these remarks, more than likely you will find more features to add and changes to make to existing ones, and you may delete redundant menu or button options. The key is to play with it, turn it inside out, stretch it, and pick it apart to see how everything works.

WIMMDI.DPR

```
{
*
*  Program:  WIMMDI.DPR
```

```
*
*  Purpose:  Main Program file.
*
*  Author:  Paul S. Penrod
*
*  Revision:
*
*  #1.00  Original Draft
*
}
program Wimmdi;
uses
  Forms,
  Main in 'MAIN.PAS' {Frame},
  Mdichild in 'MDICHILD.PAS' {Child};
{$R *.RES}
begin
  Application.CreateForm(TFrame, Frame);
  Application.CreateForm(TChild, Child);
  Application.Run;
end.
```

MAIN.PAS

```
{
*
*  Program:  MAIN.PAS
*
*  Purpose:  Parent MDI form.
*
*  Author:  Paul S. Penrod
*
*  Revision:
*
*  #1.00  Original Draft
*
}
{
```

```
*
*   Dependancies…
*
}
unit Main;
interface
uses
  SysUtils, WinTypes, WinProcs, Messages, Classes, Graphics,
Controls,
  Forms, Dialogs, Menus, MDIChild, StdCtrls, ExtCtrls;
type
  TFrame = class(TForm)
    MainMenu1: TMainMenu;
    File1: TMenuItem;
    New1: TMenuItem;
    Open1: TMenuItem;
    Exit1: TMenuItem;
    Window1: TMenuItem;
    Tile1: TMenuItem;
    Cascade1: TMenuItem;
    ArrangeIcons1: TMenuItem;
    OpenDialog1: TOpenDialog;
    Panel1: TPanel;
    DateLabel: TLabel;
    TimeLabel: TLabel;
    Timer1: TTimer;
    procedure New1Click(Sender: TObject);
    procedure StartUp(Sender: TOBject);
    procedure Exit1Click(Sender: TObject);
    procedure Tile1Click(Sender: TObject);
    procedure Cascade1Click(Sender: TObject);
    procedure ArrangeIcons1Click(Sender: TObject);
    procedure OpenWindow(Sender: TObject);
    procedure Open1Click(Sender: TObject);
    procedure Timer1Timer(Sender: TObject);
  private
    { Private declarations }
```

```
  public
    { Public declarations }
  end;
var
  Frame: TFrame;
  NewDoc: Integer;
  OldDate: TDateTime;
const
  DefaultTitle = 'DOCUMENT';
  DateFullYear = True;
  DateLeadZero = True;
  TIme24Hour = True;
  TimeLeadZero = True;
implementation
{$R *.DFM}
{
*  Procedure:  StartUp
*
*  Purpose:    Initializes objects and configures form upon
*       creation.
*
*  Arguments:  Sender: TObject
*
*  Calls:    none.
*
*  Returns:    none.
*
*  Notes:    none.
*
}
procedure TFrame.StartUp(Sender: TOBject);
begin
{
Date and Time Settings…
}
  DateLabel.Caption := DateToStr(Date);
  TimeLabel.Caption := TImeToStr(TIme);
```

```
  OldDate := Date;
{
Scale to Video display…
}
  Height := Round(Screen.Height * 0.9);
  Width := Round(Screen.Width * 0.9);
  Left := Round(Screen.Width * 0.05);
  Top := Round(Screen.Height * 0.05);
end;
{
*  Procedure:   New1Click
*
*  Purpose:     Creates a new document file to edit.
*
*  Arguments:   Sender: TObject
*
*  Calls:     none.
*
*  Returns:     none.
*
*  Notes:     none.
*
}
procedure TFrame.New1Click(Sender: TObject);
var
  Child:  TChild;
  title:  array [0..12] of Char;
  S:  array [0..12] of Char;
begin
  if NewDoc<1 then NewDoc := 1;
  Child:=TChild.Create(Self);
  Str((NewDoc/1000):4:3,s);
  StrCopy(title,DefaultTitle);
  StrCat(title,StrPos(S,'.'));
  Child.ParseFile(title);
  Child.Caption := title;
  Child.Height := Round(ClientHeight *0.7);
```

```
    Child.Width := Round(ClientWidth * 0.7);
    Child.Visible := True;
    Child.BringToFront;
    Child.Memo1.SetFocus;
    NewDoc := NewDoc + 1;
end;
{
*  Procedure:  Exit1Click
*
*  Purpose:    Exits the parent MDI forms, closes program.
*
*  Arguments:  Sender: TObject
*
*  Calls:      none.
*
*  Returns:    none.
*
*  Notes:      none.
*
}
procedure TFrame.Exit1Click(Sender: TObject);
begin
    Close;
end;
{
*  Procedure:  Tile1Click
*
*  Purpose:    Tile Children within Parent WIndow.
*
*  Arguments:  Sender: TObject
*
*  Calls:      none.
*
*  Returns:    none.
*
*  Notes:      none.
*
```

```
}
procedure TFrame.Tile1Click(Sender: TObject);
begin
  Tile;
end;
{
*  Procedure:   Cascade1Click
*
*  Purpose:     Cascade children within parent window.
*
*  Arguments:   Sender: TObject
*
*  Calls:       none.
*
*  Returns:     none.
*
*  Notes:       none.
*
}
procedure TFrame.Cascade1Click(Sender: TObject);
begin
  Cascade;
end;
{
*  Procedure:   Arrange1Click
*
*  Purpose:     Arrange icons of minimized child windows.
*
*  Arguments:   Sender: TObject
*
*  Calls:       none.
*
*  Returns:     none.
*
*  Notes:       none.
*
}
```

```
procedure TFrame.ArrangeIcons1Click(Sender: TObject);
begin
  ArrangeIcons;
end;
{
*   Procedure:   OpenWindow
*
*   Purpose:     Open file specified by OpenDialog.
*
*   Arguments:   Sender: TObject
*
*   Calls:     none.
*
*   Returns:     none.
*
*   Notes:     none.
*
}
procedure TFrame.OpenWindow(Sender: TObject);
var
  Child:  TChild;
  title:  array[0..12] of Char;
  S:  array[0..12] of Char;
begin
  if OpenDialog1.Execute then
  begin
    Child := Tchild.Create(Self);
    Child.Open(OpenDialog1.Filename);
    Child.Caption:=OpenDialog1.Filename;
    Child.ParseFile(OpenDialog1.Filename);
    Child.Visible:=True;
    Child.BringToFront;
    Child.Memo1.SetFocus;
  end;
end;
{
*   Procedure:   Open1Click
```

```
*
*  Purpose:     Event trigger for OpenWindow.
*
*  Arguments:   Sender: TObject
*
*  Calls:    none.
*
*  Returns:     none.
*
*  Notes:    none.
*
}
procedure TFrame.Open1Click(Sender: TObject);
begin
  OpenWindow(Sender);
end;
{
*  Procedure:   TImer1TImer
*
*  Purpose:     Keep date and time current on display.
*
*  Arguments:   Sender: TObject
*
*  Calls:    none.
*
*  Returns:     none.
*
*  Notes:    none.
*
}
procedure TFrame.Timer1Timer(Sender: TObject);
begin
  If OldDate <> Date then
  begin
    OldDate := Date;
    DateLabel.Caption := DateToStr(Date);
  end;
```

```
    TimeLabel.Caption := TimeToStr(Time);
end;
end.
```

MDICHILD.PAS

```
unit Mdichild;
interface
uses
  SysUtils, WinTypes, WinProcs, Messages, Classes, Graphics,
Controls,
  Forms, Dialogs, Menus, StdCtrls, ExtCtrls, Buttons, Printers;
type
  TChild = class(TForm)
    MainMenu1: TMainMenu;
    File1: TMenuItem;
    New1: TMenuItem;
    Open1: TMenuItem;
    Save1: TMenuItem;
    SaveAs1: TMenuItem;
    Exit1: TMenuItem;
    Edit1: TMenuItem;
    Cut1: TMenuItem;
    Copy1: TMenuItem;
    Paste1: TMenuItem;
    Delete1: TMenuItem;
    SelectAll1: TMenuItem;
    Character1: TMenuItem;
    Left1: TMenuItem;
    Right1: TMenuItem;
    Center1: TMenuItem;
    Font1: TMenuItem;
    WordWrap1: TMenuItem;
    Print1: TMenuItem;
    Print2: TMenuItem;
    PrintSetup1: TMenuItem;
    Panel1: TPanel;
    Memo1: TMemo;
```

```
    SaveDialog1: TSaveDialog;

    FontDialog1: TFontDialog;

    PrinterSetupDialog1: TPrinterSetupDialog;

    PrintDialog1: TPrintDialog;

    SpeedButton1: TSpeedButton;

    SpeedButton2: TSpeedButton;

    SpeedButton3: TSpeedButton;

    SpeedButton4: TSpeedButton;

    SpeedButton5: TSpeedButton;

    SpeedButton6: TSpeedButton;

    SpeedButton7: TSpeedButton;

    SpeedButton8: TSpeedButton;

    SpeedButton9: TSpeedButton;

    SpeedButton10: TSpeedButton;

    SpeedButton11: TSpeedButton;

    ColorDialog1: TColorDialog;

    ComboBox1: TComboBox;

    ComboBox2: TComboBox;

    procedure ParseFile(const path: string);

    procedure Open1Click(Sender: TObject);

    procedure Open(const path: string);

    procedure New1Click(Sender: TObject);

    procedure Exit1Click(Sender: TObject);

    procedure FormCloseQuery(Sender: TObject; var CanClose:
Boolean);

    procedure CreateBackup(const path: string);

    procedure Save1Click(Sender: TObject);

    procedure SaveAs1Click(Sender: TObject);

    procedure Cut1Click(Sender: TObject);

    procedure Copy1Click(Sender: TObject);

    procedure Paste1Click(Sender: TObject);

    procedure Delete1Click(Sender: TObject);

    procedure SelectAll1Click(Sender: TObject);

    procedure AlignClick(Sender: TOBject);

    procedure Left1Click(Sender: TObject);

    procedure Right1Click(Sender: TObject);

    procedure Center1Click(Sender: TObject);
```

```
    procedure WrapIt(Sender: TObject);
    procedure Font1Click(Sender: TObject);
    procedure PrintSetup1Click(Sender: TObject);
    procedure Print2Click(Sender: TObject);
    procedure SpeedButton6Click(Sender: TObject);
    procedure SpeedButton7Click(Sender: TObject);
    procedure SpeedButton8Click(Sender: TObject);
    procedure SpeedButton10Click(Sender: TObject);
    procedure SpeedButton11Click(Sender: TObject);
    procedure Startup(Sender: TOBject);
    procedure ComboBox1FontName(Sender: Tobject);
    procedure ComboBox2FontSize(Sender: TObject);
  private
    { Private declarations }
    fullpath: string;
    Filename: string;
    Extension: string;
    Directory: string;
    backup: string;
  public
    { Public declarations }
  end;
var
  Child: TChild;
  Const
    BackupExt = '.BAK';
    CloseText = 'Save Changes to ';
implementation
{$R *.DFM}
uses main;
{
*  Procedure:  ParseFile
*
*  Purpose:    Breaks up filename into usefull components.
*
*  Arguments:  const path: string;
*
```

```
*   Calls:      none.
*
*   Returns:     none.
*
*   Notes:     none.
*
}
procedure TChild.ParseFile(const path: string);
begin
  fullpath := path;
  filename := ExtractFileName(path);
  extension := ExtractFileExt(path);
  directory := ExtractFilePath(path);
  backup := ChangeFileExt(filename,BackupExt);
end;
{
*   Procedure:  Open1Click
*
*   Purpose:    Event trigger for Frame's OpenWindow.
*
*   Arguments:  Sender: TObject
*
*   Calls:      none.
*
*   Returns:     none.
*
*   Notes:     none.
*
}
procedure TChild.Open1Click(Sender: TObject);
begin
  Frame.OpenWindow(Sender);
end;
{
*   Procedure:  Open
*
*   Purpose:    Actually reads a file.
```

```
*
*   Arguments:   Sender: TObject
*
*   Calls:      none.
*
*   Returns:     none.
*
*   Notes:       none.
*
}
procedure TChild.Open(const path: string);
begin
  ParseFile(path);
  Memo1.Cursor := crHourGlass;
  Memo1.Lines.LoadfromFile(Filename);
  Caption := Filename;
  Memo1.SelStart:=0;
  Memo1.Modified := False;
  Memo1.Cursor := crDefault;
end;
{
*   Procedure:  New1Click
*
*   Purpose:     Event trigger for Frame's New1Click.
*
*   Arguments:   Sender: TObject
*
*   Calls:      none.
*
*   Returns:     none.
*
*   Notes:       none.
*
}
procedure TChild.New1Click(Sender: TObject);
begin
  Frame.New1Click(Sender);
```

```
end;
{
*   Procedure:   Exit1Click
*
*   Purpose:     Event trigger for frame's Exit1Click.
*
*   Arguments:   Sender: TObject
*
*   Calls:       none.
*
*   Returns:     none.
*
*   Notes:       none.
*
}
procedure TChild.Exit1Click(Sender: TObject);
begin
  Frame.Exit1Click(Sender);
end;
{
*   Procedure:   FormCloseQuery
*
*   Purpose:     Override of default function to check for *
modifed memo, prior to leaving program.
*
*   Arguments:   Sender: TObject
*
*   Calls:       none.
*
*   Returns:     none.
*
*   Notes:       none.
*
}
procedure TChild.FormCloseQuery(Sender: TObject; var CanClose:
Boolean);
var
```

```
      choice: Integer;
begin
  if Memo1.Modified then
  begin
    choice := MessageDlg(CloseText+filename+'?', mtConfirmation,
    [mbYes, mbNo, mbCancel],0);
    case choice of
      id_Yes: Save1Click(Self);
      id_Cancel: CanClose := False;
    end;
  end;
end;
{
*  Procedure:   SaveAs1Click
*
*  Purpose:     Saves file under new user specified name.
*
*  Arguments:   Sender: TObject
*
*  Calls:       none.
*
*  Returns:     none.
*
*  Notes:       none.
*
}
procedure TChild.SaveAs1Click(Sender: TObject);
begin
  SaveDialog1.DefaultExt := extension;
  SaveDialog1.FIleName := filename;
  SaveDialog1.InitialDir := directory;
  if SaveDialog1.Execute then
  begin
    ParseFile(SaveDialog1.FileName);
    Caption := filename;
    Save1Click(sender);
  end;
```

```
end;
{
*  Procedure:  CreateBackup
*
*  Purpose:     Creates a backup file.
*
*  Arguments:  Sender: TObject
*
*  Calls:     none.
*
*  Returns:     none.
*
*  Notes:     none.
*
}
procedure TChild.CreateBackup(const path: string);
begin
  DeleteFile(backup);
  RenameFile(filename,backup);
end;
{
*  Procedure:  Save1Click
*
*  Purpose:     Saves a file to disk
*
*  Arguments:  Sender: TObject
*
*  Calls:     none.
*
*  Returns:     none.
*
*  Notes:     none.
*
}
procedure TChild.Save1Click(Sender: TObject);
begin
  if filename ='' then SaveAs1Click(Sender)
```

```
      else
      begin
        CreateBackup(filename);
        Memo1.Lines.SaveToFile(fullpath);
        Memo1.Modified := False;
      end;
  end;
  {
  *  Procedure:  Cut1Click
  *
  *  Purpose:    Cut marked memo selection to clipboard.
  *
  *  Arguments:  Sender: TObject
  *
  *  Calls:      none.
  *
  *  Returns:    none.
  *
  *  Notes:      none.
  *
  }
  procedure TChild.Cut1Click(Sender: TObject);
  begin
    Memo1.CutToClipboard;
  end;
  {
  *  Procedure:  Copy1Click
  *
  *  Purpose:    Copy marked memo section to clipboard.
  *
  *  Arguments:  Sender: TObject
  *
  *  Calls:      none.
  *
  *  Returns:    none.
  *
  *  Notes:      none.
```

```
 *
 }
procedure TChild.Copy1Click(Sender: TObject);
begin
  Memo1.CopyToClipboard;
end;
{
 *  Procedure:  Paste1Click
 *
 *  Purpose:    Paste text contents of clipboard to memo.
 *
 *  Arguments:  Sender: TObject
 *
 *  Calls:     none.
 *
 *  Returns:    none.
 *
 *  Notes:     none.
 *
 }
procedure TChild.Paste1Click(Sender: TObject);
begin
  Memo1.PasteFromClipboard;
end;
{
 *  Procedure:  Delete1Click
 *
 *  Purpose:    Delete selected Memo data.
 *
 *  Arguments:  Sender: TObject
 *
 *  Calls:     none.
 *
 *  Returns:    none.
 *
 *  Notes:     none.
 *
```

```
}
procedure TChild.Delete1Click(Sender: TObject);
begin
  Memo1.ClearSelection;
end;
{
*   Procedure:  SelectAll1Click
*
*   Purpose:    Mark the entire contents of memo.
*
*   Arguments:  Sender: TObject
*
*   Calls:      none.
*
*   Returns:    none.
*
*   Notes:      none.
*
}
procedure TChild.SelectAll1Click(Sender: TObject);
begin
  Memo1.SelectAll;
end;
{
*   Procedure:  AlignClick
*
*   Purpose:    Common memo text alignment procedure.
*
*   Arguments:  Sender: TObject
*
*   Calls:      none.
*
*   Returns:    none.
*
*   Notes:      none.
*
}
```

```
procedure TChild.AlignClick(Sender: TOBject);
begin
  Left1.Checked := False;
  Right1.Checked := False;
  Center1.Checked := False;
with Sender as TMenuItem do Checked := True;
  with Memo1 do
    if Left1.Checked then
      Alignment := taLeftJustify
    else if Right1.Checked then
      Alignment := taRightJustify
    else if Center1.Checked then
      Alignment := taCenter;
end;
{
*  Procedure:  Left1Click
*
*  Purpose:    Left Justifies memo text.
*
*  Arguments:  Sender: TObject
*
*  Calls:    none.
*
*  Returns:    none.
*
*  Notes:    none.
*
}
procedure TChild.Left1Click(Sender: TObject);
begin
  AlignClick(Sender);
end;
{
*  Procedure:  Right1Click
*
*  Purpose:    Right Justifies memo text.
*
```

```
*   Arguments:  Sender: TObject
*
*   Calls:     none.
*
*   Returns:    none.
*
*   Notes:     none.
*
}
procedure TChild.Right1Click(Sender: TObject);
begin
  AlignClick(sender);
end;
{
*   Procedure:  Center1Click
*
*   Purpose:    Centers memo text.
*
*   Arguments:  Sender: TObject
*
*   Calls:     none.
*
*   Returns:    none.
*
*   Notes:     none.
*
}
procedure TChild.Center1Click(Sender: TObject);
begin
  AlignClick(Sender);
end;
{
*   Procedure:  WrapIt
*
*   Purpose:    Handles word wrapping of memo text.
*
*   Arguments:  Sender: TObject
```

```
*
*  Calls:     none.
*
*  Returns:    none.
*
*  Notes:     none.
*
}
procedure TChild.WrapIt(Sender: TObject);
begin
  with Memo1 do
  begin
    WordWrap := not WordWrap;
    if WordWrap then
      ScrollBars := ssVertical else
      ScrollBars := ssBoth;
    WordWrap1.Checked := WordWrap;
  end;
end;
{
*  Procedure:  Font1Click
*
*  Purpose:    Call FontDialog and sets memo font.
*
*  Arguments:  Sender: TObject
*
*  Calls:     none.
*
*  Returns:    none.
*
*  Notes:     none.
*
}
procedure TChild.Font1Click(Sender: TObject);
var
  old_color: TColor;
begin
```

```
  old_color := Memo1.Font.Color;
  If FontDialog1.Execute then
    Memo1.Font := FontDialog1.Font;
  Memo1.Font.Color := old_color;
end;
{
*  Procedure:  PrintSetup1Click
*
*  Purpose:    Call PrinterSetupDialog to configure printer.
*
*  Arguments:  Sender: TObject
*
*  Calls:     none.
*
*  Returns:    none.
*
*  Notes:     none.
*
}
procedure TChild.PrintSetup1Click(Sender: TObject);
begin
  PrinterSetupDialog1.Execute;
end;
{
*  Procedure:  Print2Click
*
*  Purpose:    Does the actual formatting and shoveling to *
the printer.
*
*  Arguments:  Sender: TObject
*
*  Calls:     none.
*
*  Returns:    none.
*
*  Notes:     none.
*
```

```
}
procedure TChild.Print2Click(Sender: TObject);
var
  {
    This group handles the page boundaries.
  }
  VInch: Integer;
  HInch: Integer;
  VMargin: Integer;
  TopLine: Integer;
  TopMargin: Integer;
  BotMargin: Integer;
  HMargin: Integer;
  LMargin: Integer;
  RMargin: Integer;
  TVOffset: Integer;
  TMargin: Integer;
  BotLine: Integer;
  PVOffset: Integer;
  PMargin: Integer;
  {
    This group handles the Title and Page print.
  }
  VWorkArea: Integer;
  HWorkArea: Integer;
  Indent: Integer;
  THOffset: Integer;
  PHOffset: Integer;
  TitleSize: Integer;
  PenWidth: Integer;
  {
    This group handles the data.
  }
  DeckHeight: Integer;
  PixelRatio: Integer;
  LinesPerPage: Integer;
  PageCount: Integer;
```

```
    LineOffset: Integer;
    NumCopies: Integer;
    Printed: Boolean;
    LinePrinted: Integer;
    LeftOnPage: Integer;
    LeftInDoc: Integer;
begin
{
    First, find the boundaries of the page.
    Everything is calculated based on inches
    with 8.5 x 11 paper as default.
}
    VInch := Round(Printer.PageHeight/11);
    HInch := Round(Printer.PageWidth/8.5);
    VMargin := VInch;
    TopMargin := VMargin;
    TopLine := VMargin - Round(VInch/8);
    TVOffset := VMargin - Round(VInch/4);
    TMargin := TopMargin - TVOffset;
    BotMargin := Printer.PageHeight - VInch;
    BotLine := BotMargin + Round(VInch/8);
    PVOffset := (BotMargin + Round(VInch/4)) - BotMargin;
    PMargin := BotMargin + PVOffset;
    LMargin := HInch;
    RMargin := Printer.PageWidth - HInch;
    VWorkArea := BotMargin - TopMargin;
    HWorkArea := RMargin - LMargin;
    TitleSize := 10; { Use 10 Point always }
    PixelRatio := 4; { For now 4 pixels/Point }
    Printer.Canvas.Font := Memo1.Font;
    PenWidth := Printer.Canvas.Pen.Width;
    DeckHeight := Memo1.Font.Size * PixelRatio;
    Indent := LMargin;
    LinesPerPage := Round(VWorkArea / (Memo1.Font.Size *
PixelRatio));
    PageCount := Round((Memo1.Lines.Count / LinesPerPage)+0.49);
    NumCopies := PrintDialog1.Copies;
```

```
      if PrintDialog1.Execute then
    begin
      repeat
      Printed := False;
      LinePrinted := 0;
      LeftOnPage := LinesPerPage;
      LeftInDoc := Memo1.Lines.Count;
      Printer.BeginDoc;
      repeat
      {
        Header…
      }
      Printer.Canvas.Font.Size := TitleSize;
      Printer.Canvas.TextOut(Indent,TMargin,'Filename: '+filename);
      Printer.Canvas.Pen.Width := PixelRatio * 2;
      Printer.Canvas.MoveTo(LMargin,TopLine);
      Printer.Canvas.LineTo(RMargin,TopLine);
      Printer.Canvas.Pen.Width := PenWidth;
      {
        Body of document…
      }
      LineOffset := TopMargin;
      LeftOnPage := LinesPerPage;
      Printer.Canvas.Font := Memo1.Font;
      repeat

  Printer.Canvas.TextOut(Indent,LineOffset,Memo1.Lines[LinePrinted]);
      LineOffset := LineOffset + DeckHeight;
      LinePrinted := LinePrinted+1;
      LeftInDoc := LeftInDoc - 1;
      If LeftInDoc < 1 then
      begin
        LeftOnPage := 0;
        Printed := True;
      end;
      if LeftInDoc > 0 then
        LeftOnPage := LeftOnPage - 1;
```

```
    until LeftOnPage < 1;
    {
      Footer…
    }
    Printer.Canvas.Pen.Width := PixelRatio * 2;
    Printer.Canvas.MoveTo(LMargin,BotLine);
    Printer.Canvas.LineTo(RMargin,BotLine);
    Printer.Canvas.Pen.Width := PenWidth;
    Printer.Canvas.Font.Size := TitleSize;
    Printer.Canvas.TextOut(Indent,PMargin,'Page
'+IntToStr(Printer.PageNumber)+' of '+IntToStr(PageCount));
    Printer.NewPage;
    until Printed;
    {
      Close the Document Stream…
    }
    Printer.EndDoc;
    NumCopies := NumCopies - 1;
    until NumCopies < 1;
  end;
end;
{
*  Procedure:   SpeedButton6Click
*
*  Purpose:     This one actually left justifies memo text.
*
*  Arguments:   Sender: TObject
*
*  Calls:    none.
*
*  Returns:    none.
*
*  Notes:    none.
*
}
procedure TChild.SpeedButton6Click(Sender: TObject);
begin
```

```
  with MainMenu1 do
  begin
    Left1.Checked := True;
    Right1.Checked := False;
    Center1.Checked := False;
  end;
  with Memo1 do Alignment := taLeftJustify;
end;
{
*  Procedure:   SpeedButton7Click
*
*  Purpose:     This one actually centers memo text.
*
*  Arguments:   Sender: TObject
*
*  Calls:       none.
*
*  Returns:     none.
*
*  Notes:       none.
*
}
procedure TChild.SpeedButton7Click(Sender: TObject);
begin
  with MainMenu1 do
  begin
    Left1.Checked := False;
    Right1.Checked := False;
    Center1.Checked := True;
  end;
  with Memo1 do Alignment := taCenter;
end;
{
*  Procedure:   SpeedButton8Click
*
*  Purpose:     This one actually right justifes memo text.
*
```

```
*    Arguments:    Sender: TObject
*
*    Calls:        none.
*
*    Returns:      none.
*
*    Notes:        none.
*
}
procedure TChild.SpeedButton8Click(Sender: TObject);
begin
  with MainMenu1 do
  begin
    Left1.Checked := False;
    Right1.Checked := True;
    Center1.Checked := False;
  end;
  with Memo1 do Alignment := taRightJustify;
end;
{
*    Procedure:   SpeedButton10Click
*
*    Purpose:     Sets memo foreground color.
*
*    Arguments:   Sender: TObject
*
*    Calls:       none.
*
*    Returns:     none.
*
*    Notes:       none.
*
}
procedure TChild.SpeedButton10Click(Sender: TObject);
begin
  if ColorDialog1.Execute then
    Memo1.Font.Color := ColorDialog1.Color;
```

```
end;
{
*   Procedure:    SpeedButton11Click
*
*   Purpose:      Sets memo background color.
*
*   Arguments:  Sender: TObject
*
*   Calls:      none.
*
*   Returns:      none.
*
*   Notes:      none.
*
}
procedure TChild.SpeedButton11Click(Sender: TObject);
begin
  If ColorDialog1.Execute then
    Memo1.Color := ColorDialog1.Color;
end;
{
*   Procedure:  StartUp
*
*   Purpose:      Initializes form objects and the form itself.
*
*   Arguments:  Sender: TObject
*
*   Calls:      none.
*
*   Returns:      none.
*
*   Notes:      none.
*
}
procedure TChild.Startup(Sender: TOBject);
var
  count: Integer;
```

```
  i: Integer;
  j: array[0..12] of char;
begin
{
First we grab the types of Screen Fonts available
to the Form for display.
}
  ComboBox1.Text := Memo1.Font.Name;
  count := Screen.Fonts.Count;
  for i:=0 to count-1 do
  begin
    ComboBox1.Items.Add(Screen.Fonts.Strings[i]);
  end;
{
Next we fill out the second Combo Box with valid
font sizes.
}
  Str(Memo1.Font.Size,j);
  ComboBox2.Text := j;
  for i:=6 to 72 do
  begin
    Str(i,j);
    ComboBox2.Items.Add(j);
  end;
end;
{
*  Procedure:   ComboBox1FontName
*
*  Purpose:     Sets new memo fonts from a combo box.
*
*  Arguments:   Sender: TObject
*
*  Calls:     none.
*
*  Returns:     none.
*
*  Notes:     none.
```

```
 *
procedure TChild.ComboBox1FontName(Sender: TObject);
var
  old_color:  TColor;
begin
  old_color := Memo1.Font.Color;
  Memo1.Font.Name := ComboBox1.Text;
  Memo1.Font.Color := old_color;
  Memo1.SetFocus;
end;
{
 *  Procedure:   ComboBox2FontSize
 *
 *  Purpose:     Sets memo font size from a combo box.
 *
 *  Arguments:   Sender: TObject
 *
 *  Calls:       none.
 *
 *  Returns:     none.
 *
 *  Notes:       none.
 *
}
procedure TChild.ComboBox2FontSize(Sender: TObject);
var
  size: Integer;
  ptr: Integer;
begin
  Val(ComboBox2.Text,size,ptr);
  Memo1.Font.Size := size;
  Memo1.Font.Name := ComboBox1.Text;
  Memo1.SetFocus;
end;
end.
```

CHAPTER 6

Rousting Errors with the Integrated Debugger

Here we sit. Our program is done, and we are ready to launch the new flagship product that will make us millions of dollars and bring the captains of industry to our doorstep.

Well, almost. There's a little issue with child windows. Open too many of them and you crash the program. But wait a minute! Who in his right mind wants to have dozens of windows open at the same time? Fair question. Nobody I can think of offhand. But, lurking out there in the shadows is that one user that has your name written down. This nameless user has a deft knack of finding everything you missed, and lets you know about every instance.

There is an old saw that goes, *"Never try to make anything foolproof, because fools are so ingenious."* This has never been more true, in my opinion, than with software. Users will find everything wrong with your product sooner or later. Okay, so what do we do?

185

For the child window problem, a fix is simple. You place a global in MAIN.PAS, which tracks how many windows are open, and set a limit, or just ignore it altogether as an acceptable consequence, and warn the user about opening too many child windows on machines with limited memory.

But, the real issue brought up by such a discussion centers around validating your program. There is no such thing as bug-free software. Your code may be just perfect, but the compiler, any libraries you use, any DLLs, the linker, Windows, and DOS all have problems of one sort or another. Any one of these items may be bug-free itself, but may exacerbate bad code somewhere else.

With the reality-check out of the way, it really isn't quite as bad as you might think. With all the character built into the systems we use, things still run, answers still come out correctly, and life goes on. The key to your program's success and the trust that people will place in it centers on how well it operates, as described by you, and how well it performs the functions intended. This you have control over. Probably the most useful tool you will find in the plethora of development goodies at your disposal is the debugger.

Using Delphi's Integrated Debugger

As we discussed in Chapter 3, testing code should happen at three levels: function, module, and environment. Because of the object-oriented nature of Delphi's version of PASCAL, these divisions for testing occur at natural partitions in the code. For the most part, you will probably find yourself (at least in this environment) testing at the function level.

Preparing the Code for Debugging

Before you can use the integrated debugger, or for that matter, the Turbo Debugger for Windows, the compiled code needs to have debugging information included. With symbolic information included, either debugger will let you walk through your source code while the program is executing. This is really a big help to you as the programmer, since source code is much easier to understand and follow than the machine code the computer enjoys digesting.

To do this in Delphi:

1. With a project loaded in Delphi, Select the **Options** main menu item, and choose **Project** from the drop list.
2. Select the tab labeled **Compiler** from the **Project Options** window (Figure 6.1). You will notice inside the Debugging group, a list of three check boxes:
   - Debugging Information
   - Local Symbols
   - Symbol Info

Debug Information Directive

Choosing this option from the Compiler page tells Delphi's compiler to generate debugging information for each module in the project. Codewise, this directive would appear in each unit as **{$D+}** (turn on debug information) or **{$D-}** (turn off debug information).

When turned on, the debug information directive causes the compiler to generate a line-number table for each procedure to map object code addresses to source text. If an error occurs at runtime, the debugger can go right to the source line that generated the offending code. This is a really big help if you are not clear what the problem is from the onset. Many times, just seeing what line of source code is at the heart of the problem is all that is necessary to figure out what to do, or where to go next to fix things.

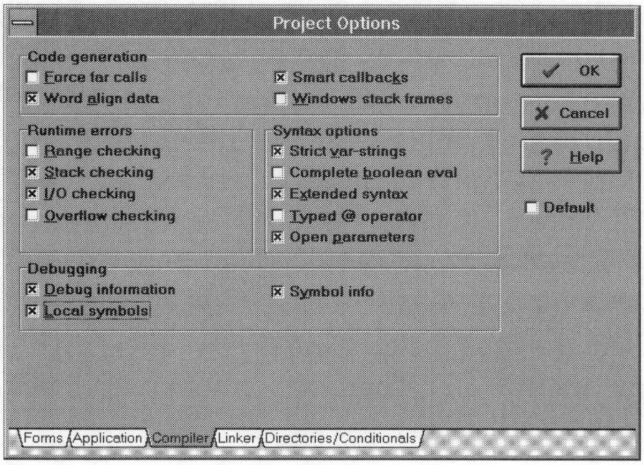

Figure 6.1
The Project
Options window.

Local Symbols Directive

Choosing this option from the Compiler page tells Delphi's compiler to generate debugging information for all local identifiers within each module in the project. Codewise, this directive would appear in each unit as {$L+} (turn on local symbol generation) or {$L-} (turn off local symbol generation).

When this option is turned on for a unit, Delphi's compiler generates a symbol table to give the debugger access to all identifiers within the unit that are local to the procedure or to the implementation part of the unit. In other words, no global declarations are covered here, either to the module or to the program as a whole.

What is unique about this directive is that these local variables are not only visible, but modifiable as well. This can be very important if you need to test different values on the fly for a local variable during a debugging session. In a sense, these local identifiers are much like local or automatic variables in C. If declared in procedures, these variables exist on the stack only during the execution of the procedure or function itself. Once the procedure or function is completed and returns to the calling procedure, these variables are destroyed.

Symbol Information Directive

Choosing this option from the Compiler page tells Delphi's compiler to generate debugging information for all identifiers within each module in the project. Codewise, this directive would appear in each unit as {$Y+} (turn on symbol generation) or {$Y-} (turn off symbol generation).

When this option is turned on for a unit, Delphi's compiler generates a symbol table that provides line numbers to all symbols within the module, where they are declared, and where they are referenced. When this information is available, the Object Browser can display reference information and symbol definitions within the unit itself.

3. Select the tab labeled **Linker** from the **Project Options** window (Figure 6.2). There are only two options that you will

generally concern yourself with on this page, the **Map File** option, and the **Debug in EXE** option.

Debug in EXE Option

As far as the integrated debugger is concerned, this option has no effect on its operation, as the symbol tables are taken from intermediate files, not from the EXE, while the debugger runs. However, if you want to run your code with the Turbo Debugger for Windows (a stand-alone debugger), then you must select this option; otherwise, the debugger will not find the information it needs to run properly.

A quick side note is in order. If you do select this option, your EXE will grow significantly larger. Instead of generating intermediate files for use in debugging and using those separately, the Linker rolls all that information right into your EXE file. IF you don't want your program to take up lots of room in memory after you are through testing it, you need to recompile your project with all debug options turned off to remove the extraneous information.

Map File Options

Surprisingly enough, this option is not necessary for the debugger to do its job. However, it can be very helpful to advanced programmers in their debugging; plus, the Turbo Debugger for Windows can also make use of it. Table 6.1 lists the four Map File options.

Figure 6.2
Selecting the
Linker.

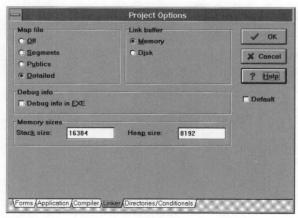

Table 6.1	Map File Options
Off	The linker does not produce a Map File.
Segments	The Linker creates a Map File that has: • Program Start Address • List of segments • Linker Warning and Error messages
Publics	The Linker creates a Map File that has: • Program Start Address • List of segments • Linker Warning and Error messages • Alphabetically sorted public symbols
Detailed	The Linker creates a Map File that has: • Program Start Address • List of segments • Linker Warning and Error messages • Alphabetically sorted public symbols The Linker also creates an additional segment map that contains: • Group • Module information • Segment • Address • Length (in bytes)

A Sample Map File

Following is a sample Map File created by compiling the WIM-MDI Editor with all the debugging options turned on:

Start	Length	Name	Class
0001:0002	007FH	Wimmdi	CODE
0001:0081	14A3H	Mdichild	CODE
0001:1524	0675H	Main	CODE
0001:1B99	0D73H	Printers	CODE
0001:290C	0564H	TypInfo	CODE
0001:2E70	0075H	WinProcs	CODE
0002:0002	4623H	Dialogs	CODE
0003:0002	2E03H	Buttons	CODE
0004:0002	1A4CH	ExtCtrls	CODE
0004:1A4E	223FH	Menus	CODE
0005:0002	3FCBH	StdCtrls	CODE
0006:0002	6D10H	Graphics	CODE
0007:0002	6954H	Controls	CODE

Start	Length	Name	Class
0008:0002	686DH	Forms	CODE
0009:0002	526DH	Classes	CODE
000A:0002	3005H	SysUtils	CODE
000B:0002	19DFH	System	CODE
000C:0000	0F54H	DATA	DATA

Address	Publics by Value
0001:0002	@
0001:28E3	@
0001:290C	GetTypeData
0001:2921	GetEnumName
0001:294D	GetEnumValue
0001:29A1	GetPropInfo
0001:2A0F	GetPropInfos
0001:2A75	IsStoredProp
0001:2AC0	GetOrdProp
0001:2B50	SetOrdProp
0001:2BD0	GetStrProp
0001:2C2A	SetStrProp
0001:2C99	GetFloatProp
0001:2D11	SetFloatProp
0001:2DA9	GetMethodProp
0001:2E09	SetMethodProp
0001:2E70	GlobalAllocPtr
0001:2E92	GlobalReAllocPtr
0001:2EC3	GlobalFreePtr
0002:451A	MessageDlg
0002:454A	MessageDlgPos
0002:45EF	@
0003:06AC	DrawButtonFace
0003:2DE5	@
0004:0B07	Frame3D
0004:1F72	ShortCutToText
0004:21FC	TextToShortCut
0004:3C3E	@
0006:0D00	ColorToRGB

Address	Publics by Value
0006:0D9E	PaletteChanged
0006:0E00	ColorToIdent
0006:0E63	IdentToColor
0006:2407	MemAlloc
0006:4C9C	FreeMemoryContexts
0006:6B5F	InitGraphics
0007:0AE1	InitWndProc
0007:0BA3	FindControl
0007:0C25	CursorToIdent
0007:0C8F	IdentToCursor
0007:0D02	GetShortHint
0007:0D5C	GetLongHint
0007:0DB5	GetCaptureControl
0007:0E06	SetCaptureControl
0007:0EE6	FindDragTarget
0007:6939	@
0008:0E14	DisableTaskWindows
0008:0EF7	EnableTaskWindows
0008:11B1	DoneCtl3D
0008:11CE	Subclass3DDlg
0008:1228	MakeObjectInstance
0008:1344	FreeObjectInstance
0008:138C	AllocateHWnd
0008:140B	DeallocateHWnd
0008:1436	KeysToShiftState
0008:148B	KeyDataToShiftState
0008:14CF	IsAccel
0008:1529	GetParentForm
0008:1582	ValidParentForm
0009:06AF	Point
0009:06C9	Rect
0009:06EF	Bounds
0009:077C	GetClass
0009:081C	FindClass
0009:08DF	RegisterClass
0009:099B	RegisterClasses

Address	Publics by Value
0009:0A77	RegisterIntegerConsts
0009:0AB9	ReadComponentRes
0009:0BB6	LineStart
0009:1D60	NewStrItem
0009:1DAB	DisposeStrItem
0009:5225	@
000A:04CD	AddExitProc
000A:0530	NewStr
000A:057D	DisposeStr
000A:05AA	AssignStr
000A:05E1	AppendStr
000A:060E	CompareStr
000A:063D	CompareText
000A:068E	AnsiCompareText
000A:06C5	IsValidIdent
000A:074A	IntToStr
000A:077B	StrToInt
000A:07CC	LoadStr
000A:07F1	FmtLoadStr
000A:0842	FileOpen
000A:086A	FileCreate
000A:0891	DeleteFile
000A:08B5	RenameFile
000A:08EE	ChangeFileExt
000A:096A	ExtractFilePath
000A:09BD	ExtractFileName
000A:0A13	ExtractFileExt
000A:0A88	StrLen
000A:0A9F	StrEnd
000A:0AB6	StrMove
000A:0ADB	StrCopy
000A:0AFD	StrECopy
000A:0B20	StrLCopy
000A:0B48	StrPCopy
000A:0B66	StrPLCopy
000A:0B8B	StrCat
000A:0BAE	StrComp

Address	Publics by Value
000A:0BD7	StrIComp
000A:0C1B	StrScan
000A:0C43	StrRScan
000A:0C6A	StrPos
000A:0CBD	StrPas
000A:0CDE	StrAlloc
000A:0D0B	StrBufSize
000A:0D25	StrNew
000A:0D72	StrDispose
000A:0D96	StrFmt
000A:0DDE	Format
000A:0E16	FmtStr
000A:0EC1	EncodeTime
000A:0EFB	DecodeTime
000A:10A4	EncodeDate
000A:10D7	DecodeDate
000A:120C	DayOfWeek
000A:1237	Date
000A:126A	Time
000A:1910	DateTimeToString
000A:1933	DateToStr
000A:1958	TimeToStr
000A:197D	GetProfileStr
000A:19BA	GetProfileChar
000A:1AF9	GetFormatSettings
000A:1D0E	ExceptObject
000A:1D22	ExceptAddr
000A:1DDE	ShowException
000A:23C5	EnableExceptionHandler
000A:24C9	@
000A:24D9	FormatBuf
000A:280D	FloatToText
000A:2A7C	FloatToTextFmt
000A:2D2D	FloatToDecimal
000A:2E4C	TextToFloat
000C:004C	MsgDlgButtonStyle
000C:004D	MsgDlgGlyphs

Address	Publics by Value
000C:004E	MsgDlgBtnSize
000C:0736	CreationControl
000C:073A	VBXHook
000C:073E	VBXPropMsg
000C:0852	Ctl3DBtnWndProc
000C:0856	Ctl3DDlgFramePaint
000C:085A	Ctl3DCtlColorEx
000C:09EC	ProcessorExceptHook
000C:09F0	EmptyStr
000C:09F2	NullStr
000C:0B30	ExceptList
000C:0B32	RaiseList
000C:0B34	ExceptProc
000C:0B38	ErrorProc
000C:0B3C	ExceptionClass
000C:0B40	ExceptDebugPtr
000C:0B44	ExitProc
000C:0B48	ExitCode
000C:0B4A	ErrorAddr
000C:0B4E	PrefixSeg
000C:0B50	InOutRes
000C:0B52	RandSeed
000C:0B56	SelectorInc
000C:0B58	HeapCheck
000C:0B5C	HeapError
000C:0B60	Test8086
000C:0B61	FileMode
000C:0B62	HPrevInst
000C:0B64	HInstance
000C:0B66	CmdShow
000C:0B68	CmdLine
000C:0B6C	HeapList
000C:0B6E	HeapLimit
000C:0B70	HeapBlock
000C:0B72	HeapAllocFlags
000C:0B94	Child

Address	Publics by Value
000C:0B98	Frame
000C:0B9C	NewDoc
000C:0B9E	OldDate
000C:0CCE	NewStyleControls
000C:0CEC	Application
000C:0CF0	Screen
000C:0CF4	HintWindows
000C:0D0E	Printer
000C:0D12	CurrencyString
000C:0D1A	CurrencyFormat
000C:0D1B	NegCurrFormat
000C:0D1C	ThousandSeparator
000C:0D1D	DecimalSeparator
000C:0D1E	CurrencyDecimals
000C:0D1F	DateSeparator
000C:0D20	ShortDateFormat
000C:0D30	LongDateFormat
000C:0D50	TimeSeparator
000C:0D52	TimeAMString
000C:0D5A	TimePMString
000C:0D62	ShortTimeFormat
000C:0D72	LongTimeFormat
000C:0D92	ShortMonthNames
000C:0DC2	LongMonthNames
000C:0E82	ShortDayNames
000C:0E9E	LongDayNames

```
Line numbers for Wimmdi(WIMMDI.DPR) segment Wimmdi
10 0001:0002  11 0001:003E   12 0001:0056   13 0001:006E
14 0001:0079
Line numbers for Mdichild(MDICHILD.PAS) segment Mdichild
111 0001:05C9 112 0001:05D8  113 0001:05EE  114 0001:060F
115 0001:0630 116 0001:0651  117 0001:067B  120 0001:067F
121 0001:0689 122 0001:069A  125 0001:069E  126 0001:06A8
127 0001:06B7 128 0001:06C8  129 0001:06E5  130 0001:06F8
131 0001:0709 132 0001:071A  133 0001:072B  136 0001:072F
137 0001:0739 138 0001:074A  141 0001:074E  142 0001:0758
```

```
143 0001:0769 148 0001:0780 149 0001:078F 151 0001:07A2
153 0001:07DA 154 0001:07DD 155 0001:07F4 158 0001:0800
161 0001:0804 162 0001:080E 163 0001:082C 164 0001:084A
166 0001:0862 168 0001:0877 169 0001:088F 170 0001:08A2
172 0001:08B2 175 0001:08B6 176 0001:08C0 177 0001:08CE
178 0001:08E5 181 0001:08E9 182 0001:08F3 185 0001:090D
186 0001:0920 187 0001:093D 189 0001:094E 192 0001:0952
193 0001:095C 194 0001:096B 197 0001:096F 198 0001:0979
199 0001:0988 202 0001:098C 203 0001:0996 204 0001:09A5
207 0001:09A9 208 0001:09B3 209 0001:09C2 212 0001:09C6
213 0001:09D0 214 0001:09DF 217 0001:09E3 218 0001:09F1
219 0001:0A02 220 0001:0A13 221 0001:0A24 222 0001:0A44
223 0001:0A52 224 0001:0A61 225 0001:0A6F 226 0001:0A7E
227 0001:0A8C 228 0001:0A9B 229 0001:0AA7 232 0001:0AAB
233 0001:0AB5 234 0001:0AC5 237 0001:0AC9 238 0001:0AD3
239 0001:0AE3 242 0001:0AE7 243 0001:0AF1 244 0001:0B01
247 0001:0B05 248 0001:0B13 250 0001:0B21 251 0001:0B34
252 0001:0B3F 253 0001:0B4A 254 0001:0B56 256 0001:0B6E
261 0001:0B72 262 0001:0B80 263 0001:0B9A 264 0001:0BB9
265 0001:0BCC 266 0001:0BEB 267 0001:0C04 270 0001:0C08
271 0001:0C12 272 0001:0C21 321 0001:0C55 327 0001:0C64
328 0001:0C88 329 0001:0CAC 331 0001:0CB2 332 0001:0CB8
333 0001:0CD6 334 0001:0CF4 336 0001:0CFD 337 0001:0D0E
338 0001:0D2C 339 0001:0D56 341 0001:0D5F 342 0001:0D65
344 0001:0D76 345 0001:0D7F 347 0001:0D88 348 0001:0D8D
349 0001:0D92 350 0001:0DB8 351 0001:0DD5 352 0001:0DEE
353 0001:0DF4 354 0001:0E24 355 0001:0E5D 357 0001:0E6C
360 0001:0E82 361 0001:0E86 362 0001:0E8B 363 0001:0E91
364 0001:0EAA 369 0001:0EB5 370 0001:0ED2 371 0001:0F0C
372 0001:0F2C 373 0001:0F48 374 0001:0F64 380 0001:0F81
381 0001:0F87 382 0001:0F8D 384 0001:0FB3 385 0001:0FEE
386 0001:0FF7 387 0001:0FFE 389 0001:1005 391 0001:100B
392 0001:1010 395 0001:1014 396 0001:101A 398 0001:1021
402 0001:1027 403 0001:1047 404 0001:1063 405 0001:107F
406 0001:109C 407 0001:10B9 408 0001:1120 409 0001:112B
413 0001:1134 414 0001:113F 415 0001:1146 417 0001:114F
421 0001:1153 422 0001:1161 424 0001:1169 425 0001:117A
```

```
426 0001:118B 429 0001:119C  430 0001:11AD  433 0001:11B1
434 0001:11BF 436 0001:11C7  437 0001:11D8  438 0001:11E9
441 0001:11FA 442 0001:120B  445 0001:120F  446 0001:121D
448 0001:1225 449 0001:1236  450 0001:1247  453 0001:1258
454 0001:1269 457 0001:126D  458 0001:1277  459 0001:128A
460 0001:12AD 463 0001:12B1  464 0001:12BB  465 0001:12CE
466 0001:12ED 472 0001:12F1  480 0001:1300  481 0001:1328
482 0001:133C 484 0001:1352  485 0001:1382  491 0001:138A
492 0001:13AE 493 0001:13CF  495 0001:13D9  496 0001:13ED
497 0001:1415 498 0001:141B  503 0001:141F  504 0001:142E
505 0001:1448 506 0001:1470  507 0001:1489  508 0001:149B
514 0001:149F 515 0001:14AE  516 0001:14D0  517 0001:14E6
518 0001:150E 519 0001:1520
Line numbers for Main(MAIN.PAS) segment Main
58 0001:175B  63 0001:176A   64 0001:1794   65 0001:17BE
69 0001:17CA  70 0001:17F9   71 0001:1828   72 0001:1857
73 0001:1886  80 0001:1898   81 0001:18A7   82 0001:18B4
83 0001:18D0  84 0001:18EB   85 0001:18FA   86 0001:1915
87 0001:1931  88 0001:194D   89 0001:197B   90 0001:19A9
91 0001:19B5  92 0001:19BF   93 0001:19D1   94 0001:19D8
97 0001:19DC  98 0001:19E6   99 0001:19F0   102 0001:19F4
103 0001:19FE 104 0001:1A08  107 0001:1A0C  108 0001:1A16
109 0001:1A20 112 0001:1A24  113 0001:1A2E  114 0001:1A38
121 0001:1A3C 122 0001:1A4A  124 0001:1A62  125 0001:1A7E
126 0001:1A96 127 0001:1AAE  128 0001:1AC6  129 0001:1AD2
130 0001:1ADC 132 0001:1AEE  135 0001:1AF2  136 0001:1AFC
137 0001:1B0C 140 0001:1B10  141 0001:1B1F  143 0001:1B35
144 0001:1B41 147 0001:1B6B  148 0001:1B95
Program entry point at 0001:0002
```

Testing
Procedures and Functions

Now that our project is compiled with debug information, we can
tour the code in grand style. We shall investigate some of the different things the debugger will let you do that you will find useful
for testing functions and procedures.

By the way, everything we do at this level applies to the project level of testing as well. There are just some things the debugger does that are more useful at this level of detail, and vice versa.

Our first stop on the tour is at *breakpoints.*

Breakpoints—Stop Signs on the Highway

The breakpoint's sole purpose is to stop things—like your program when it reaches a certain point during execution. Think of it as a brick wall in the middle of the road. Whether your program pulls up short or runs headlong into it, it stops.

Delphi's breakpoints are just a little different in this respect. Not only can they stop your program, but they also do it with flair. More on this later. For now, we need to get the breakpoint basics first, such as setting, deleting, disabling, and enabling.

Setting a Breakpoint

There are three ways to set a breakpoint: The easiest is to use your mouse on the line of code in the source window that you want to set your breakpoint at. Move the mouse to the far left corner of the window and press the left mouse button. The line of code will be highlighted and a little stop sign will appear to the left of the code (Figure 6.3).

The second way to set a breakpoint requires the following:

1. Move the cursor in the source window to the line where you want to place the breakpoint.

2. From the **Run** menu option of Delphi's main menu, select **Add Breakpoint** from the drop list.

3. The **Edit Breakpoint** window will appear (Figure 6.4). Press **ENTER** or select the **NEW** button to add the breakpoint to the list of active breakpoints. Again, the line of code selected previously will be highlighted with the little stop sign to the left.

   As a test, run the program. When the program gets to the line you placed the breakpoint on, it stops and waits there for you to take action. From here you can edit, reset the program, look at variables, let the program continue to run, or stop the run entirely.

Figure 6.3
Setting a break-
point.

```
┌─────────────────────────────────────────────────────┐
│ ─              MAIN.PAS                      ▼  ▲     │
│   end;                                            ↑  │
│                                                      │
│   procedure TFrame.New1Click(Sender: TObject);       │
│   var                                                │
│       Child:    TChild;                              │
│       title:    array [0..12] of Char;               │
│       S:        array [0..12] of Char;               │
│   begin                                              │
│ ●     If NewDoc<1 then NewDoc := 1;                  │
│       Child:=TChild.Create(Self);                    │
│       Str((NewDoc/1000):4:3,s);                      │
│       StrCopy(title,DefaultTitle);                   │
│       StrCat(title,StrPos(S,'.'));                   │
│       Child.ParseFile(title);                        │
│       Child.Caption := title;                        │
│       Child.Height := Round(ClientHeight *0.7);      │
│       Child.Width := Round(ClientWidth * 0.7);       │
│       Child.Visible := True;                         │
│       Child.BringToFront;                            │
│       Child.Memo1.SetFocus;                          │
│       NewDoc := NewDoc + 1;                          │
│   end;                                               │
│                                                      │
│   procedure TFrame.Exit1Click(Sender: TObject);      │
│   begin                                              │
│       Close;                                         │
│   end;                                               │
│   procedure TFrame.Title1Click(Sender: TObject);  ↓  │
│ 81: 1  Modified  Insert          ←│             │→    │
│ \Main/\Mdichild/\Wimmdi/                             │
└─────────────────────────────────────────────────────┘
```

A third method involves the keyboard only:

1. Move the cursor in the source window to the line you want the breakpoint to reside on.

2. Press **CTRL-F8**. The breakpoint will appear on that line. If you press **CTRL-F8** again on the same line, the breakpoint goes away. Keep this in mind for later.

A word of caution: If the spot you select for your breakpoint is a blank line, a declaration, or a comment, (in other words, a nonexecuting line of code), when you run your program, the debugger will complain about your breakpoint being invalid (Figure 6.5).

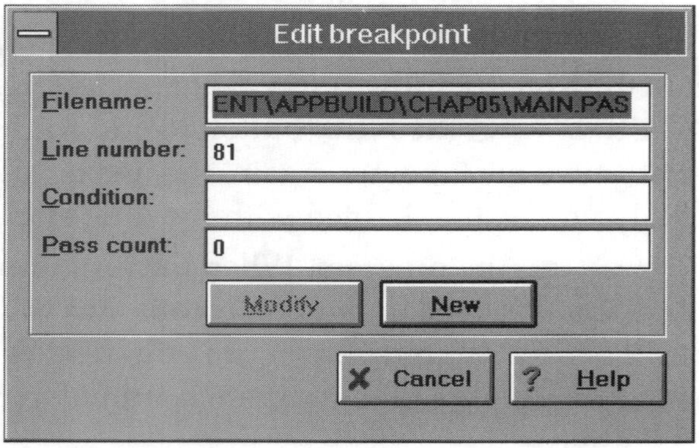

Figure 6.4
The Edit break-
point window.

```
┌─────────────────────────────────────────────────────┐
│ ─              Edit breakpoint                       │
│                                                      │
│   Filename:     │ENT\APPBUILD\CHAP05\MAIN.PAS│       │
│                                                      │
│   Line number:  │81                        │         │
│                                                      │
│   Condition:    │                          │         │
│                                                      │
│   Pass count:   │0                         │         │
│                                                      │
│              ┌─────────┐    ┌─────────┐              │
│              │ Modify  │    │  New    │              │
│              └─────────┘    └─────────┘              │
│                                                      │
│           ┌──────────┐   ┌──────────┐                │
│           │ X Cancel │   │ ? Help   │                │
│           └──────────┘   └──────────┘                │
└─────────────────────────────────────────────────────┘
```

Figure 6.5
Invalid
breakpoint.

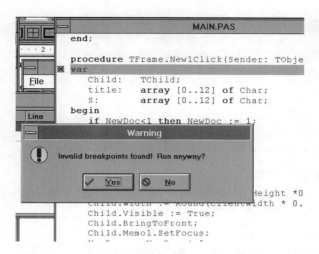

This could be a problem, since we have not learned to delete a breakpoint yet (next section). But, not to worry, as you can continue to run your program, and the debugger will disable the breakpoint so that it does not pose a problem to your program.

One other gotcha is the issue of *dead code*. Dead code is defined as executable lines of code that never execute. The program never gets around to it, because something in the logic tells the program counter, Hey! don't hang with these guys, they're a bad bunch. So your breakpoint and your forgotten code sit there looking lost and forlorn—as do you for that matter, wondering why that part of your program never seems to make an appearance.

During the link step, the linker sees that you forgot to call this block of code, but doesn't care that that's what you meant to do and flags it as dead code. The debugger, ever vigilant, marks your breakpoint as invalid because of the linker and goes on about its business.

Deleting a Breakpoint

There are a few ways you can delete a breakpoint when you no longer need it.

To delete a breakpoint the easy way:

> Using the left mouse button, select the left-hand side of the line the breakpoint resides on. The breakpoint will disappear and the line will appear normal again.

Figure 6.6
Deleting a
breakpoint
using the
breakpoint list.

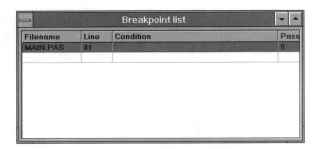

Or:

Place the cursor on the source line with the breakpoint and hit **CTRL-F8**. This will toggle the breakpoint off. Hit it again and it magically comes back.

To delete a breakpoint the hard way:

1. From Delphi's main menu, select the **View** option.
2. Select **Breakpoints**. The Breakpoint list will appear (Figure 6.6).
3. Select from the list the breakpoint you wish to delete.
4. Press the **Delete** key. The entry in the Breakpoint list window will disappear and the source code line highlighted with the breakpoint will return to normal.

Disabling a Breakpoint

Disabling a breakpoint lets you bypass it to execute your program, but lets it stick around in case you need it again.

To disable a breakpoint:

1. From Delphi's main menu, select the **View** option and select **Breakpoints** from the drop list. The Breakpoint list will be displayed on the screen.
2. Using the right mouse button, select the breakpoint you wish to disable. The Breakpoint list SpeedMenu will appear (Figure 6.7).
3. Select **Disable Breakpoint** from the SpeedMenu. The breakpoint in the source window will change color to show it is now disabled.

   As a variation on a theme, you could select **Disable All Breakpoints**, and every breakpoint listed would become inactive.

Figure 6.7
Disabling a
breakpoint.

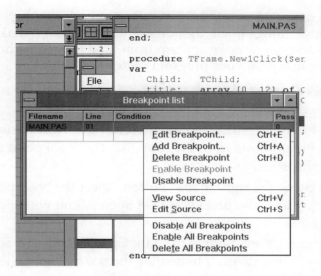

Enabling a Breakpoint

The nice thing about disabling a breakpoint rather than deleting it is that you can enable it for use later.

To enable a breakpoint:

1. From Delphi's main menu, select the **View** option and select **Breakpoints** from the drop list. The Breakpoint list will be displayed on the screen.

2. Using the right mouse button, select the breakpoint you wish to enable. The Breakpoint list SpeedMenu will appear.

3. Select **Enable Breakpoint** from the SpeedMenu. The breakpoint in the source window will change color back to active status to show it is now enabled.

   As a variation on a theme, you could select **Enable All Breakpoints**, and every breakpoint listed would become active.

Advanced Breakpoints— Viewing and Modifying

A good part of the time, you will use one, maybe two or three breakpoints to halt execution so that you can single-step through parts of a procedure and watch variables change values, or logic be executed. However, there are those occasions when you are doing enough things in enough different places that it makes sense to be able to peek or poke at them from time to time without interfering too much with your program under test.

Viewing a Breakpoint

You can easily view all your current breakpoints:

1. From Delphi's main menu, select the **View** option and select **Breakpoints** from the drop list. The Breakpoint list will be displayed on the screen.

2. Using the right mouse button, select the breakpoint you wish to view. The Breakpoint list SpeedMenu will appear (Figure 6.8).

3. Select **View Source** from the SpeedMenu. The source window will update itself to display the source code where the selected breakpoint is located. It should be noted that the Breakpoint list is still kept as the active window, so if you want to see the entire source window, you need to select it so that it sits on top of all the other Delphi windows you currently have open.

Editing a Breakpoint

1. From Delphi's main menu, select the **View** option and select **Breakpoints** from the drop list. The Breakpoint list will be displayed on the screen.

Figure 6.8
The Breakpoint list SpeedMenu.

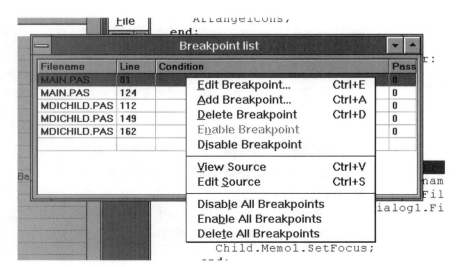

2. Using the right mouse button, select the breakpoint you wish to view. The Breakpoint list SpeedMenu will appear.

3. Select **Edit Source** from the SpeedMenu. The source window will update itself to display the source code where the selected breakpoint is located (Figure 6.9). Instead of letting the Breakpoint list sit on top as the active window, Delphi gives control and focus to the source window, so you can directly modify the code where the breakpoint is. If you do modify anything and then press **F9** to run the program, Delphi will recompile the changed unit before running the program.

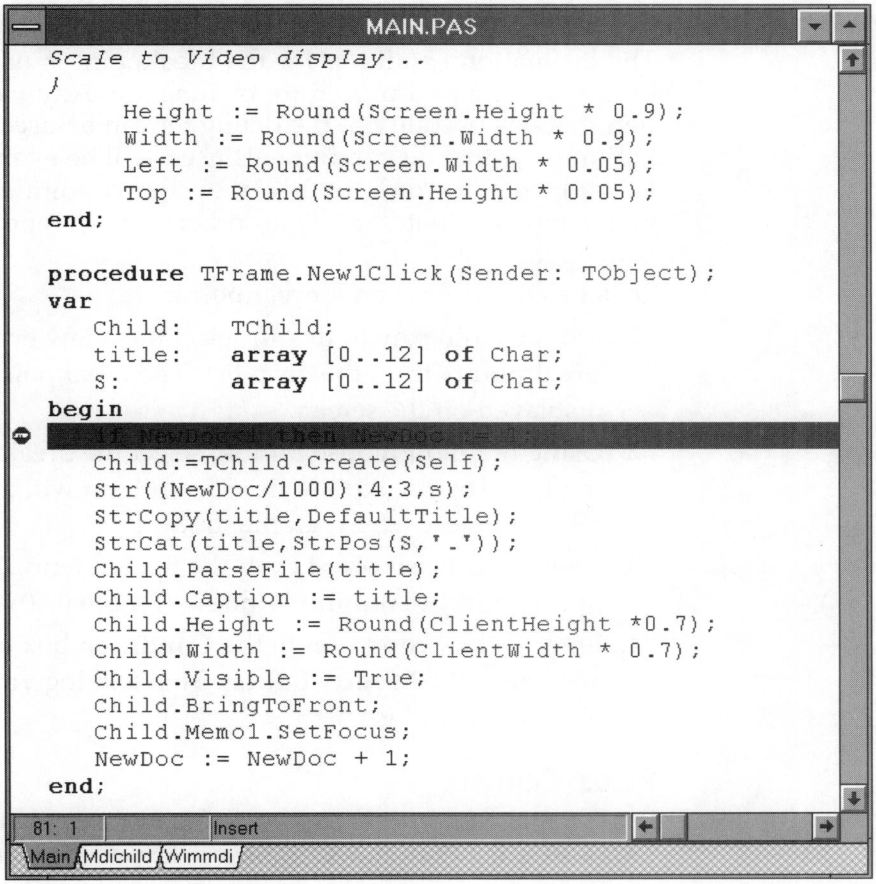

Figure 6.9

The source code with a breakpoint inserted.

```
                            MAIN.PAS
Scale to Video display...
}
     Height := Round(Screen.Height * 0.9);
     Width := Round(Screen.Width * 0.9);
     Left := Round(Screen.Width * 0.05);
     Top := Round(Screen.Height * 0.05);
end;


procedure TFrame.New1Click(Sender: TObject);
var
    Child:    TChild;
    title:    array [0..12] of Char;
    S:        array [0..12] of Char;
begin
    if NewDoc = 1 then NewDoc := 1;
    Child:=TChild.Create(Self);
    Str((NewDoc/1000):4:3,s);
    StrCopy(title,DefaultTitle);
    StrCat(title,StrPos(S,'.'));
    Child.ParseFile(title);
    Child.Caption := title;
    Child.Height := Round(ClientHeight *0.7);
    Child.Width := Round(ClientWidth * 0.7);
    Child.Visible := True;
    Child.BringToFront;
    Child.Memo1.SetFocus;
    NewDoc := NewDoc + 1;
end;
```

```
81: 1              Insert
Main  Mdichild  Wimmdi
```

Advanced Breakpoints—Breaking with Flair

Delphi breakpoints will not only stop program execution, but they can also be made smart enough to respond to some special conditions so that they stop the program only under the right set of circumstances, instead of indiscriminately.

Conditional Breaking

The first useful thing that comes to mind is evaluating counters and values based on loops. For instance, if I wanted to see the fourth character located by a loop that scans a string, I could tell the breakpoint to stop the program when my counter "I" was equal to 4. Once the breakpoint activated, I could check the string pointer and see what part of the string it was looking at and whether it was looking in the right place.

The evaluation condition for the breakpoint is not just limited to local variables of a procedure or function. Any variable or condition that has visibility to the debugger can be used or created. The limitation is that all conditionals used will be evaluated as True or False. In other words, if **I=4,** then the condition to activate the breakpoint evaluates to **True**; otherwise, it reports **False** to the debugger.

To set a conditional on a breakpoint:

1. From Delphi's main menu, select the **View** option and select **Breakpoints** from the drop list. The Breakpoint list will be displayed on the screen.

2. Using the right mouse button, select the breakpoint you wish to view. The Breakpoint list SpeedMenu will appear. Please refer to Figure 6.8 for an illustration.

3. Select **Edit Breakpoint** from the SpeedMenu. This will bring up the **Edit Breakpoint** window (Figure 6.10).

4. Enter a valid condition in the **Condition** box of the window, and select the **Modify** button. This will log your changes in the Breakpoint list.

Pass Counts

Pass counts are a specialized form of conditional breaking, because program execution, not variables or expressions, controls its acti-

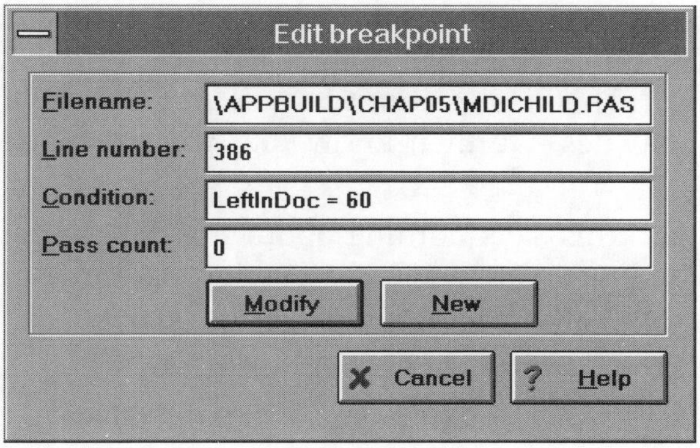

Figure 6.10
The
Edit Breakpoint
window.

Edit breakpoint

Filename:	\APPBUILD\CHAP05\MDICHILD.PAS
Line number:	386
Condition:	LeftInDoc = 60
Pass count:	0

Modify   New

X Cancel   ? Help

vation. Essentially, you tell the debugger how many times you want the program to pass over a particular breakpoint before the breakpoint is activated and stops program execution. For instance, if I wanted to look at what happens in a printed report procedure after the fifth line is sent to the printer, all I have to do is set a breakpoint at that line and tell the debugger to let the program pass by this breakpoint five times before stopping it. Every time thereafter, the breakpoint will stop the program every time it is encountered.

Where a feature like this is most useful is when you need to find a subtle bug. I'll give you a scenario: Let's suppose that you need to execute a function five times that calculates a number for you. Let's also suppose that the results generated from the inclusion of this function and several others are not coming out as expected. Let's also say that we have tested this function and we know the results it produces are accurate. Confused? Hang in there for a moment. Now, we know that the program runs without obvious error, since it generates results for us. So, we have several possibilities. One, the function in question is getting bad data, or two, it is not being called as many times as we expected, or it is not being called in the right order.

Let's do the simplest yet most subtle test first to demonstrate a use of the pass count. How many times does our function get called? By setting a breakpoint on that function and then telling the debugger we want to stop the program at the fifth time through the function, we now can verify the accuracy of our logic. If our program calls the function five times, we will see the program halted by the breakpoint on the fifth pass. If the program calls the function more than five times, then we will get halted each and every time past that point. This lets us count how far off we are. If the breakpoint never activates, we then know that we call the function too few times.

Mind you, this says nothing about the data being generated, but that is another matter. We are making sure that our logic is good before worrying about accuracy elsewhere.

To set a conditional on a breakpoint:

1. From Delphi's main menu, select the **View** option and select **Breakpoints** from the drop list. The Breakpoint list will be displayed on the screen.

2. Using the right mouse button, select the breakpoint you wish to view. The Breakpoint list SpeedMenu will appear.

3. Select **Edit Breakpoint** from the SpeedMenu. This will bring up the **Edit Breakpoint** window (Figure 6.11).

4. Enter the number of times you want to let the program pass the breakpoint before it activates, in the Pass Count box of the window, and select the **Modify** button. This will log your changes in the Breakpoint list.

A Pass Count Side Note   To fine-tune the pass count, you can combine it with a conditional expression in the **Condition** box of the **Edit Breakpoint** window (Figure 6.12). By doing so, you can refine your testing, or control testing of complex logic. Either way,

Figure 6.11
The Edit
Breakpoint
window.

Edit breakpoint
Filename: \APPBUILD\CHAP05\MDICHILD.PAS
Line number: 386
Condition:
Pass count: 5
Modify   New
✗ Cancel   ? Help

it's a combination you will find yourself using more and more as you get more comfortable with the debugger.

Watching Your Variables

Tracing program logic is great. It reveals many things about how your program behaves, but it falls short in a critical area—variables. Many times, logic is pragmatically controlled by the values that certain variables take on. This is a form of *conditional branching*.

As an example, let's revisit the child window problem that started this chapter. If, for instance, we wanted to place a limit of 10 open child windows at any one time in the program, we would create a variable that kept track of how many windows were open. If the number of open windows exceeds 10, then we need to have code that handles that condition. Blocking out the logic should look something like this:

```
if OpenWindows>10 then ProcessError(TOOMANYWINDOWS)
else
begin
{ Create a new child Window}
{Assign a default Name to it }
{Do any initialization needed to setup the window}
{Display it in the parent }
OpenWindows := OpenWindows + 1;
end;
```

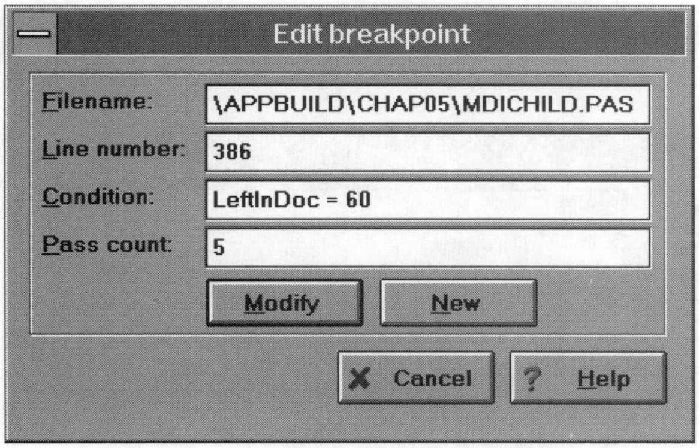

Figure 6.12
Condition box in the Edit breakpoint window.

As you can see, the only time the procedure **ProcessError()** gets called is when the variable OpenWindows exceeds the value of 10.

Okay, so the logic looks flawless. But how do we really know that this is going to work. We could test it by creating lots of windows on the fly, and verify that we could no longer do so after 10 of them are open. That's the easy way in this case. But many types of logic testing are not quite that simple. Instead of just one condition that can force a program to branch in its execution, there may be two or more that must be satisfied before a branch occurs. This leaves you with more detail to keep track of, and more opportunity for mistakes along the way. Using watch expressions not only saves you time, but also can save you many a headache.

Now that we're done with the sales pitch, let's look at how we can use watches in our debugging.

Creating Watches

There are several ways to create a watch. We'll cover a couple of them here.

Method #1:

1. Before running your program, choose **Run** from Delphi's main menu.

2. From the drop list, choose the **Add Watch** option. The Watch Properties window (Figure 6.13) will be displayed on the screen.

3. Enter the name of the variable you wish to track, and select the data type (default usually works).

Figure 6.13
The Watch Properties window.

Method #2:

1. Place the cursor on the variable you wish to watch. Press the right mouse button and the Code Editor SpeedMenu will appear.

2. Select the **Add Watch At Cursor...** option. The Watch Properties window will appear (Figure 6.14). If you are happy with the default data type, or you have selected the right data type for the watch, then press **Enter.** Each time you enter a new watch, it is placed in the Watch List window.

A Closer Look at the Watch Properties Window

The Watch Properties window is where all the action takes place, at least on your part. I'll quickly run through each of the options available to you, as there will be times when leaving a watch with default formatting is not enough.

Repeat Count

This option really has application only to data structures, such as arrays, strings, and so on. The purpose is to limit the number of elements of that structure being displayed at any one time. For instance, if you have an array of characters 30 elements deep and you want to look only at the first 10, you would enter 10 into the Repeat Count edit box, and the first 10 consecutive characters of that array will be displayed for that watch. By default, the watch will display all elements of a data structure (such as a string, array, etc.).

Digits

This option controls how many digits of precision you want to display floating-point values with. This makes sense if you want to look at the 15th place to the right of the decimal, or you want to

Figure 6.14
The Watch List window.

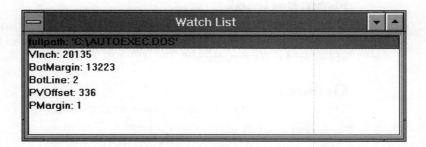

fullpath: "C:\AUTOEXEC.DOS"
VInch: 20135
BotMargin: 13223
BotLine: 2
PVOffset: 336
PMargin: 1

keep things short and sweet and just look at two decimal places. The default is seven digits.

Enabled

This check box is important. By having it checked, the watch stays active and visible to you. If, however, you want to dispense with looking at certain watches for the moment, but you don't want to have to re-create them, then uncheck the box. Like magic, Delphi removes them from sight in the Watch List window so that they don't clutter up the display.

Watch Property Format Types

Displaying watches will show the data you asked for, but not necessarily in the way you wish to see it. In order to present data more the way you might want to see it, the Watch Properties window provides a number of ways to customize the type of data output.

Character

This data type displays the watch in question as ASCII data. Delphi will also show the special characters that represent the control codes for ASCII 0 to 31. Control characters, such as Carriage Returns, Linefeeds, and Tabs, will be displayed in C syntax, such as \r, \f, \t, \n, and so on.

String

Displays data type as a string of characters. This format will also display the ASCII control codes in C syntax.

Decimal

This format displays values in decimal form—primarily suited for Integer data types. It works for both variables and data structures.

Hexadecimal

This format displays values in hexadecimal form with a prepended 0x—primarily suited for Integer data types. It works for both variables and data structures.

Ordinal

This format shows integer values as ordinals.

Pointer

This format shows pointers in segment:offset notation, including additional information about the address pointed to. You can see the region of memory in which the segment is located and the name of the variable at the offset address.

Record

This format shows the field names of a data structure or record, plus the associated values. For instance, if I had a data structure that contained the fields A,B,C that had the values 5,15, and 25 currently assigned to them, the output in the Watch List window would look like A:5,B:15,C:25 instead of 5,15,25.

Default

Selecting this shows the values in the format that most closely matches the data type of the watch expression you are tracking. You will probably use this one more than all the others.

Memory Dump

Selecting this check box forces the displayed data for that watch into a memory dump format (size in bytes of expression, starting address, and bytes displayed as two hexadecimal digits). By modifying the selected display format to something like Character, String, Decimal, or Hexadecimal, you will change the displayed bytes' formatting.

Deleting Watches

Once you are done using a watch, it's a good idea to get rid of it so that you have room to display another in the Watch List window without having to scroll past a bunch of unnecessary watches looking for it.

You can delete watches one of three ways:

1. Select a watch from the Watch List and press the **Del** key. A confirmation message box (Figure 6.15) will ask you if you really want to do this. If you do, then press the **OK** button and the watch will disappear from the Watch List.

2. Select a Watch from the Watch List and bring up the SpeedMenu by pressing the right mouse button with the

Figure 6.15
Delphi asks for
confirmation
when you delete
a watch.

mouse located in the Watch List. Select the **Delete Watch**
option from the menu. Again, the confirmation message box
will appear and ask if you really want to do this.

3. Select a Watch from the Watch List and bring up the
SpeedMenu by pressing the right mouse button with the
mouse located in the Watch List. Select the **Delete All
Watches** option from the menu. This lets you dump all of
your watches at the same time. Once again, the confirmation
message box will appear and ask if you really want to do this.

Modifying Your Data

Previously, we looked at how to watch data and stop our program
at different points and for different reasons. The next item on
the list of "It would be really wonderful if I could..." has to do
with modifying your data without having to change code and
recompile.

Delphi allows you to do this, but this is by no means completely
comprehensive, nor is it a cure-all. Two things that Delphi will not
allow you to do are:

• Evaluate local or static variables when they are not visible from
the current program execution point. In other words, if you
can't see it, neither can Delphi.

• Function and Procedure calls. What is really nice about changing data values on the fly is that you can control some of your
logic and test things before you change code and recompile.
Basically it's a time saver. You don't need it, but there are times
you will sing its praises and be glad it was there.

Evaluate/Modify Dialog

The Evaluate/Modify dialog box is your one-stop shop to handle all the poking about you will do with variables and data in the program under test.

You can bring up the dialog box in one of two ways:

1. In the Code window, press the right mouse key and the SpeedMenu will appear. Select the **Evaluate/Modify** option, and the dialog box will appear (Figure 6.16).

2. From Delphi's main menu, select the **Run** option. From the drop list, select the **Evaluate/Modify** option, and the dialog box will appear.

Changing Values

Now that we have a dialog box up, we need to make it useful. We evaluate expressions by entering them in the **Expression** edit box and pressing the **Evaluate** button. This displays the value associated with our expression in the **Result** display box.

To change the value of our expression, we would modify the contents of the **New Value** edit box and press the **Evaluate** button (Figure 6.17). This forces the expression to change its runtime value. It's important to remember that no permanent changes have taken place in your code. This you must do when you edit. Any changes you make to variable values are lost when the program concludes its run.

Figure 6.16
The Evaluate/Modify dialog.

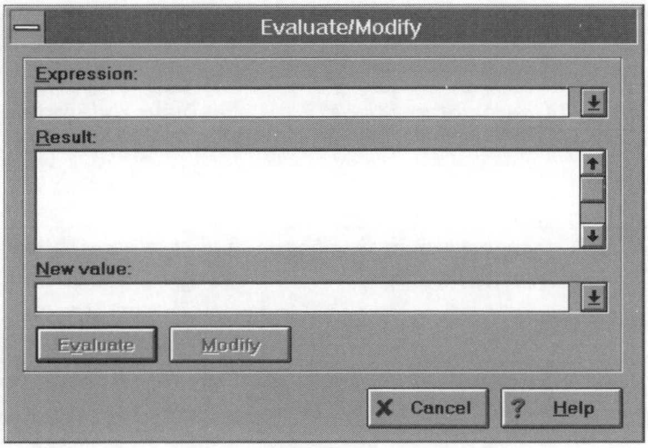

Figure 6.17
The Evaluate/
Modify dialog.

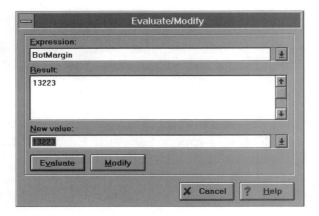

Formatting Evaluation Output

Just like the Watch List, you can format the displayed output of each variable or structure you evaluate. This is done by placing a comma and then the format modifier after the variable or data structure listed in the Expression edit box. Table 6.2 describes briefly each valid display format modifier, what data types it works with, and what you can expect to see.

Character	Affected Data Types	What It Does
Table 6.2 Display Format Modifiers and Their Data Types		
C	Character or String	This data type displays the watch in question as ASCII data. Delphi will also show the special characters that represent the control codes for ASCII 0 to 31. Control characters, such as Carriage Returns, Linefeeds, and Tabs, will be displayed in C syntax such as \r, \f, \t, \n, and so on.
S	Character or String	Displays data type as a string of characters. This format will also display the ASCII control codes in C syntax.
D	Integers (including those in data structures)	This format displays values in decimal form—primarily suited for Integer data types. It works for both variables and data structures.
H or X	Integers	This format displays values in hexadecimal form with a prepended 0x—

Table 6.2 Continued		
Character	**Affected Data Types**	**What It Does**
		primarily suited for Integer data types. It works for both variables and data structures.
F*n*	Floating-Point (all types)	This format displays floating-point numbers to *n* significant digits from a range of 2 to 18. If *n* is not specified, then the default value is seven digits.
*n*M	All data types	This format displays a memory dump starting at the address of the expression and continuing for *n* bytes. If *n* is not specified, then it dumps the entire object being evaluated. So, if you have a large array or data structure and you invoke this format—ZING! Off you go to the races.
P	Pointers	This format shows pointers in segment:offset notation; including additional information about the address pointed to. You can see the region of memory in which the segment is located and the name of the variable at the offset address.
R	Structures/Unions	This format shows the field names of a data structure or record, plus the associated values. For instance, if I had a data structure that contained the fields A,B,C that had the values 5,15, and 25 currently assigned to them, the output in the Watch List window would look like A:5,B:15,C:25 instead of 5,15,25.

Other Useful Features

Previously, we covered many of the features of the debugger that you will find yourself using constantly—especially at the procedure level. The other features presented in this section not only apply to function level testing, but help in doing higher-level testing as well.

The Call Stack

Chasing logic bugs can become exasperating sometimes. Even though you might know the value of the flag that put you in the current procedure, how you got there can sometimes be a complete mystery—especially if you are using breakpoints to stop the program, and are not stepping through the code line by line.

The call stack provides a big picture road map localized to show just where you were a short while ago. Basically, knowing the sequence of when procedures got called and where you sit now in the program code tells you a lot about how the program is currently behaving. In fact, it may be the only piece of information that clues you in on just where the problem is.

To bring up the Call Stack window:

1. From Delphi's main menu, select the **View** option.
2. Select the **Call Stack** option from the drop list. The Call Stack window will then be displayed (Figure 6.18).

What's in the Call Stack Window When viewing the Call Stack, the most used information will be the procedures and the order in which they appear in the window. The procedure that contains the program pointer will be listed at the top, with each previous function call listed beneath in the order in which it was called. Another piece of useful information is the argument data supplied with each call. Each call comes with details about the arguments passed to the function from the caller. This is useful if you want to monitor what was passed in.

Figure 6.18
The Call stack window.

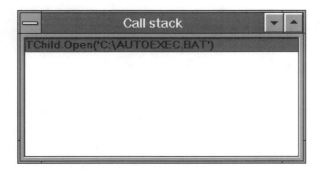

A Free Ride on the Stack   Poking at the Call Stack is more of an advanced level of debugging, but for the novice, the Call Stack can be a free ticket to viewing and editing code under test.

To View or Edit code courtesy of the Call Stack:

1. From Delphi's main menu, select the **View** option.

2. From the drop list, select the **Call Stack** option. The Call Stack window will be displayed.

3. Highlight the function call you want to go to.

4. Press the right mouse button with the mouse in the Call Stack window to bring up the SpeedMenu.

5. Select the **View Source** option if you want to look at the code, or select the **Edit Source** option if you want to make changes and recompile your program on the fly.

   Poking at the Call Stack is also useful if you accidentally trace into a function that you wanted to skip over.

To back up to where you were do the following:

1. From Delphi's main menu, select the **View** option.

2. From the drop list, select the **Call Stack** option. The Call Stack window will be displayed.

3. Double-click the mouse on the function call that called the function you are now in (the second function listed from the top of the window).

4. The Code window will become active. At this point, place the cursor on the instruction just below the function call you wandered into and press the **F4** key. This will take the program pointer to the cursor and bypass the function call.

General Protection Faults

This bugaboo causes lots of grief. Usually, if you caught one of these, you lost your application at best, or the whole Windows environment at worst.

Delphi provides some protection against GPFs by trapping them when they occur. As an added bonus, the Code window comes to the front and the program pointer lands on the offending line of code that generated the GPF. This gives you the opportunity to see what caused the problem, instead of feeling around blindly for it.

When this situation does occur, you must reset the program so that you can fix it without crashing it and possibly Delphi. To do this, press the **CTRL-F2** key sequence or:

1. From Delphi's main menu select the **Run** option.
2. Select the **Program Reset** option from the drop list. The program will then be reset and Delphi will go back into edit mode.

One word of caution. As nifty as Delphi is about catching GPFs (which is no mean feat), there are times when it will miss one and Windows will get hold of it. Depending on what caused the problem, you will either have to shut down Delphi, or worst case, you will have to leave Windows and reboot, depending on the seriousness of the problem.

Run To, Step Into, and Step Over

Our last look at the debugger will consist of looking at three really useful methods of tracing your program execution.

Run To Delphi's debugger, just like the Turbo Debugger for Windows, lets you pick a spot within a procedure with the cursor, and runs the program pointer to that point before stopping. This is really useful when you need to skip such things as small loops and statements, but using a breakpoint would not be practical. One good example of the need for this kind of program execution is in a real-time process.

There are occasions when you need to run a tiny block of code to coax a problem to show itself. If you were to step through it line by line, the program will execute slowly enough that you never see the conflict. Breakpoints may help but many times get in the way as they set up permanent roadblocks that must be dealt with.

Anyway, to run to the cursor, move the cursor to a spot in the code where you want the program to stop, and press the **F4** key. The program will zip along until it comes to the line with the cursor on it.

Step Into   The **F7** key lets you walk your source code one line at a time. When it comes to a function or procedure call that is part of your source, the program and code editor will track into that procedure so that you can follow along. This type of tracing is for detail execution, when you want to see *all* your logic.

Step Over   Like the **F7** key, the Step Over function (**F8** key) executes your code one line at a time. The difference is that when it comes to a function call that is part of your code, it runs the call at full speed instead of tracing into it.

This type of tracing is for detail execution, when you want to confine yourself to a procedure or section of code.

CHAPTER 7

Data Types, Variables, and Constants

Starting with this chapter and in the next two that follow, we will explore Object Pascal starting from the inside and working our way out. First, we will look at data types, variables, and constants. In Chapter 8, we will cover language constructs that focus on the procedure and function. In Chapter 9, we will discuss organizing our data, procedures, and functions into units and programs.

In these chapters, I want to cover aspects of Object Pascal by relating it to C where appropriate. Surprisingly enough, there is much similarity between C and Object Pascal; more so than in times past with the traditional UCSD Pascal parent language. By taking this approach, we should be treading some familiar ground while learning new things. The goal is to help make the transition from C to Delphi's Object Pascal as easy as possible. So, without further adieu, let's get started.

Data: The Basis of Our World

The essence of programming is data. The whole purpose of writing a computer program in the first place is to manipulate a set of data to achieve some desired results. But data does not come in a one-size-fits-all variety. We have whole numbers, rational numbers, characters, strings, binary sets, aggregate sets, and unions. The list goes on. Each of these kinds of data is of different sizes and means different things.

One thing we do know about our data is that it tends to naturally occur in sets. Letters form words, which form sentences, which form paragraphs. Numbers form mathematical equations, and provide a convenient means of measuring or describing something in a most precise and compact fashion, as compared to words. So too in programming, we create sets of data to help us keep track of the kinds of data we have and what they mean.

Data Types: The Foundation

Sets of data on a computer take on a unique hue and color all their own. This is primarily due to the computer's limited ability to count. If you are new to programming, that last statement probably sounded a bit unbelievable. Let me explain.

We all have what I like to call a *natural counting index*. Since we use our hands to count, the normal inclination is to group things according to the number of fingers we have. This provides us with a visible reminder and a ready means to group things. So counting by tens comes pretty automatically (except for uncle Zeek who has that sixth pinkie).

Anyway, the computer doesn't have any fingers or toes to help it out, so it relies on something else—the binary switch.

A computer for all intents and purposes is an expensive collection of microscopically small switches that do nothing more than turn themselves ON or OFF in pretty patterns that mean something. This binary flip-flopping from ON to OFF and back again yields a natural counting index of 2. So, the path of least resistance is to represent all data types in binary notation. For instance, counting to 10 in binary would look something like Table 7.1.

Table 7.1 Decimal Numbers and Their Binary Equivalents

Decimal	Binary
0	0
1	1
2	10
3	11
4	100
5	101
6	110
7	111
8	1000
9	1001
10	1010

If we kept going, the binary numbers would quickly get so large as to be virtually unreadable. Fortunately for the computer, this is not a problem.

As a further means of keeping things straight and manageable (this again is purely for our benefit), binary data is organized in powers of 2. For instance, a *nibble* is 4 binary digits long, a *byte* is 8 binary digits. These groupings are labeled *data types*, because they have specific meaning and attributes. A nibble has a data set represented by decimal numbers between 0 and 15. A byte, between 0 and 255, inclusive.

Okay, so what? We can count, but that doesn't explain characters, strings and such. Well, the trick here is to take a large enough group of binary digits so that you can provide a unique value to each member of your data set that you want represented. In the case of ASCII characters, the byte is just large enough, as there are 128 basic ASCII characters, giving a total of 256 unique members of the set.

This method represents how basic data types are defined. As we discuss the simple data types, notice how the counting sets of each type is a power of 2.

In Object Pascal there are three basic types of data:

- Simple Data Types
- Derived Data Types
- Data Structures

Simple Data Types

Simple data types are just that. These types are represented by binary digit groupings. Change the number of binary digits in the group and you change the data set represented by that type.

Delphi (this version for Windows 3.x) is based on 16-bit code, so we will compare our sample C data types with that in mind. Table 7.2 shows the Object Pascal predefined data types, equivalent C data types (if applicable), and their data set range. As you can tell, not all Pascal types have an equivalent C data type.

Table 7.2 Object Pascal Predefined Data Types		
C Data Type	**PASCAL Data Type**	**Dataset Range and Size in Memory**
	Boolean	1 byte—Evaluates to TRUE or FALSE
	ByteBool	1 byte—0=FALSE, nonzero=TRUE
	WordBool	2 bytes—0=FALSE, nonzero=TRUE
	LongBool	4 bytes—0=FALSE, nonzero=TRUE
Unsigned Char	Char	1 byte—0 to 255, inclusive, this type evaluates to ASCII and extended ASCII, as defined for the IBM PC
Integer	Integer	2 bytes—Dataset ranges from −32768 to 32767
Char	Shortint	1 byte—Dataset ranges from −128 to 127
Long	Longint	4 bytes—Dataset ranges from −2147483647 to 2147483647
Unsigned Short	Byte	1 byte—0 to 255, inclusive
Unsigned Int	Word	2 bytes—0 to 65535, inclusive
Char*	Pchar	Pointer to a NULL terminated string
Void*	Pointer	An untyped pointer
	Real	6 bytes—Rational number that has a fractional part with 11 to 12 significant digits; dataset ranges from $2.9 \times 10E-39$ to $1.7 \times 10E38$
Float	Single	4 bytes—Rational number that has a fractional part with 7 to 8 significant digits; dataset ranges from $1.5 \times 10E-45$ to 3.4×1038

Table 7.2 *Continued*		
C Data Type	Pascal Data Type	Dataset Range and Size in
Double	Double	8 bytes—Rational number that has a fractional part with 15 to 16 significant digits; dataset ranges from 5x10E–324 to 1.7x10E308
Long Double	Extended	10 bytes—Rational number that has a fractional part with 19 to 20 significant digits; dataset ranges from 3.4x10E–4932 to 1.1x10E4932
	Comp	8 bytes—This is an integral data type that has 19 to 20 significant digits; dataset ranges from–2^63 –1 to 2^63–1
	String	A sequence of characters that can have up to 255 members in the string

Operators

This is as good a place as any to stop for a moment and talk about data operations; more specifically, those Pascal atoms that allow logical, bitwise, and relational operations between data elements to take place. Bear in mind that while we will focus our examples primarily on Integer types, the application of an operator is good for all types unless specifically stated.

Arithmetic Operators

Pushing number values around is done primarily with arithmetic operators. These operators let you define mathematical statements. For higher level math functions, there are library functions that provide the operations necessary to give the proper result.

Addition (+)   This operator is valid for Integer, Real, and cardinal types. It provides the sum of an addition equation.

Integer Division (DIV)   This operator is valid for Integer and cardinal types. It provides a dividend based on a whole number divide. There is no remainder or fractional part retained from the operation. For example:

2 DIV 3 returns a value of 0 as the fractional remainder is thrown away. But, the equation **9 DIV 3** returns a value 3 as the dividend.

Modulus (MOD)   This operator is valid for Integer and cardinal types. It provides the remainder from a divide equation. For instance:

3 MOD 2 returns a value of 1; where as **9 MOD 3** would return a value of 0; as 3 divides perfectly into 9.

Multiplication (*)   This operator is valid for Integer, Real, and cardinal types. It provides the results of a multiplication equation.

Real Division (/)   This operator is valid for Integer, Real, and cardinal types. It provides a dividend and a fractionalized remainder (if any) in the form of a Real number from the divide operation. Going back to our Integer **DIV** problems:

2/3 would yield a result of 0.66667, and

9/3 would still return 3.0, since it is a perfect division.

Sign Inversion (−)   This operator is valid for Integer and Real types. It provides the reverse of the existing sign of a value. Simply put, it multiplies the value given by −1. One word of caution: This operator cannot be used with Byte and Word data types, as they are defined as unsigned and therefore have no negative values.

Bitwise Operators

Bitwise operators let you diddle directly with the bits inside of the data type.

NOT   This operator flips all bits to their opposite value within a variable. In C, the ~ operator is the equivalent and is used to do a one's complement.

Consider the variable Test:

```
VAR
  Test : Byte;
  Test1 : Byte;
  Test := 0;
  Test1 := NOT Test;
```

If we evaluate Test1, we find that Test1 is equal to 255. In binary, the two variables look like:

```
Test - 00000000
  Test1 - 11111111
```

AND This operator evaluates two sets of binary bits. In C, the &
operator is the equivalent used for a bitwise AND. The truth table
for AND looks like:

```
0 AND 0 = 0
0 AND 1 = 0
1 AND 0 = 0
1 AND 1 = 1
```

AND is used most frequently if you want to mask a bit to either
turn it OFF, or see if it is turned ON. For example, consider the
variables:

```
VAR
  Test : Byte;
  Test1 : Byte;
  Test2 : Byte;
  Test : = 255;
  Test1 := Test AND 32;
  Test2 := Test AND 223;
```

In the case of Test1, we are testing to see if bit 4 of the variable Test
is turned on. Looking at the bits, we can demonstrate it this way:

```
    11111111  Test
AND 00100000 (32)
------------------
    00100000  Test1
```

As you can see, we masked the original value for the bit and we got
back a nonzero answer that tells us that bit 4 is indeed turned on.

In the next case, with Test2, we are turning off bit 4.

```
    11111111  Test
AND 11011111 (223)
------------------
    11011111  Test2
```

OR This operator evaluates two sets of binary bits. In C, the |
operator is the equivalent used for a bitwise OR. The truth table for

OR looks like:

```
0 AND 0 = 0
0 AND 1 = 1
1 AND 0 = 1
1 AND 1 = 1
```

OR is used most frequently for turning things on. Consider the variable Test:

```
VAR
  Test  : Byte;
  Test1 : Byte;
  Test  : = 0;
  Test1 := Test AND 32;
```

In the case of Test1, we are forcing bit 4 to turn on. Looking at the bits we can demonstrate it this way:

```
      00000000   Test
 AND 00100000   (32)
--------------------
      00100000   Test1
```

XOR This operator evaluates two sets of binary bits. In C, the ^ operator is the equivalent used for a bitwise XOR. The truth table for XOR looks like:

```
0 AND 0 = 0
0 AND 1 = 1
1 AND 0 = 1
1 AND 1 = 0
```

XOR turns on bits, if and only if the bits they are compared to are different. Consider the variable Test:

```
VAR
  Test  : Byte;
  Test1 : Byte;
  Test  : = 127;
  Test1 := Test AND 120;
```

In the case of Test1, we are looking for the difference in the bits. This is the equivalent of subtraction. Looking at the bits, we can demonstrate it this way:

```
    01111111  Test
AND 01111000  (32)
------------------
    00000111  Test1
```

SHL   This operator multiplies in powers of 2 by shifting all bits to the left a specified amount. In C, the << operator is the equivalent used for a **SH**ift **L**eft. Consider the variable Test:

```
VAR
  Test : Byte;
  Test1 : Byte;
  Test := 31;
  Test1 := Test SHL 2;
```

If we look at Test in binary, we see the value 00011111 (31). Now by shifting all the bits left 2 places, Test1 takes on the binary value of 01111100, or 124. If we multiply 31 by 4 (2 to the 2nd power) we end up with 124.

SHR   This operator divides in powers of 2 by shifting all bits to the right a specified amount. In C, the >> operator is the equivalent used for a **SH**ift **R**ight. Consider the variable Test:

```
VAR
  Test : Byte;
  Test1 : Byte;
  Test := 124;
  Test1 := Test SHR 2;
```

If we look at Test in binary, we see the value 01111100 (124). Now by shifting all the bits right 2 places, Test1 takes on the binary value of 00011111, or 31. If we divide 124 by 4 (2 to the 2nd power), we end up with 31.

Relational Operators

Relational operators have only one function in life. They compare things and give you their opinion (True or False) as to whether the items are alike or dissimilar. Table 7.3 lists the relational operators that are implemented in Object Pascal. I should mention that we just talked about the bitwise operators in the previous section, and the operators dealing with sets are described again in the section on sets. The rest in this list should be fairly self-explanatory.

Table 7.3 Object Pascal Relational Operators

Operator	Symbol	Operand (Data)Type
Equality (equals)	=	Numbers, Pointers, Records, Sets, and Strings
Inequality (not equals)	<>	Numbers, Pointers, Records, Sets, and Strings
Greater than	>	Scalars and Strings
Less than	<	Numbers and Strings
Greater than or equal to	>=	Numbers and Strings
Less than or equal to	<=	Numbers and Strings
Member of a Set	IN	Sets
Left Set a subset of Right Set	<=	Sets
Right Set a subset of Left Set	>=	Sets
Conjunction	AND	Boolean
Disjunction	OR	Boolean
Exclusive OR	XOR	Boolean
Negation	NOT	Boolean

Derived Data Types

One of Pascal's strengths is the ability to create data types to fit the problem being solved. These derived data types are created from the existing simple types. In some cases, you may end up creating another data type from a variation on an existing simple type. We'll focus on several different kinds of derived types:

• Custom
• Enumerated

- Sets
- Strings
- Subranges

Custom Data Types: Rolling Your Own

This is one of the easiest types to create, and is very important for two reasons: First, creating a custom type can lend more readability to your code and the problem addressed by it. For example, let's say we needed to create a program to handle simple money transactions of less than $10,000. Since we don't have any fractional calculations to deal with (such as compound interest), we'll keep our accuracy by using a Long Int to store money values in. The other condition that will exist in our program is that our variables that deal with money and the values in them will get passed around between at least two units or modules.

In C, we would use the **typedef** keyword in an **#include** file to identify our new data type, as follows:

```
typedef long MONEY;
```

In Object Pascal, we would create a **TYPE** section in our program, as follows:

```
TYPE
   MONEY = Long Int;
```

If the **TYPE** section already existed, then we would just add the definition to it.

As an aside, I should note that even though you have defined a *new* data type here, just as in C, the compiler does not allocate any space for it in an executable. It is only after you have declared a variable or structure that uses this data definition that the compiler will set aside space in the executable.

Now when we go to define our variables based on MONEY, it looks something like this:

For C:

```
foo()
{
```

```
    MONEY pennies, nickels, dimes;

    ...

}
```

For Pascal:

```
procedure foo ()
var
   pennies : MONEY;
   nickels : MONEY;
   dimes : MONEY;
begin

   ...

end;
```

Now the variables themselves were obvious as to what they represented, but stop for a minute and consider the possibility of a large project. I've been involved in several projects where variables got such names as MOD301XV2. While it is defined in the project as the "Variable named 'XV2' for temporary storage as defined for module 301", to the average person, this is not obvious. In fact, this kind of naming convention resulted in a lot of stress for the maintenance programmers, because they didn't have a clue to what was going on without lots of research and questions. On top of that, to make it more generic, MOD301XV2 might be define as a **long**. Well, at least we know two things about it: There are no fractional values, and you won't get a number higher than $2^{31}-1$.

Now, if MOD301XV2 was defined as a **MONEY** type, then we instantly know that any place we find it involves monetary calculations and data. The name is still awful, but the type gives us a much better picture as to its use.

The second reason that you would want to create a custom data type has more to do with objects than with traditional variables. This goes back to the concept of inheritance in Chapter 1. It's much easier to take an object type that is close to what we want and modify a copy of it to suit our needs. Probably the most visible example has to be the **Tform** object.

When you build a program on a form, you take the default **Tform** and add things to it. In the case of the following example (from the

WIM-MDI Editor), we are adding menu items, dialogs, timers, labels, panel, and event handlers to the object **TFrame**:

```
type
TFrame = class(TForm)
MainMenu1: TMainMenu;
File1: TMenuItem;
New1: TMenuItem;
Open1: TMenuItem;
Exit1: TMenuItem;
Window1: TMenuItem;
Tile1: TMenuItem;
Cascade1: TMenuItem;
ArrangeIcons1: TMenuItem;
OpenDialog1: TOpenDialog;
Panel1: TPanel;
DateLabel: TLabel;
TimeLabel: TLabel;
Timer1: TTimer;
procedure New1Click(Sender: TObject);
procedure StartUp(Sender: TOBject);
procedure Exit1Click(Sender: TObject);
procedure Tile1Click(Sender: TObject);
procedure Cascade1Click(Sender: TObject);
procedure ArrangeIcons1Click(Sender: TObject);
procedure OpenWindow(Sender: TObject);
procedure Open1Click(Sender: TObject);
procedure Timer1Timer(Sender: TObject);
```

When you are done here, you still have a form, but it looks and behaves differently from a default **Tform** object.

Subranges

Subranges are a form of data set that is not found in C. The unique thing about subranges over data sets is that they are specifically closed sets of ordinal type. Instead of wasting a paragraph trying to describe it, I'll just show you:

```
TYPE
  letters 'A'..'Z';
```

```
digits '0'..'9';
percentage 0..100;
```

The first thing you notice is that **letters** and **digits** have single quotes around the first and last arguments. This identifies to the compiler that these subranges are of type **Char**, as they specify the ASCII representation of these letters and digits. **Percentage**, however, denotes a subrange type of **Integer**, as the actual values of 0 to 100 make up the data set. The .. tells the compiler to include all values in between, plus the first and last argument, as part of that data set.

Subranges are very useful if you want to limit the number of choices that can be made in certain instances. For example, if you were writing a program to evaluate test scores that had a valid range of 0 to 100 points, then a subrange would be helpful in limiting the data that made it into the students' records.

Of course, there is a price to pay for this filter of convenience. At compile time, if you have range checking {$R} turned on, the compiler will evaluate all data assignments to the subrange. If any data assigned falls outside of the defined data set, then the compiler will complain to you about it.

While this is good at catching some of the mistakes in the code, it does not get all of them. At runtime, if out-of-bounds data show up, the program generates an exception that must be handled—or the program just stops. This necessitates writing an exemption handler to catch any problems that might occur. Let's use our test grade example to demonstrate how we might use a subrange:

```
TYPE
  valid_scores 0..100;
procedure test_score(grade : Integer)
var
  English_test : valid_scores
begin
  try
    English_test := grade;
  except
    on ERangeError do writeln("ERROR: Test Score out of
range (0...100)");
```

```
    end;
end;
```

Notice that we **try** to assign **grade** to **English_test** first. If that fails because the score was out of range, then the program executes the code located in the **except** portion of the block.

Enumerated Types

Enumerated types are specialized data sets. These data sets contain a list of items, but the only values that exist are derived from an item's position in the list. In other words, if I had a series of 10 items and I referenced the seventh one, that item would carry a value of 7. As we will see in a minute, these values allow for some pretty nifty tricks. But, first we need to create a list. Going back to our money example, let's create an enumerated list of coinage:

```
TYPE
    coins = (penny, nickel, dime, quarter, half_dollar, dollar);
```

In C, the equivalent would look like:

```
enum coins {penny, nickel, dime, quarter, half_dollar, dollar};
```

From the placement in the list, each of these items has the following value:

penny	0
nickel	1
dime	2
quarter	3
half_dollar	4
dollar	5

This is very useful if we want to index into an array or data structure. For instance, let's say we have an array of money:

```
money : Array[penny..dollar] of Integer;
```

which looks like:

```
int money[dollar];
```

in C, and we want to assign a count of 165 quarters to this array. We can do this by saying:

```
money[quarter] := 165;
```

in Pascal, or

```
money[quarter] = 165;
```

in C.

Evaluating Enumerated Types

Object Pascal provides ways to evaluate an enumerated type to help you find your way around the list. First and foremost, you can compare elements of an enumerated list, as they are fixed in position and value. Comparing two values like this will result in a Boolean TRUE or FALSE, depending on the comparison.

As an example, if we take the previously defined money list, we find that:

```
penny > dime
```

will evaluate to FALSE, whereas

```
penny < dollar
```

will return TRUE. This is also the case with C.

Object Pascal does not stop there. It includes additional functionality that utilizes enumerated types. These functions are:

Ord()   This function returns the positional value of an enumerated type within a list. From the money list, **Ord(penny)** would yield 0, while **Ord(dime)** yields 2.

Odd()   This function returns a Boolean **TRUE** or **FALSE** to indicate whether the argument is an odd number. **Ord(nickel)** would return **TRUE**, while **Ord(dime)** would return **FALSE**.

Pred()   This function returns the preceding value in the list. Thus **Pred(dime)** would return the value **nickel**, and **Pred(dollar)** would return the value **half_dollar**.

Succ()   This function returns the next value in the list. This means **Succ(dime)** would return the value **quarter**, and **Succ(penny)** gives the value **nickel**.

A word of caution about **Pred()** and **Succ()**. When you are evaluating the item that begins the list, **Pred()** will return an undefined value, as there is nothing prior to the beginning of the list for **Pred()** to find. The same is true of **Succ()**, but at the end of the list.

Sets

Sets are collections of items that are simple types. These sets are not necessarily progressive in their elements. For example, the set 0..9 is progressive, but the set 0,4,3,7,6,2,8,9 is not. That's what differentiates a set from a subrange.

A set defined in Object Pascal would look like:

```
VAR
   Vowels : SET of Char;
   Vowels := ['A','E','I','O','U'];
```

One other aspect of sets that should be mentioned is that in Object Pascal, sets are limited in definition. They can be derived only from simple types that have 256 or fewer values in their range. Thus the types **Char** and **Byte** qualify, but the type **Integer** does not; given that its range spans 65,536 different numbers. However, you can define a subrange of a type, such as **Integer**, as long as the number of unique values is less than 256. For example:

```
TYPE
   TestRange = 0..100;
Var
   EnglishTest : SET of TestRange;
```

Using a set based on an **Integer** here is valid, because the subrange **TestRange** contains less than 256 unique values.

When creating a set, it is not necessary to delineate every member of that set. If applicable, you can define a range of elements as part of the group, just like you were defining a subrange. For instance, the set HexNumbers can be defined like this:

```
Var
   HexNumbers : SET of Char;
HexNumbers := [
'0','1','2','3','4','5','6','7','8','9','A','B','C','D','E','F'];
```

Or like this:

```
HexNumbers := ['0'..'9','A','B','C','D','E','F'];
```
or like this:
```
HexNumbers := ['0'..'9','A'..'F'];
```

In other words you can mix and match, as long as you define all the members of your set properly. C does not have sets *per se,* the closest thing being an array. But that's for later.

Object Pascal not only allows the creation of sets, but lets you operate on them as well. The two types of operations permitted are *relational* and *set builder* operations. Let's look closer at both to find out what we can do with our sets.

Relational Set Operations   Relational operators work on sets in much the same way that they work on single values. However, instead of evaluating individual values, these operators concern themselves with set membership. In other words, the relational operator does not care if set A has numbers greater in value than those in set B; rather, it cares if there are any numbers in set A found in set B, and so on.

IN   This operator returns **TRUE** if the specified element is present in the set being compared to; otherwise, the operator returns **FALSE**. Let's say we have a set of valid responses that a user could give to answer questions posed to them. We'll define this set as:

```
VAR
  Responses: SET of Char;
  Answer : Char;
  Responses := [ 'A'..'D','Y','N','Q','a'..'d','y','n','q'];
```

Now we need to evaluate the user's response by comparing their answer with the valid ones in the set. We can do this the hard way by coding a **CASE** statement that looks something like:

```
CASE Answer OF
'A','a','B','b', 'C','c','D','d':  EvaluateAnswer;
'Y','y','N','y', 'Q', 'q':    EvaluateAnswer;
```

```
else
   BogusAnswer;
```

In C, it would look something like:

```
switch(toupper(Answer))
{
   case 'A':
   case 'B':
   case 'C':
   case 'D':
   case 'Y':
   case 'N':
   case 'Q':
      EvaluateAnswer();
      break;
   default:
      BogusAnswer();
      break;
}
```

and so on, until we have covered all the values contained in the set Responses.

One problem, though. What happens when we change the values in the set Responses? For that matter, why do we even have the set? We're not even using it at the moment. These are valid questions. I'll answer them this way.

We've just demonstrated that we don't need the set **Responses** to evaluate the variable **Answer.** However, we do have a chore on our hands anytime we have to change the valid responses; especially if we have to evaluate **Answer** in more than one spot. This is where **IN** comes to the rescue. We can check for a valid response this way:

```
IF Answer IN Response THEN EvaluateAnswer ELSE BogusAnswer;
```

This is much more readable. On top of that, this code has no data dependencies, and is controlled by the set Responses. So, when we change the data set Responses, that change is reflected at every point in the program that contains this code. Sure beats hacking files all day long and missing something.

= This operator returns **TRUE** only if the two sets being compared contain the exact same elements; otherwise, it returns **FALSE**. For example, consider three sets A, B, and C, as follows:

```
VAR
  A : Set of Byte
  B : Set of Byte
  C : Set of Byte
  A := [0,1,2,3,4,5,6,7,8,9];
  B := [0,1,2,3,4,5,6,7,8,9];
  C := [0,2,4,6,8,1,3,5,7,9];
```

Now, if we evaluate them:

```
if A = B then writeln("Sets A and B are equal");
if B = C then writeln("Sets B and C are equal");
if A = C then writeln("Sets A and C are equal");
```

we will find that all three sets are equal, even though set C has its elements ordered differently.

<> This operator returns **TRUE** if the two sets being compared do not contain exactly the same elements for each; otherwise, it returns **FALSE**. Consider the sets A, B, C, D, and E:

```
VAR
  A : Set of Byte
  B : Set of Byte
  C : Set of Byte
  D : Set of Byte
  E : Set of Byte
  A := [0,1,2,3,4,5,6,7,8,9];
  B := [0,1,2,3,4,5,6,7,8,9];
  C := [0,2,4,6,8,1,3,5,7,9];
  D := [0,2,4,6,8];
  E := [0,1,2,3,4,5,6,7,8,10];
```

If we evaluate them as:

```
If A<>B then writeln("Sets A and B not equal");
```

```
If A<>C then writeln("Sets A and C not equal");
If A<>D then writeln("Sets A and D not equal");
If A<>E then writeln("Sets A and E not equal");
```

we will discover that:

```
Set A equals set B (Both sets the exact same)
Set A equals set C (Exact same elements, order does not matter)
Set A not equal to set D (Set D missing elements in set A)
Set A not equal to set E (Set E contains a different element
than set A)
```

<= This operator returns TRUE if all the elements in the set on the left of the operator are present in the set on the right of the operator; otherwise, it returns FALSE. Consider the sets A, B, C, D, E, and F:

```
VAR
  A : Set of Byte
  B : Set of Byte
  C : Set of Byte
  D : Set of Byte
  E : Set of Byte
  F : Set of Byte
  A := [0,1,2,3,4,5];
  B := [0,1,2,3,4,5,6,7,8,9];
  C := [0,2,4,6,8,1,3,5,7,9];
  D := [0,1,2,3,4,5];
  E := [0,1,2,3,4];
  F := [0,2,4,6,8,10];
  G := [4,5,6,7,8];
```

If we evaluate them as:

```
If A <= B then writeln("Set A is a subset of B");
If A <= C then writeln("Set A is a subset of C");
If A <= D then writeln("Set A is a subset of D");
If A <= E then writeln("Set A is a subset of E");
If A <= F then writeln("Set A is a subset of F");
If A <= G then writeln("Set A is a subset of G");
```

we will discover that:

```
Set A is a subset of B (B is a superset of A)
Set A is a subset of C (C is a superset of A, order of elements
doesn't matter)
Set A is a subset of D (Set D identical to set A)
Set A is not a subset of E (Set E is actually a subset A)
Set A is not a subset of F (Elements in both sets are different)
Set A is not a subset of G (Set G smaller than A, and has dif-
ferent elements).
```

>=   This operator returns TRUE if all the elements in the set on the right of the operator are present in the set on the left of the operator; otherwise, it returns FALSE. Consider the sets A, B, C, D, E, and F:

```
VAR
   A : Set of Byte
   B : Set of Byte
   C : Set of Byte
   D : Set of Byte
   E : Set of Byte
   F : Set of Byte
   A := [0,1,2,3,4,5];
   B := [0,1,2,3,4,5,6,7,8,9];
   C := [0,2,4,6,8,1,3,5,7,9];
   D := [0,1,2,3,4,5];
   E := [0,1,2,3,4];
   F := [0,2,4,6,8,10];
   G := [4,5,6,7,8];
```

If we evaluate them as:

```
If B <= A then writeln("Set A is a subset of B");
If C <= A then writeln("Set A is a subset of C");
If D <= A then writeln("Set A is a subset of D");
If E <= A then writeln("Set A is a subset of E");
If F <= A then writeln("Set A is a subset of F");
If G <= A then writeln("Set A is a subset of G");
```

we will discover that:

```
Set A is a subset of B (B is a superset of A)
Set A is a subset of C (C is a superset of A, order of elements
doesn't matter)
Set A is a subset of D (Set D identical to set A)
Set A is not a subset of E (Set E is actually a subset A)
Set A is not a subset of F (Elements in both sets are different)
Set A is not a subset of G (Set G smaller than A, and has dif-
ferent elements).
```

Set Builder Operations   Set Builder Operations are used to test and change the values of data within sets. The operators take sets as arguments and return sets as answers.

Set Difference (Exclusion)   Conceptually, the idea of set difference is related to mathematical subtract, but with a twist. Essentially, it boils down to removing all common elements contained in the subtrahend from the initial set. Consider the sets A through I:

```
VAR
  A : Set of Byte
  B : Set of Byte
  C : Set of Byte
  D : Set of Byte
  E : Set of Byte
  F : Set of Byte
  G : Set of Byte
  H : Set of Byte
  I : Set of Byte
  A := [0,1,2,3,4,5,6,7,8,9];
  B := [0,1,2,3,4,5];
  C := [0,2,4,6,8,10,12,14];
  D := A - B;
  E := A - C;
  F := B - A;
  G := B - C;
```

```
H := C - A;
I := C - B;
```

When we evaluate sets D through I, we get these results:

```
Set D = [6,7,8,9]
Set E = [1,3,5,7,9]
Set F = [] (nothing)
Set G = [1,3,5]
Set H = [10,12,14]
Set I = [6,8,10,12,14]
```

Set Intersection   Intersecting two sets of data leaves a third set composed of only those members held in common from both original data sets. Consider the sets A through F:

```
VAR
  A : Set of Byte
  B : Set of Byte
  C : Set of Byte
  D : Set of Byte
  E : Set of Byte
  F : Set of Byte
  A := [0,1,2,3,4,5,6,7,8,9];
  B := [0,1,2,3,4,5];
  C := [0,2,4,6,8,10,12,14];
  D := A * B;
  E := A * C;
  F := B * C;
```

When we evaluate sets D through F, we get these results:

```
Set D = [0,1,2,3,4,5]
Set E = [0,2,4,6,8]
Set F = [0,2,4]
```

Set Union   The union of two sets takes the members held in common and the unique members of each set, and forms a larger set.

Consider the sets A through F:

```
VAR
  A : Set of Byte
  B : Set of Byte
  C : Set of Byte
  D : Set of Byte
  E : Set of Byte
  F : Set of Byte
  A := [0,1,2,3,4,5,6,7,8,9];
  B := [0,1,2,3,4,5];
  C := [0,2,4,6,8,10,12,14];
  D := A + B;
  E := A + C;
  F := B + C;
```

When we evaluate sets D through F, we get these results:

```
Set D = [0,1,2,3,4,5,6,7,8,9]
Set E = [0,1,2,3,4,5,6,7,8,9,10,12,14]
Set F = [0,1,2,3,4,5,6,8,10,12,14]
```

It should be noted that even though an identical member may occur in both original data sets, it will still appear only once in the new set formed by the union. By definition, a set describes only whether a member value is present in that data set. If it is present, it occurs only once, regardless of how many data sets contain the same member value.

Strings

Strings in Object Pascal are not the same as NULL-terminated strings in C. Other than strings being a run of characters, that's where the similarity ends.

Pascal strings have a maximum length of 255 characters. When declaring a string, if you do not specify a length, then the length defaults to the maximum. The reason for the limited size has to do with the first element of the array. In Pascal, element 0 contains the logical length (how many actual characters the string contains at the moment) of the string. The physical length of a string is how much memory it actually takes up while it exists. Since strings are composed of Chars, that have a maximum of 256 unique values, then element 0 cannot contain any number larger than 255.

To give you a better idea of how this all plays together, strings are typically defined like this:

```
VAR
  MyString : String
  MyString80 : String[80];
  MyString := 'Test String';
  MYString80 := 'Test String';
```

The first definition (MyString) uses the string data type in the default configuration. Thus, the physical size of MyString is 256 bytes—one for the length, and 255 for data. The second definition (MyString80) used a numeric modifier to reduce the physical size of the string to 81 characters—80 for data, and the first element for the length. So, when defining specific string lengths, unlike C, you don't have to count one extra for a string terminator or the logical size.

String Procedures and Functions

One of the bonuses that comes with Object Pascal strings is that of built-in procedures and functions for string manipulation. We'll take a quick look at these.

```
FUNCTION Length(Source : STRING) : Integer;
```

Length   This function returns the logical length of a Pascal string located in element 0 of the source string. For example:

```
VAR
  HowLong : Integer;
  MyString : String;
  MyString := "How long is this string?";
  HowLong := Length(MyString);
```

Or we could use it in a FOR statement, like so:

```
procedure SimpleEncode( str : String)
VAR
```

```
    I : Integer;
BEGIN
  FOR I := 1 to Length(str) DO
    str[I] := (str{i} * 2) + 10;
END;
```

A second method for getting the length of an Object Pascal string is to simply look at element 0 of the string in question. Because of Pascal's strong type checking, we just can't simply say:

```
  HowLong := MyString[0];
```

The compiler would complain about trying to make a number out of a character. Instead we use the ORD() function, like so:

```
  HowLong := ORD(MyString);
```

```
FUNCTION Concat(str1 [, str2,…, strn]: STRING) : STRING;
```

Concat   Like **goto** in C, Concat is really a legacy function to provide backward compatibility with older versions of Pascal. Concat's purpose is to take two or more strings and combine them into one large string. Strings that are combined together to make a string longer than the physical length that the destination will allow for are truncated off from the right to fit inside the destination string.

Here is an example of each:

```
VAR
  ShortString : String[25];
  LongString : String;
  Destination : String[30];
BEGIN
  ShortString := "This is a short string ";
  LongString := "that got way too long for the destination.";
  Concat(Destination,ShortString,LongString);
END
```

Destination now contains the string:

```
"This a short string that "
```

Now let's change things around a bit:

```
VAR
   ShortString: String[25];
   Destination : String;
BEGIN
   ShortString := "This is a short string."
   Concat(Destination,
      ShortString,
      "Me Too..",
      " And me!",
      " And don't forget me!");
END;
```

Notice, you can pass in raw strings to the function. Destination now contains:

```
"This is a short string. Me Too.. And me! And don't forget me!"
```

The second method for concatenating strings is to simply add them together, like so:

```
   Destination := ShortString + LongString;
```
or
```
   Destination := ShortString + "Me Too.." + " And me!" + " And
don't forget me!";
```

```
PROCEDURE Delete(str : STRING; start, length : Integer);
```

Delete   The Delete procedure removes characters from anywhere within a string. It does this by accepting a target string, a valid starting position within the target string, and a number of characters to delete.

Here's a useful procedure, **Const**, to demonstrate Delete with:

```
   DontPrint : SET of Char = [#0..#30,' '];
PROCEDURE Whack(str : STRING);
BEGIN
   while (Length(str) > 0) AND (str[1] IN DontPrint) do
```

```
      Delete(str,1,1);
END;
```

Any string passed to this procedure will have prepended non-printing and control characters whacked off from the left.

```
FUNCTION Pos(match : STRING; str : STRING) : Integer;
```

Pos   The purpose of **Pos** is to locate a substring within a larger target string and return the starting position of the first occurrence that it finds. This is similar to **strstr()** in C. For example:

```
VAR
   Single : Char;
   match: String;
   str : String;
   start : Integer;
BEGIN
   Single := 'x';
   match := "fox";
   str := "The quick brown fox jumps over the lazy dog."
   if (start=Pos(Single,str))  0 then
     Writeln('Found ',Single,' at ',start);
   if (start=Pos(match,str))  0 then
     Writeln('Found ',match,' at ',start);
END;
```

```
FUNCTION Copy( str : STRING; Start,Length : Integer) : STRING;
```

Copy   The **Copy** function returns a substring of a larger target string that begins at the position pointed to by **Start**, and is **Length** characters long.

Here is a function that uses copy to extract the DOS logical drive from a pathname:

```
FUNCTION GetDrive(path : STRING) : STRING;
BEGIN
  if Pos(':',path)  2 then GetDrive := '' else
    GetDrive := Copy(path,1,2,);
END;
```

By definition, a complete file pathname under DOS starts with a logical drive letter and a colon. So if **Pos()** sees the colon in any other position other than second, or cannot find it, we want **GetDrive** to return a NULL string to let the caller know we came up empty-handed; otherwise, we want to send back a substring composed of the first two characters in the file pathname.

```
PROCEDURE Insert(Source : STRING; Dest : STRING; start : Integer);
```

Insert The **Insert** procedure takes a **Source** string and inserts it into the **Dest** string at the position in **Dest** pointed to by **start**. A word of caution. If the new **Dest** string is longer than what **Dest** is physically sized for, then the extra is truncated. For example:

```
VAR
  str : STRING;
  str1 : STRING;
BEGIN
  str := " blue";
  str1 := "Look, it's a whale!";
  Insert(str,str1,13);
END;
```

Once **Insert** has been called, **str1** now reads: **"Look, it's a blue whale!"**

```
PROCEDURE Str(X [: Width [: Decimals ]]; var S);
```

Str The **Str** procedure is a generic string-to-number converter that works for Integers and Real numbers. In C, the closest analogous function would be **sprintf()**.

The optional **Width** parameter tells **Str** how wide to make the string to hold the number. If you specify **Decimals**, then **Str** assumes that **X** was previously defined as a Real number. Let's look at an example of two:

```
VAR
  I : Integer;
  R : Real;
  Number : STRING;
```

```
BEGIN
  I := 12345;
  R := 12345.678
  Str(I:3,Number);
```

This produces a string of **12345** even though the Width is smaller than the string logically sized to.

```
  Str(I:5,Number);
```

This produces a string of **12345**. The Width and logical string size are equal.

```
  Str(I:8,Number);
```

This produces a string of **12345**. The number is right-justified in the new string as spaces are used to pad the string to the defined logical width.

```
  Str(R,Number);
```

This produces a string of **1.2345678000E+04**. By default, Reals are displayed in scientific notation in strings 18 characters wide.

```
  Str(R:9:3,Number);
```

This produces a string of **12345.678**. The number of decimal places is taken out of the width, just like the **%7.2f** format argument for **sprintf()**.

```
  Str(R:12:4,Number);
```

This produces a string of **12345.6780**. The number is right-justified in the new string as spaces are used to pad the string to the defined logical width. If the number of decimal places is larger than the displayed fractional portion of the Real, then zeroes are appended.

```
PROCEDURE Val(S; var V; var Code: Integer);
```

Val   The **Val** procedure takes a string representation of a signed whole number and converts it to either an Integer or a Real. The variable **Code** contains the status of the operation when completed. If successful, Code will be set to zero. If there is a problem evaluating the string, then Code will be set to point to the character in the string that caused the problem. If the string is NULL-terminated, then the value of Code should be reduced by 1 to account for zero offset. For example:

```
VAR
  ValueStr : String;
  I : Integer;
  Status : Integer;
BEGIN
  ValueStr := "12345";
  Val(ValueStr,I,Status);
END;
```

Data Structures

Besides the derived data types already discussed, there are two data structures that I want to touch on for a brief moment: *arrays* and *records*. They are not the only data structures in Object Pascal, but of all the others, except possibly STRINGS, you will use these two the most in your coding.

Arrays

Arrays, as in C, are collections of data elements (all of the same type) that are bound by a single identifier. Just as with C, Pascal arrays reference individual members of the array by indexing from item 0. Strings are the noted exception here as they keep their logical string lengths in element 0, so they reference from an offset of 1.

Array elements can be composed of just about any data type. In fact, you can define arrays with very complex derived data types of your own making, such as records, other arrays, and other data structures. Let's take a look at some examples:

```
TYPE
  rec_type = RECORD
    field1 : Integer;
    field2 : Integer;
    field3 : Integer;
    END
SubRange = 1..100;
```

```
Array1 : ARRAY[10] of Char;
Array2 : ARRAY[10] of STRING;
Array3 : ARRAY[0..10,0..10] of Integer; {10x10}
Array4 : ARRAY[10] of rec_type;
Array5 : ARRAY[10] of SubRange;
```

I could list off dozens of different ways to declare arrays. The key here is to think about the problem you are trying to solve. By doing that, the form of the array (should one be necessary) will suggest itself very quickly.

While array declaration may seem limitless, indexing into them is not. There are some restrictions on indexing that you should be aware of:

1. Array index data types must be one of the following:
   - A member
   - A subrange of an ordinal type
   - An ordinal type such as:

     Integer

     ShortInt

     Byte

     Word

     Char

     Boolean
   - A programmer-defined enumerated type
2. Array index data types may not be any of these:

   Floating point

   LongInt

   Comp

Some things to be aware of when declaring arrays and coding for them:

1. Dimensioning arrays larger than two or three dimensions is a waste of RAM, not to mention difficult to keep track of in terms of coding and indexing. Try breaking things up into simpler pieces, or using other data structures, such as records, to supplement.

2. Arrays are static in size in Pascal. Once you declare an array's size, that's it. You cannot fiddle with its structure like you can in C to some extent via pointers and **malloc()**.

3. At runtime, initialize your arrays to some preset value. Pascal makes no attempt to clear memory that is occupied by data. This should be a habit already ingrained if you have worked with multiple C compilers in the past. Some initialized memory to zero; others let the variables and structures assume the values from the garbage on the stack and in memory. Never assume you have a clean array when you first start up.

A quick and dirty way to initialize arrays in Object Pascal is to use the **FillChar** procedure:

```
procedure FillChar(var X; Count: Word; value);
```

For example:

```
VAR
   Items : ARRAY[1000] of Integer;
BEGIN
   FillChar(Items, SizeOf(Items), 0);
END;
```

Records

Pascal records are collections of data items that can be of different types. Just keep in mind that Pascal records are like structures in C.

The best way to describe a record to you is to show you one:

```
TYPE
   PhoneEntry = RECORD
     FirstName : String[40];
     LastName : String[40];
     Address1 : String[40];
     Address2 : String[40];
     City : String[40];
     State : String[2];
     ZipCode : LongInt;
```

```
    HmPhone : String[20];
    WkPhone : String[20];
  END
```

Now that we have defined **PhoneEntry**, we can use it as a new data type so that we can track the entire record as a single entity, instead of explicitly pushing around all the fields in the record. We can declare a record, like any other derived data type:

```
Var
  MyList : PhoneEntry;
```

By declaring **MyList**, the compiler will now set aside space in the program for the variable **MyList** that has a physical size of one PhoneEntry record.

Referencing the fields within the record is done with a dot (.) modifier. So, just like in C, if we want to look at each of the fields within **MyList**, it would look something like:

```
MyList.FirstName
MyList.LastName
MyList.Address1
MyList.Address2
MyList.City
MyList.State
MyList.ZipCode
MyList.HmPhone
MyList.WkPhone
```

Using WITH to Hide Record Details   Normally, you would have to explicitly reference the record name of each field to identify it to the compiler, but Object Pascal provides another method—the **WITH** statement that removes the need to do so.

WITH is another one of those conveniences for programmers to help them keep their code organized and clean. It also saves typing the record name over and over again during long stretches of field updates. The syntax for **WITH**, looks like:

```
WITH <record names> DO
  BEGIN
```

```
<statements>
END;
```

BEGIN and **END** are required only if you have more than one statement to associate to **WITH**. When you list the record name in the **WITH** statement, any field references associated to the **WITH** statement do not require the record name in order to be resolved.

Here are two examples, one done straight up, the other using **WITH**:

Example #1:

```
procedure AddRecord()
BEGIN
    MyList.FirstName := "John"
    MyList.LastName := "Doe"
    MyList.Address1 := "123 Maple Drive."
    MyList.Address2 := "Apt # 5"
    MyList.City    := "Your Town"
    MyList.State := "OR"
    MyList.ZipCode := "97201"
    MyList.HmPhone := "(503)555-1234"
    MyList.WkPhone := "(503)555-4321"
END;
```

Example #2:

```
procedure AddRecord()
BEGIN
    with MyList DO
    BEGIN
        FirstName := "John"
        LastName := "Doe"
        Address1 := "123 Maple Drive."
        Address2 := "Apt # 5"
        City := "Your Townv"
        State := "OR"
        ZipCode := "97201"
        HmPhone := "(503)555-1234"
        WkPhone := "(503)555-4321"
```

```
   END;
END;
```

I personally like **WITH** for this, because it removes a lot of superfluous detail from the code, and I don't have to type so much.

Variables

Variables are the workhorse of the Pascal program. You will use
more of these than any other construct. Basically, variables represent blocks of reserved space that the executable program sets aside
at runtime to store data in. The names given to variables tell us
what purpose the data it stores will serve, while the declaration of
type tells the compiler how much room to set aside for the data
occupying that space.

Declarations and Naming

There are two points of view when it comes to using variables—
yours and the compiler's. To the compiler, the variable name is
rather meaningless outside of name uniqueness. It serves only to
mark the spot where memory will be reserved for data storage. It
really does not know or care what the data will be used for. What
is most important to the compiler is how much space to set aside
for the variable, based on type.

To the programmer, the size and type of said variable is important
only in terms of the kind of data (numbers, letters, strings, etc.) that
will be put there. We are really more interested in the abstract problem that will be solved using this variable and the data it will contain. To us, it is more important to have a recognizable name than
worry about memory size.

Understanding both sides will help you create better programs.
When naming a variable, there are some points to keep in mind:

1. Pick a name that means something to you now, and that will
   again six months from now. Names such as A, B, X, or Y are
   valid, but try to guess what kind of data they hold while not
   looking at anything else. You can't; there is nothing distinc-
   tive about these names.

   Names, such as TaxRate, DayOfWeek, Friction, Temperature,

and GrossReceipts, not only identify the data used in solving a problem, but they also give a clue as to the type of data that is stored there and the possible range of values, and they define the problem more fully when viewed in context.

2. Make sure that variables visible to each other do not have the same name. For instance, don't declare something like:

```
VAR
   temp : Char;
   temp : Integer;
```

It won't work, and the compiler will complain. Also, Delphi recognizes only the first 63 characters of a variable name. Even if you actually want to name your variables that long, be careful to distinguish between them within the 63-character limit; otherwise, to the compiler, you will again have a situation where it thinks you have duplicate names. For example:

```
VAR
ThisVariableIsIdenticalToAnotherOneBecauseWeAreNotUniqueWithin6
3Characters : Char
ThisVariableIsIdenticalToAnotherOneBecauseWeAreNotUniqueWithin6
3Characters_2 : Char
```

will fetch a complaint from the compiler.

3. Variable names must start with a letter (A, B, C, etc.) or an underscore (_). Anything else is not valid. Numbers, underscores, and letters can appear in any order after the first letter of the name. But symbols, such as @, #, $, %, and so on, are not allowed. For instance:

```
_InitSystem : Integer;
AnotherVar : Integer;
Club54 : Char
C_syntax : Boolean
```

are valid variable names, while

```
@#$%#%@# : Integer;
```

```
98BottlesOfBeer : SET of Integer
Percent%Return : Real
Money$ : Real
```

are examples of invalid variable names.

4. You cannot use any Pascal reserved words to name your variable. Following is the list of words that are off limits:

and	in	string
as	inherited	then
asm	inline	to
array	initialization	try
begin	interface	type
case	is	unit
class	label	until
const	library	var
constructor	mod	while
destructor	nil	with
div	not	xor
do	object	
downto	of	
else	or	
end	packed	
except	procedure	
exports	program	
file	property	
finally	raise	
for	record	
function	repeat	
goto	set	
if	shl	
implementation	shr	

5. Don't use already defined data types (no matter how tempt-

ing) as variable names. This includes such words as Char, Byte, Word, Integer, LongInt, Real, Single, Double, Comp, String, Array, and so on. Using one of these names for a variable results in the loss of that data type to your program.

Type Casting

One of the biggest annoyances about Pascal to a C programmer, besides lack of pointer manipulation, is type casting. Because of the strong type checking that is inherent in Pascal, the compiler will typically complain if you do something like throw an Integer value at a Byte or Char to lop off the top 8 bits. While such constructs are nonportable by comparison to **AND**ing with **$FF**, it does demonstrate the philosophy of C that you, the programmer, already know what the rules are concerning data types, and that you know how to break them to make things work. Working without safety nets gets to be an everyday affair. Of course, the bugs and crashes on occasion can get frequent and/or spectacular during development.

Getting back to the original topic, Object Pascal provides two methods of type casting: using the manipulation operators **IS** and **AS**, and value type casting.

IS and AS

The **IS** and **AS** operators allow the safe casting of objects from one type to another. The **IS** operator looks at the object on its left and compares it with the object type on the right. If the object on the left is the same object type, or is descended from the object type, or is assignment-compatible, then it returns **True**. For example, the code:

```
if Sender is Tbutton then
  SetColors;
else
  IgnoreAction;
```

checks the object **Sender** (which is the means of passing about object information in Delphi) to see if the object in question is a button. Now, **Sender** is an object of type **TObject**. **TObject** is the parent object from which all other Delphi objects are derived. So,

Sender by its very nature is assignment-compatible with everybody (Delphi objects, anyway).

So, if the object being passed in **Sender** is of type **TButton**, then the IF statement evaluates to True and the procedure SetColors is executed. If any other object types come through, the IF evaluates to False, as the comparison failed.

The **AS** operator does the actual type casting of objects from one to the other. Looking at Sender again, we can say:

```
Sender AS Tbutton
```

Here, **AS** combines the **IS** test for assignment compatibility with the actual type cast. It is equivalent to saying:

```
if Sender is TButton then
   TButton(Sender);
else
   Raise EinvalidCast;
```

This is actually better than just straight casting TButton(Sender), since **AS** gives you the opportunity to generate and handle an exception when the type cast will fail.

Going back to the WIM-MDI Editor, we have already used the **AS** operator in dealing with menu items. We wrote the following procedure to handle text alignment as it appears in the **memo** object:

```
procedure TChild.AlignClick(Sender: TObject);
begin
Left1.Checked := False;
Right1.Checked := False;
Center1.Checked := False;
with Sender as TMenuItem do Checked := True;
with Memo1 do
  if Left1.Checked then
  Alignment := taLeftJustify
else if Right1.Checked then
  Alignment := taRightJustify
else if Center1.Checked then
  Alignment := taCenter;
end;
```

The first thing we do when entering the procedure is turn all check marks off for these menu items. Since we are about to select an alignment and we don't know what it is just yet, this makes good sense. The next thing we do is make the actual type cast:

```
with Sender as TMenuItem do Checked := True;
```

By casting **Sender** as a **TMenuItem**, we now point at the menu item that generated the event we are now handling. We now set the **Checked** attribute to True, so that a check mark shows up right next to the menu item that generated the event we are handling. This one line of code handles all the menu items that come by way of **Sender**. The important thing to remember is that by typecasting Sender, we were able to *see* who called us and therefore make the changes necessary to that object.

Value Typecasting

The second method of typecasting resembles the way it is done in C. Essentially, value typecasting changes one type of expression into another. The limitations on this are that the expressions must be of ordinal or pointer type for this to work. The syntax looks like:

```
<data types> (argument)
```

which is similar to C's

```
(data type)argument
```

and identical to C's

```
<data types> (argument)
```

Table 7.4 shows some examples with their C equivalents.

Table 7.4 Value Typecasting	
Pascal	C
Char(65)	(char)65 or char(65)
Integer('D')	(int)'D' or int('D')

Constants

Constants are Pascal's way of keeping programmers from making a bigger mess than they already have. These expressions, quite simply, are self-documenting place holders for data in the code. They serve no other useful purpose than for our benefit in tracking details.

Constants replace in the source code what I like to call *magic numbers*. These magic numbers are raw data that show up in a function or procedure, or that wander about as a global data element somewhere. If documented properly, the number 5 would mean something specific to you as the programmer reading the code. But many times, 5 just sits there and stares at you like a cow at a passing train. Of course, you stare back in likewise fashion and eventually curse the person who wrote the code if you can't figure out what it's doing there and why.

Case in point. The equation:

```
RATE := 1400 * 0.005123496;
```

doesn't do a whole lot for me when I see it. All I know is that some kind of rate is calculated from multiplying two numbers together. Now, poking around in the preceding code and the code following this line may provide the answers I am looking for, but then again, it may also be just as revealing.

But, if I define a constant that tells me what the numbers represent, then the equation takes on new meaning. For instance, if we rewrote the code to look like:

```
RATE := MinMonthlyIncome * BaseTaxRate;
```

and added the constants:

```
MinMonthlyIncome = 1400
BaseTaxRate = 0.005123496
```

to the program, then the line of code becomes self-documenting and we don't have to scrounge around looking for a definition. It's right there.

One last point I want to make about the use of constants: If you have some value that is used all over your program, then define a constant for it and use that instead. You will thank yourself later when you need to make a change to that value and there are 57 different places where that value crops up. Changing the value of the constant definition ensures that all 57 instances will be correct. You will also save time, as you won't have to wade through the code locating and changing the old value to the new. And you will almost never catch all of them the first time in the code. This means you will spend yet more time poking at the code trying to find the stray that got by you the first time.

Types of Constants

Constants in Object Pascal are generally simple data types, such as bytes, chars, integers, reals, longs, booleans, literals, and words. Derived types, such as strings, enumerated types, and sets, are also supported.

Constants are simple to create. They take on the data type of the data they are assigned to. That being the case, let's look at some samples:

```
CONST
    Drive = 'A';        {Constant is a Char }
    OK = True;          {Constant is a Boolean}
    Port = $278         {Constant is a Hex value}
    PI = 3.1742         {Constant is a Real}
    ValidResp = ['Y','N']  {Constant is a set}
    Temp = 78           {Constant is an Integer}
    Null = ''           {Constant is a NULL string}
    Version = 'V1.00E'    {Constant is a string}
    BigBucks = 98765432    {Constant is a Long Int}
```

In C, these would be defined as:

```
#define Drive    'A'
#define OK      True
#define PORT    0x278
#define PI     3.1742
#define ValidResp  "YN"     /* Close approximation. */
#define Temp    78
#define NULL     ""
#define Version  "V1.00E"
#define BigBucks  98765432
##end##
```

8

Object Pascal Language Elements

Computer languages are composed of several basic elements:

- A symbol set
- Variables and constants
- Data types and structures
- Operators
- Execution constructs

While many of these vary greatly from language to language, there is a certain commonality that can be found amongst all computer languages. For example, in C we might see the statement:

```
if ( A < B)
{
    do_something_with_A();
    clean_up();
```

```
}
else
  make_A_less_than_B();
```

If we rewrite this in Object Pascal, it might look like:

```
IF A < B THEN
BEGIN
  DoSomeThingWithA;
  CleanUp;
END;
ELSE
  MakeALessThanB;
```

If we rewrite it a third time in Visual Basic, we might see:

```
If A < B
  DoSomethingWithA
  CleanUp
Else
  MakeALessThanB
End If
```

And finally, if we really get fancy and write it in Intel Assembly, we might see:

```
  Mov AX,_B
  Mov BX,_A
  Sub AX,BX
  JC Reduce_A  ; IF A < B
  call _DoSomethingWithA  ; A is less than B
  call _CleanUp  ; so we execute these calls.
  JMP $+6  ; skip over the ELSE condition.
Reduce_A:
  call _MakeALessThanB  ; here is our ELSE condition.
...
```

In all the preceding examples, we kept seeing the variables A and B evaluated for some kind of action to be taken. In each case, it was just expressed differently on paper. To go back to our original premise, each language expresses the same logic of execution, but under its own set of rules and conditions. Now we'll take a look at some of the elements that make up the Object Pascal language and see how they are used.

Special Symbols

Previously, if you did any of the projects, or looked at some of the code in the book, you noticed that Object Pascal has an affinity for letters, numbers, and lots and lots of semicolons. Basically, Object Pascal will respond to all ASCII letters and numbers, plus punctuation marks and other symbols that fall into the *special symbols* category.

Okay, so what are special symbols? Glad you asked. Special symbols are those symbols and punctuation marks in the ASCII character set that have a predefined meaning when read by the compiler. They get their meaning from the definition given to them by Borland when they wrote the compiler. For instance, if we were to sit down to write our own compiler, we could make the $ symbol stand for multiplication instead of *. So, in our PASCAL, 3$4 would be read by the compiler as 3 times 4. In other words, we have defined our meaning for this symbol ahead of time. The only problem we now have is that when we attempt to compile some-one else's PASCAL code with our compiler, it bombs. But, that's a story for another day.

The following single characters are special symbols:

```
+ - * / = < > [ ] . , ( ) : ; ^ @ { } $ #
```

Sometimes these symbols can be combined to mean other things:

```
<= >= := .. (* *) (. .)
```

(The last two sets mark comments.)

Operators and Precedence

Operators are a funny category of data. They include both special symbols and reserved words. Here is a list of operators for Object

Pascal:

Special Symbols:

```
@ * / + - = <> >= <= > <
```

Reserved Words:

```
AND, OR, XOR, NOT, DIV, MOD, AS
```

The other unique thing about operators is that they indicate some kind of manipulation of one or more pieces of data. As you can tell from the list, operators tend to concern themselves with mathematical and boolean operations on data. If you need additional explanation on how they are used, you can find it in Chapter 7, "Data Types, Variables, and Constants."

Whenever operators are used in an expression, there tends to be more than one involved. This can get confusing not only to the eyeball processor, but also to the compiler when it comes to interpreting the statement. There needs to be a hierarchy of precedence when it comes to unraveling a compound operation.

For instance, consider the C statement:

```
if(!(year%4) && !(year%100) || !(year%400))
   leap = YES;
```

Here we calculate a leap year. Notice the use of parentheses to separate operations. They do make it readable, but also serve to ensure that operations done on the variable **YEAR** are done in the proper sequence.

In Object Pascal, we could rewrite this statement to become:

```
IF(NOT(Year MOD 4)) AND
   (NOT(Year MOD 100)) OR
   (NOT(Year MOD 400)) THEN
      Leap := YES;
```

Table 8.1 shows the order of precedence (from high to low) in which operators will be executed as they are encountered (from left to right) in an expression:

Table 8.1 Order of Precedence for Executing Operators	
Operators	Category
@ NOT	Unary operators
* / DIV MOD AS AND SHL SHR	Multiply, Divide, Modulus, typecasting, and bitwise operators.
+ - OR XOR	Add and subtract, plus OR and XOR
= <> > < <= >= IN IS	Relational and Type comparisons, and set membership

When combining these operators with parentheses in a compound statement, the rules are that the operations most deeply nested within parentheses are done first, until all operations are completed to the outside of the parentheses. To give you some idea of how this all works, let's go back to our Object Pascal statement of:

```
IF(NOT(Year MOD 4)) AND
   (NOT(Year MOD 100)) OR
   (NOT(Year MOD 400)) THEN
     Leap := YES;
```

The compiler will resolve this equation as follows:

1. The operation Year MOD 4 is done first, and the results are passed to the NOT operator waiting outside the innermost parentheses.

2. The NOT operator evaluates the results of Year MOD 4, and awaits the results of the other side of the AND operation.

3. The operation Year MOD 100 is done, and the results are passed to the waiting NOT operator waiting outside the innermost parentheses.

4. The NOT operator evaluates the results of Year MOD 100 and passes its value to the AND operator.

5. Now the AND operator has two values to operate on. If the value from the first equation evaluates True along with the value of the second equation, then we continue on to the OR portion of the compound statement, with the results of our AND operation waiting in the wings. Otherwise, we quit right here not having satisfied our requirements.

6. The operation Year MOD 400 is done, and the results are passed to the waiting NOT operator waiting outside the innermost parentheses.

7. The NOT operator evaluates the results of Year MOD 100 and passes its value to the OR operator.

8. OR now uses this value and the results of the previous AND operation to do its operation. If the results are True, then we have successfully completed the compound statement, and the IF statement that contains it will result in True. Otherwise, we return False to the IF statement, which then fails the conditional.

Sounds complicated? At first glance it does, but after thinking about it for a while you will come to appreciate the ability to evaluate many operations in a single statement.

Reserved Words

Like special symbols, reserved words have a predefined meaning assigned to them when the compiler is built. In essence they are the nouns, verbs, adjectives, adverbs, and prepositions that we use to build sentences so that we can *speak* PASCAL to the machine and tell it exactly what we want.

Just as we distinguish words into groups, such as nouns and verbs, we also separate reserved words based upon their action or the designation they give. There are several distinct categories that reserved words fall into. They are:

• Block Statements
• Data
• Decision Making
• Declarative
• Execution
• Objects
• Operators

Table 8.2 shows the Object Pascal reserved words for Delphi listed by category.

Table 8.2 Object Pascal Reserved Words	
Category	**Reserved Words**
Block Statements	ASM, BEGIN, END
Data	ARRAY, CONST, FILE, NIL, OF, RECORD, SET, SHL, SHR, STRING, TYPE
Decision Making	CASE, ELSE, IF, THEN
Declarative	EXPORTS, FUNCTION, IMPLEMENTATION, INLINE, INITIALIZATION, INTERFACE, LABEL, LIBRARY, PACKED, PROCEDURE, PROGRAM. PROPERTY, UNIT, USES, VAR
Execution	DO, DOWNTO, EXCEPT, FINALLY, FOR, GOTO, RAISE, REPEAT, TO, TRY, UNTIL, WHILE, WITH
Objects	CLASS, CONSTRUCTOR, DESTRUCTOR, INHERITED, OBJECT
Operators	AND, AS, DIV, IN, IS, MOD, NOT, OR, XOR

Statements

If you've come this far from the beginning of the chapter, you will notice that we are building outward—starting with letters and symbols, then words. Now we can take the words and make sentences out of them, called statements.

Assignment Statements

Assignment statements are the simplest statements to build. Composed of a data element on the left side and an expression on the right, this statement manipulates data directly. For example:

```
Count := 4;
```

assigns the value 4 to the variable Count. We could also perform an arithmetic operation on Count, like so:

```
Count := Count + 4;
```

If we extend this out and do a complex math equation, we could break it into a series of small, simple assignment statements:

```
FreeBlock := FreeSectors;
FreeBlock := FreeBlock * BytesPerSector;
FreeBlock := FreeBlock DIV 1024;
```

or combine the operations into a single compound statement, like so:

```
FreeBlock := (FreeSectors * BytesPerSector) DIV 1024;
```

In all cases, the results are always assigned to the data element on the left side.

Block Statements

Block statements are another way of combining simple statements into a single executable block. You will find block statements mostly in decision statements, such as IF and CASE, as well as looping execution statements, such as DO, FOR, REPEAT, and TRY.

ASM

This is an advanced block statement that many programmers will never use. Delphi does such a good job at providing resource support that you would rarely need to use assembly language in your code. But nonetheless, the one time you need it, you will sing praises about the folks that put it there.

There are only two reasons I can think of as to why you would want to have any assembly language in your code at all:

1. You need the ultimate in speed that Assembly Language can provide.
2. You need to poke at the PC's hardware directly, or address a driver of some sort.

Anyway, to do this, you start a block using the ASM reserved word, and complete it with the END reserved word and a semicolon. Here is an example that turns off the Num Lock key on the keyboard:

```
ASM
  Mov   AX,$40
  Mov   ES,AX
  Mov   AX,$17
```

```
    Mov   BX,AX   { Point to the keyboard flag at 40:17 }
    Mov   AX,ES:BX   { Get the keyboard flag }
    And   AX,$DF   { Turn off Num Lock bit }
    Mov   ES:BX,AX   { Put back the modified flag }
END;
```

Borland C has a similar ASM construct. It looks almost the same, but requires a **#pragma inline** so that the compiler will invoke the built-in assembler. So, using the Borland C compiler, our ASM would look like:

```
#pragma inline
ASM
{
  Mov   AX,0x40
  Mov   ES,AX
  Mov   AX,0x17
  Mov   BX,AX   /* Point to the keyboard flag at 40:17 */
  Mov   AX,ES:BX   /* Get the keyboard flag */
  And   AX,0xDF   /* Turn off Num Lock bit */
  Mov   ES:BX,AX   /* Put back the modified flag */
};
```

BEGIN / END

The BEGIN / END block statement is one that you will use constantly. Its function is to group a series of simple statements into a large statement that acts as a single statement. In some ways, it is analogous to the C braces that are used to group statements together. BEGIN / END statements are mostly found in two places:

• Inside decision making statements

• Inside procedures and function

For example, we can do more than one thing inside of an IF statement, like so:

```
IF Sender = Memo1 THEN
BEGIN
  Memo1.Font := SelectedFont;
  Memo1.Color.Foreground := NewFGColor;
  Memo1.Color.Background := NewBGColor;
```

```
    Memo1.Alignment := taAlignLeft;
END;
```

Without the BEGIN / END statement, we would be limited to creating four IF statements and executing each operation on the Memo1 object individually.

We can also nest BEGIN / END statements, like so:

```
IF Sender = Memo1 THEN
BEGIN
  Memo1. Font := SelectedFont;
  IF ColorChanged THEN
  BEGIN
    Memo1.Color.Foreground := NewFGColor;
    Memo1.Color.Background := NewBGColor;
  END;
  Memo1.Alignment := taAlignLeft;
END;
```

Decision Making Statements

There are times in the code when you want to take action based upon how a variable or equation is evaluated. For instance, let's say that we are keeping track of how many times we cycle through a loop, adding characters to a string. When we have added at least five characters to the loop, we want to update our display to let the user know how far we have gotten, then continue adding characters again.

Basically, we have a decision to make. Object Pascal provides two statements that let us branch in our execution: the CASE and the IF / THEN / ELSE statements.

IF / THEN / ELSE

The IF / THEN / ELSE statement provides a means to make simple choices; namely, two at a time. However, the IF statement is not limited to just two choices, as we will soon see.

IF provides for Boolean evaluation. It basically says, If my evaluation statement resolves to True, then I will do something and continue on. If an ELSE is tacked on to the end of the IF statement, then we might say, If my evaluation statement resolves to True, then I will do something; otherwise, I will do something else before continuing on.

Here are some examples:

```
IF Count = 5 THEN Done := True;
```

As long as Count is less than 5, nothing happens. Once count reaches the value of 5, then the Boolean variable **Done** takes on the value of True.

```
IF Count = 5 THEN Done := True ELSE Done := False;
```

In this statement, we are explicitly telling the program that we will perform some kind of operation on the Boolean variable **Done**, depending on the value of **Count**.

Now let's throw in a compound statement:

```
IF Count = 5 THEN
BEGIN
  Done := True;
  SetColors;
  UpdateScreen(Count);
END;
```

Now when we evaluate **Count** and it is equal to 5, all the statements between BEGIN and END will execute every time; otherwise, nothing happens. We can even add a compound statement to the ELSE clause:

```
IF Count = 5 THEN
BEGIN
  Done := True;
  SetColors;
  UpdateScreen(Count);
END;
ELSE
BEGIN
  Done := False;
  UpdateTickDisplay;
```

```
    MoveVisualPointer;
END;
```

One last trick that the IF / THEN / ELSE statement allows for: You can daisy chain IF statements through the ELSE clause. This lets you continue to evaluate only on the previous condition checked returning False. For example:

```
IF Count = 5 THEN Done := True
ELSE IF ScreenUpdate THEN UpdateTickDisplay
ELSE IF BufferEmpty THEN ReadFile ELSE WriteBuffer;
```

CASE

The CASE statement is similar in nature to the **switch** statement in C. The biggest difference, outside of syntax, is that CASE statements are more limited in evaluation value range. While a **switch** statement works on the basis of an integer value (16 bits usually), the CASE statement requires that all values be in the range of CHAR, BYTE, or Integers between 0 and 255.

While this may seem like a limitation, the CASE statement makes up for it in other ways. For instance, CASE is more flexible in coding choice evaluation. It derives this flexibility from the use of sets and grouping choices on a single line. Let's say we have a set of valid menu choices that we can make. If we code them explicitly, we would end up with something like:

```
CASE Choice OF
    '1':  EvaluateChoice;
    '2':  EvaluateChoice;
    '3':  EvaluateChoice;
    '4':  EvaluateChoice;
    '5':  InitializeFunction;
    '6':  InitializeFunction;
    '7':  InitializeFunction;
    '8':  InitializeFunction;
    '9':  InitializeFunction;
    'A':  DoThis;
    'B':  DoThis;
    'C':  DoThis;
```

```
   'D':   DoThis;
   'E':   DoThis;
END;
```

This is very similar to C's **switch** statement, which requires discrete conditions. Written in C, we would see the CASE statement written this way:

```
switch(Choice)
{
  case '1':
    EvaluateChoice();
    break;
  case '2':
    EvaluateChoice();
    break;
  case '3':
    EvaluateChoice();
    break;
  case '4':
    EvaluateChoice();
    break;
  case '5':
    InitializeFunction();
    break;
  case '6':
    InitializeFunction();
    break;
  case '7':
    InitializeFunction();
    break;
  case '8':
    InitializeFunction();
    break;
  case '9':
    InitializeFunction();
    break;
  case 'A':
```

```
      DoThis();
      break;
   case 'B':
      DoThis();
      break;
   case 'C':
      DoThis();
      break;
   case 'D':
      DoThis();
      break;
   case 'E':
      DoThis();
      break;
}
```

In either case, that's a lot of coding. It also is unnecessary coding, as there are more efficient and readable ways to write this. Now, if we group choices together by the procedures they call, we could write something like:

In Object Pascal:

```
CASE Choice OF
   '1','2','3','4':   EvaluateChoice;
   '5','6','7','8','9':   InitializeFunction;
   'A','B','C','D','E':   DoThis;
END;
```

By comparison in C:

```
switch(Choice)
{
   case '1':
   case '2':
   case '3':
   case '4':
      EvaluateChoice();
      break;
   case '5':
```

```
case '6':
case '7':
case '8':
case '9':
  InitializeFunction();
  break;
case 'A':
case 'B':
case 'C':
case 'D':
case 'E':
  DoThis();
  break;
}
```

This looks much better. Another way we could have written this just as concisely in Object Pascal is to use sets to group the data. Now our CASE statement looks like:

```
CASE Choice OF
  '1'..'4':  EvaluateChoice;
  '5'..'9':  InitializeFunction;
  'A'..'E':  DoThis;
END;
```

There is no equivalent to sets in C.

While our CASE statement handles lots of valid choices well, what happens when the variable Choice wanders in with data that is unaccounted for? Aha! We have found a hole in our menu evaluation logic! Not to worry, though; CASE provides a way to handle this through the use of the ELSE reserved word.

Just like with the IF statement, matching an evaluation condition returns a True to the CASE statement. However, ELSE provides a catchall for everything that returns False. The equivalent in C's **switch** statement is the **default** keyword.

By adding an ELSE clause to cover bad selections, our CASE statement now looks like:

```
CASE Choice OF
  '1'..'4':  EvaluateChoice;
```

```
'5'..'9':  InitializeFunction;
'A'..'E':  DoThis;
ELSE Writeln('Bad Choice. Try Again.');
END;
```

Our C equivalent would now look like:

```
switch(Choice)
{
  case '1':
  case '2':
  case '3':
  case '4':
    EvaluateChoice();
    break;
  case '5':
  case '6':
  case '7':
  case '8':
  case '9':
    InitializeFunction();
    break;
  case 'A':
  case 'B':
  case 'C':
  case 'D':
  case 'E':
    DoThis();
    break;
  default:
    printf("Bad Choice. Try Again\n");
    break;
}
```

Remember, whenever you add an ELSE clause to a CASE statement, place it after all the evaluation statements.

Execution Statements

Execution statements direct the action of manipulating data, such as filling an array of numbers one at a time, or printing a buffer, or invoking an error condition. Mostly, these types of statements find their best use in directing repetitive tasks; although a few of them, such as RAISE, have a very specific function.

Let's look at how Object Pascal directs the action.

DO

While this reserved word does not exist by itself in Object Pascal, it is very important to the WHILE, FOR, WITH, and ON statements. Basically, DO is the action part of these statements, and executes if the condition attached to these statements holds True.

Some quick examples of DO:

```
WHILE Done = False DO SomethingUseful;
FOR I := 1 TO 100 DO array[I] := Sin(I);
WITH Memo1 DO Font := SelectedFont;
ON EINVALID DO Halt;
```

FOR

The FOR statement is geared primarily for loop execution when the number of iterations through the loop is known in advance, or can be calculated beforehand at runtime. The control variable that FOR uses to keep track of how many times through the loop it has executed must be an ordinal (whole number) data type. FOR loops in PASCAL are actually much closer to BASIC's FOR loops than they are for C.

In C's FOR loop, all three arguments are options. In fact, when they are not declared at all (**FOR(;;)**), this creates an infinite loop that is broken only by exiting the program, or using a return, break, or goto statement. On the other hand, if you are really clever, it is possible to write an entire C program embedded in a FOR loop without having to put any statements inside the block portion of the loop.

Even though Object Pascal's FOR loop is not as flexible as C's, it nonetheless is quite serviceable for what it is called upon to do.

To count upward (or forward, as the case may be), FOR is declared like so:

```
FOR Count := 1 TO 15 DO array[Count] := GetChar;
```

Or like:

```
FOR Count := 1 TO 15 DO
BEGIN
   array[Count] := GetChar;
   Writeln('I have collected ',Count,' of 15 Characters.');
END;
```

In each of these loops the variable Count controls the number of times that array can collect a character. In this case, **array** will collect 15 characters before leaving the FOR loop.

The key factor here is the value of Count. By default, if we do not modify Count, then Count will automatically increment by one each time through the loop. Now, this does not mean that Count is sacred; in fact, if you want to get clever, you can modify Count in the body of the loop to force the FOR statement to cycle more or fewer times than the initial limit of 15 implies. But you must be careful about this, as each time you cycle through the loop, Count will be incremented by one whether you want it to or not.

Now, suppose we want to exit our loop prematurely because we got a <CR> from the keyboard. Well, we could do it this way:

```
FOR Count := 1 TO 15 DO
BEGIN
   array[Count] := GetChar;
   if array[Count] = $D THEN Count := 15
   ELSE
   Writeln('I have collected ',Count,' of 15 Characters.');
END;
```

This method is valid, but there is a problem. If we ever decide to change the number of times we go through the FOR loop, or use a different variable other than Count as our conditional, then we need to change this in two places, not one. Not good coding practice. Instead, FOR provides a little trapdoor called Break that lets us out early. So, instead we can write the loop this way:

```
FOR Count := 1 TO 15 DO
BEGIN
  array[Count] := GetChar;
  if array[Count] = $D THEN Break
  Writeln('I have collected ',Count,' of 15 Characters.');
END;
```

Now, when we receive a <CR>, we can leave the loop immediately without having to change Count, cycle back to the top, and drop out.

One last goodie here: FOR loops can count backward by replacing TO with DOWNTO, like so:

```
FOR Count := 15 TO 1 DO
BEGIN
  array[Count] := GetChar;
  if array[Count] = $D THEN Break;
  Writeln('I have ',(15-Count),' of 15 Characters.');
END;
```

The FOR loop now stuffs **array** from the back to the front so that if we were to print it out, we would see all of our collected characters printed in reverse order.

GOTO

This is a legacy execution statement that is carried forward from days of yore. In the past, GOTO was used as a means of forcing program execution to a particular point in the code without qualifying it. The code pointed to by GOTO was prefixed by a label that included a semicolon, like so:

```
JUMP1: Writeln('This is a jump point for a GOTO');
```

Now, if we take the previous FOR loop example and rewrite it to include a GOTO statement, it would look something like this:

```
FOR Count := 15 TO 1 DO
BEGIN
```

```
    array[Count] := GetChar;
    if array[Count] = $D THEN GOTO JUMP1;
    Writeln('I have ',(15-Count),' of 15 Characters.');
END;
```

Now a quick word about labels and GOTO's limitation. First, any label referenced by GOTO must be in the same code block. Just like C, a GOTO cannot force the program to jump outside a procedure or function. The second issue that must be dealt with is that any labels referenced in Object Pascal must be declared within the same procedure before being referenced, like so:

```
procedure Foo();
BEGIN
label   JUMP1;
FOR Count := 15 TO 1 DO
BEGIN
    array[Count] := GetChar;
    if array[Count] = $D THEN GOTO JUMP1;
    Writeln('I have ',(15-Count),' of 15 Characters.');
END;
JUMP1: Writeln('This is a jump point for a GOTO');
END;
```

C uses the same syntax for its labels but does not require that they be explicitly declared first; only that they exist within the body of the function where they are referenced and that their names are unique.

REPEAT

The REPEAT statement is the equivalent of C's DO loop. The loop is executed one time before the conditional is evaluated with the UNTIL clause. If the conditional is True, then execution falls out of the loop; otherwise, the loop continues to execute until the conditional is satisfied.

Unlike FOR loops, REPEAT loops by definition can execute indefinitely. These kinds of loops are good for repeating tasks in which you don't know ahead of time how many times you want to repeat, but you want to at least do them one time. For instance, we collect keys from the keyboard until we found a <CR> by doing this:

```
VAR
  key:  Char;
REPEAT
  key := GetChar;
  Writeln('key is ',key);
UNTIL key = $D;
```

The same thing in C would look like this:

```
char key;
do {
  key = getch();
  printf("Key is %c\n",key);
} while (key != 0xD);
```

TRY

The TRY statement is unique among the execution statements. TRY and its clauses EXCEPT and FINALLY allow the use of protected code within Object Pascal. So just what is protected code, you ask?

Essentially, protected code is written such that during execution, if an error designated as an exception occurs, then the program has a method to deal with the problem and continue running. Okay, so what's an exception?

In Delphi, an *exception* is an object that provides a method of handling problems that are usually fatal errors. It allows you to remove quite a bit of error-handling from your application code and reference it only when you really need to. Some examples of errors that are exceptions are:

- Out of Memory errors
- File I/O errors
- Invalid Pointer errors
- Divide by Zero errors
- Numbers Out of Range
- Integer Overflow
- Type Conversion errors

- Undefined Instruction errors
- Floating-point Number Overflow
- Floating-point Number Underflow
- General Protection Faults
- Stack Faults
- Page Faults
- Hardware errors
- Operating System errors

In fact, since exceptions are objects within Delphi, it is not too difficult to create your own and make use of the built-in error-handling system already in place. Basically, you will use TRY in one of two situations.

The first place you might use TRY is when you want to catch a specific error before it becomes a problem. For instance, let's say that you have a block of code that requires a divide. Now logically, we would expect all data that gets used in the divisor to be nonzero; otherwise, our results are undefined and the program generates an EDivByZero exception telling you so.

Consider the code:

```
Avg := dividend DIV divisor;
```

Now, if we set **divisor := 0**, then the program blows up. But if we code it as follows using the EXCEPT clause with TRY:

```
try
  Avg := dividend DIV divisor;
except
  on EDivByZero do Avg := 0;
end;
```

we now avoid the problem by providing a valid value for **Avg**. Instead of that, you could generate a message box and tell the user what the problem is, or do just about anything within reason to take care of the problem. The payoff here is that you, the programmer, are in control of how the program responds and you surrender error-handling to the operating system only when you have to.

NOTE

The EXCEPT clause only provides a place to handle exceptions, it does not guarantee that anything will be done unless you specifically trap the exception and write code to handle it.

The other situation you might find yourself in, where you need to handle problems gracefully, is when you are handling resources dynamically and an error condition occurs. By cleaning up stray resources when a problem occurs, you create less problems for all concerned in the long run; especially since some resources, such as memory, can wreak havoc on the operating system, forcing you to reboot and lose *all* your data, not just some of it.

Probably one of the best illustrations of resource protection occurs in memory management. A good way to make problems for DOS and/or Windows is to allocate a block of memory and then never free it. Over time, this gets in the way of the memory manager, and other problems surface because DOS can't find enough contiguous memory to allocate for other data structures. Eventually, given sufficient time and program usage, it leads to a system crash. Here is an example:

```
VAR
    ptr     : Pointer;
    divisor : Integer;
    answer  : Integer;
BEGIN
answer := 0;
divisor := 0;
GetMem(ptr, 4096);      {allocate a buffer of 4K }
answer := 12345 DIV divisor;      {generates the exception}
FreeMem(ptr,4096);      {free the buffer }
END;
```

In this case, when execution hits the division problem, the program will bomb on a Divide by Zero error. Now, notice that we previously allocated a buffer of 4K. We never got the chance to clean up after ourselves, so now we face the problem of having a possible 4K buffer allocated to nothing, with no way to recover it without rebooting the system.

To fix the problem with the buffer, we can recode using TRY with the FINALLY clause:

```
VAR
  ptr     : Pointer;
  divisor : Integer;
  answer  : Integer;
BEGIN
answer := 0;
divisor := 0;
GetMem(ptr, 4096);      {allocate a buffer of 4K }
try
  answer := 12345 DIV divisor;   {generates the exception}
finally
  FreeMem(ptr,4096);   {free the buffer }
end;
END;
```

The FINALLY clause forces execution of the statements within its block regardless of the error generated within the TRY block. This lets us free the buffer before the program dives headlong into the bit bucket, and wipes out any pointers that referenced that allocated section of memory.

WHILE

WHILE works like the REPEAT statement, except it tests the conditional before executing the loop. Doing it this way allows you to bypass the loop if you do not need to use it. As with REPEAT, a WHILE statement is by design a potential infinite loop to be used for those situations where you do not know or cannot calculate ahead of time how many times you must execute the loop. C's **while** statement operates identically to Object Pascal's WHILE. Here's an example:

```
VAR
  key: Char;
  key = '';
  WHILE key <> $D DO key := GetChar;
```

The C equivalent would look like:

```
char key;
  while((key = getch()) != 0xD);
```

WITH

The WITH statement is used to abstract detail in the code so that it becomes more readable. Coupled with the DO statement, it forms a block of code that operates on the fields of a record, or upon the properties and methods of an object.

Here is a sample record denoting a phone entry:

```
TYPE
  PhoneEntry = RECORD
    FirstName  : String[40];
    LastName   : String[40];
    Address1   : String[40];
    Address2   : String[40];
    City  : String[40];
    State  : String[2];
    ZipCode  : LongInt;
    HmPhone  : String[20];
    WkPhone  : String[20];
  END
```

If we were to add data to a record of this type, without WITH it would look like this:

```
Var
  MyList  : PhoneEntry;
procedure AddRecord()
BEGIN
  MyList.FirstName  := "John"
  MyList.LastName  := "Doe"
  MyList.Address1  := "123 Maple Drive."
  MyList.Address2  := "Apt # 5"
  MyList.City  := "Your Town"
  MyList.State  := "OR"
```

```
      MyList.ZipCode   := "97201"
      MyList.HmPhone   := "(503)555-1234"
      MyList.WkPhone   := "(503)555-4321"
END;
```

Notice that each field must be explicitly addressed as an element of the record MyList. Now, if we were to use WITH, we could rewrite it like so (this version looks much cleaner):

```
procedure AddRecord()
BEGIN
  with MyList DO
  BEGIN
    FirstName   := "John"
    LastName    := "Doe"
    Address1    := "123 Maple Drive."
    Address2    := "Apt # 5"
    City   := "Your Town"
    State   := "OR"
    ZipCode   := "97201"
    HmPhone   := "(503)555-1234"
    WkPhone   := "(503)555-4321"
  END;
END;
```

As for objects, a good example can be found in the WIM-MDI Editor created in Chapter 5. The procedure that sets the Text alignment for the Memo object and places the check marks on the drop menu items uses WITH to abstract the properties for the Memo. In the following, the bold text shows the code involved.

```
procedure TChild.AlignClick(Sender: TOBject);
begin
  Left1.Checked   := False;
  Right1.Checked   := False;
  Center1.Checked   := False;
with Sender as TMenuItem do Checked   := True;
    with Memo1 do
      if Left1.Checked then
        Alignment   := taLeftJustify
      else if Right1.Checked then
```

```
        Alignment   := taRightJustify
    else if Center1.Checked then
        Alignment   := taCenter;
end;
```

As an example, if we did not use the WITH statement, we would have to rewrite that section of code to look like:

```
if Memo1.Left1.Checked then
    Memo1.Alignment   := taLeftJustify
else if Memo1.Right1.Checked then
    Memo1.Alignment   := taRightJustify
else if Memo1.Center1.Checked then
    Memo1.Alignment   := taCenter;
```

Functions, Procedures, and Units

In previous chapters, we talked about the letters, words, and sentences that make up the language we call Object Pascal. Now, we are going to start putting these together in useful groupings to make paragraphs and chapters of the book that is our program or project.

The Block—The Smallest Aggregate

Many languages require you to think through a problem and express it on a statement-by-statement basis with no method of grouping that allows for common functionality. BASIC, in its original form, is a perfect example. Each statement was usually preceded by a line number to mark its location relative to every other statement in the program. Looping and branching somewhere was based on a specific line number to go to. This meant for most BASIC programs that any statement was a candidate to be looped or branched to. Procedural programming of this type may be adequate for small problems and jobs, but when the size of the program starts stretching across a number of files, there is a dire need for some form of grouping that helps keep the smaller functions together and readable. Enter the *block.*

The block is the basis for grouping and organization in Object Pascal. All procedures, functions, and units are based in whole or in part on this one simple structure. The basic block uses the **BEGIN/END** construct like this:

```
BEGIN
  <statement 1>
  <statement 2>
  <statement 3>
  ...
END;
```

Between the construct is a series of statements that group together to solve a problem. It can be any kind of problem; it doesn't matter. The point is that the solution cannot be constructed and executed unless the statements are grouped together to guarantee that when they are executed, all of them are executed and in a certain order.

One interesting thing about PASCAL blocks is that you can nest a block inside another, like so:

```
BEGIN
  <statement 1>
  <statement 2>
  BEGIN
    <statement 1>
    <statement 2>
    ...
  END;
  <statement 3>
  <statement 4>
  ...
END;
```

You can find representations of this inside of procedures and functions that contain IF, WHILE, FOR, and other branching and looping statements. In fact, Object Pascal will let you take the concept of embedded blocks even further and define procedures inside of procedures and functions. This touches upon the issue of the visibility or scope of a procedure or function. We will cover this a bit later.

We will demonstrate the concept of the program block as we talk about functions and procedures. Remember, too, that this concept also applies at the unit level and the program level. Each piece solves a larger part of the problem.

Procedures and Functions

Procedures are one of the most applied and simplest of the *paragraphs* that you will use in writing your PASCAL *book* with Delphi. In fact, it may be the only block structure you deal with in some cases. Delphi does so much of the work for you that many times all that is needed is to have the event handler procedures fill in which statements to make them work the way you want to. But, we will discuss that later.

Procedures in PASCAL are like VOID functions in C. They do not return a value of any kind to a calling statement. The basic structure of a procedure/function looks like:

```
PROCEDURE <name>(<parameters>)
<declarations>
BEGIN
<statements>
END;
```

The equivalent in C would look like:

```
void <function name> (<parameters>)
{
<declarations>
<statements>
}
```

As you can see, they are fairly similar in construction. By default, in C any function that is not specifically declared to return any data type will return a signed integer. Procedures by definition have no mechanism to return data of any type. Functions, on the other hand, will always return data of the type specified in the function declaration. Following is a template of a function:

```
FUNCTION <name>(<parameters>) : <return data type>
<declarations>
BEGIN
<statements>
<name> := <data>;
{ or you could say }
Result := <data>;
END;
```

In C, the equivalent would look like:

```
<return data type> <name> (<parameters>)
{
<declarations>
<statements>
  return(<return data type>); /* This is optional */
}
```

Now for some differences between C functions and Object Pascal functions:

- Return values in C functions are optional. Even though a C function is declared to be of some type other than void, it is not required to explicitly assign a return value to a variable, or return data at all to a caller. However, the compiler, if it is a more recent one, will complain that the function should return a value. This is a warning message only and is not fatal until you forget and try to set a variable equal to whatever the function returns. Sometimes the results get quite interesting.

- Delphi's Object Pascal, on the other hand, won't let you be so casual about functions. It expects to see a return value, and will complain loudly and refuse to compile any further until you comply. Functions must return a value that is of the same data type as the declared return data type of the function.

- Object Pascal returns data in two ways. In C, you call **return()** to send information back to the calling function. In Object Pascal, you can do this in one of two ways. The first is the more conventional method, which involves assigning the return value back to the original function, like so:

```
FUNCTION Squared(Value: Integer) : LongInt;
VAR
  x: LongInt;
BEGIN
  x := Value * Value;
  Squared := x;
END;
```

Now when we use this function in a program make a call like:

```
  Y := Squared(Data);
```

- The variable Y now contains the squared value of the variable **Data**.
- The second method of returning a value from a Delphi Object Pascal function is the built-in variable called **Result**. This variable is included for use in Delphi functions for programmer ease of use. Some people will find this more readable. Instead of assigning values to the function name, you just assign them to **Result** and be done with it. If we rewrite our **Squared** function to use **Result**, we would get this:

```
FUNCTION Squared(Value: Integer) : LongInt;
VAR
  x: LongInt;
BEGIN
  x := Value * Value;
  Result := x;
END;
```

- Which method you use is a matter of personal choice. However, be aware that if you are writing a function that may move to another PASCAL compiler, it would be better to use the traditional method, as the other PASCAL compiler and earlier Borland PASCAL compilers do not support this language extension.

Naming Procedures and Functions

When naming a procedure or function, there are some points to keep in mind:

1. Pick a name that means something to you now and will again six months from now. Names such as A, B, X, or Y are valid, but try to guess what these functions do without looking up the actual source code and reading it first. Names such as TaxRate, Area, FormatDisk, PrintReport, and SquareRoot identify what kind of data the function returns or processes, or what the procedure does.

2. Do not create two functions or procedures with the same name. It won't work, and the compiler will complain. Delphi recognizes only the first 63 characters of an identifier, function, procedure, or variable name. Even if you actually want to have a name that long for your function or procedure, you must make it unique within the 63-character limit; otherwise, to the compiler, you will again have a situation where it thinks you have duplicate names. For example:

```
PROCEDURE
ThisProcedureIsIdenticalToAnotherOneBecauseWeAreNotUniqueWithin
63Characters( Data: Char);
PROCEDURE
ThisProcedureIsIdenticalToAnotherOneBecauseWeAreNotUniqueWithin
63Characters_2(Data: Char);
```

will fetch a complaint from the compiler.

3. Function names, just like variable names, must start with a letter (A, B, C, etc.) or an underscore (_). Anything else is not valid. Numbers, underscores, and letters can appear in any order after the first letter of the name, but symbols, such as @, #, $, %, and so on, are not allowed. For instance:

```
FUNCTION _InitPrinter( PrinterPort : Integer) : Boolean;
PROCEDURE PrintALine( Line : Integer);
FUNCTION MakeDollarAmount100( Pennies : LongInt) : Pointer;
FUNCTION Check_C_syntax (Line : STRING ) : Boolean;
```

are valid function and procedure names, while

```
PROCEDURE @#$%#%@#( lang : STRING);
PROCEDURE 98BottlesOfBeer( bottles : SET of Integer);
FUNCTION Percent%Return (Dollars : Real) : Real;
FUNCTION Money$ (Amount : Real) : Boolean;
```

are examples of invalid function and procedure names.

4. You cannot use any PASCAL reserved words to name your function or procedure. Table 9.1 lists the words that are off limits.

Table 9.1 PASCAL Reserved Words (in alphabetical order)

and	in	then
as	inherited	to
asm	inline	try
array	initialization	type
begin	interface	unit
case	is	uses
class	label	var
const	library	while
constructor	mod	with
destructor	nil	xor
div	not	
do	object	
downto	of	
else	or	
end	packed	
except	procedure	
exports	program	
file	property	
finally	raise	
for	record	
function	repeat	
goto	set	
if	shl	
implementation	string	

Parameter Passing: Values and Variables

We've talked previously about returning results of functions, and the structure of blocks, procedures, and functions, but not about how we enter the data.

Parameter-passing to functions and procedures happens the same way and comes in two forms: passing by value, and passing by reference.

Here is a quick synopsis of how it's done and why it's important to distinguish between the two methods.

Passing by Value

Passing by value means just that. The program pushes a value on the stack before calling the function or procedure that will use it as one of its arguments. Once the function or procedure is invoked, it takes all its arguments off the stack so that it can begin to work with them.

The declaration necessary to do this can be found in the header of the function and procedure. It looks something like:

```
PROCEDURE <name> (<variable name> : <data type>);
FUNCTION <name> (<variable name> : <data type>) : <return type>;
```

Let's peek at the syntax between the parentheses. All parameters that will be passed in from the outside must be declared within the parentheses; no exceptions. C requires a similar construct. For example, in the older style of coding, we might represent parameters thus:

```
main(argc,argv)
int argc;
char **argv;
```

whereas in more modern notation, it looks more like PASCAL:

```
main(int argc, char **argv)
```

In each case, we have declared that function **main()** when invoked will expect to receive on the stack an integer value and a pointer to an array of strings. PASCAL works in a similar syntactical fashion:

```
<variable name> : <data type>
```

This declaration is the structure for all local declarations on the stack for any procedure and function. We can have one declaration or many. Usually it is wise to keep the number of data items passed to a function or procedure down to a reasonable number, keeps things readable. When the amount of discrete data gets too large to be manageable, then using records, structures, and objects to get data inside becomes desirable.

<variable name> represents any valid identifier, whether is it a variable or a constant value. The key to identifying it is with the **<data type>** modifier. The **<data type>** modifier identifies to the compiler how much space to set aside on the stack when it comes time to whip this bad boy into action. Without telling the compiler how much room you need for data on the stack, you leave the program open to clobbering itself. Here's why.

In the Intel DOS/Windows environment, whenever a function or procedure of some type gets called, the program counter has to remember what it was doing and where before it runs off someplace else. The program remembers its place by placing a *bookmark* on the stack so that it can come back to where it was. Essentially, this book mark consists of the return address of the currently executing function or procedure, and any values or data from local variables created in that function. Well, as a matter of course, these local variables are already there on the stack; the program just throws the return address on top of them.

Here's a quick sample of what that would look like on a stack. Let's suppose we are in a function and working away on some data that was created and/or passed in from somewhere else. If we were to look at the top of our stack, we would see our local data elements there, complete with their current values.

Local Data element #1

Local Data element #2

Local Data element #3

(etc.)

Now, let's say we need to call a function somewhere else within the program. The first thing the program does is save the position it currently points at in the program to the stack by placing it on top of the data elements already there:

Return Address

Local Data element #1

Local Data element #2

Local Data element #3

(etc.)

Now the program loads any arguments that need to be passed onto the stack, on top of the return address:

New Local Data element #1

New Local Data element #2

New Local Data element #3

(etc.)

Return Address

Old Local Data element #1

Old Local Data element #2

Old Local Data element #3

(etc.)

We now enter the function, and the program picks off the data elements and creates any other local variables and constants it needs:

Created Data element #1

Created Data element #2

Created Data element #3

Local Data element #1

Local Data element #2

Local Data element #3

(etc.)

Return Address

Local Data element #1

Local Data element #2

Local Data element #3

(etc.)

We work through this function and reach the end. It is time to return to our calling function. But how? Our return address is buried under all the new data and references that sit on the top of the stack. Not to worry; the program has been keeping track of all of this and knows exactly how much to take off the stack to get to our return address. This is based upon the data types declared for all the variables created by the function, and all the arguments passed in. Without too much ceremony, the program jettisons the data off the stack from the function we are leaving, and grabs the return address. It then uses this address to point itself back to where it left off. Our stack now looks like this again:

Local Data element #1

Local Data element #2

Local Data element #3

(etc.)

If the program did not know how much memory to set aside on the stack for arguments and local variables, it could easily look in the wrong place and use a data value as the return address, and never return to the right place. The program crashes with a stack fault.

Getting back to the issue of passing by value, Object Pascal does this in one of two ways: constant values and local values.

Constant Values   Constant values are raw numbers, strings, and other pieces of data that are literally passed across the stack to the function or procedure. They are copies of the data that sits in a variable or data element somewhere that is invisible to the routine.

The values can be used in calculations, manipulations, comparisons, and just about anything else you can do with data, except you cannot modify it. While I can change the value of a variable named X from 2 to 3, I cannot change the constant value 2 to the constant value 3.

To pass a value to an Object Pascal function or procedure, we use the key word CONST. For example, consider the function:

```
FUNCTION scale( value: Integer, scaler:CONST) : LongInt;
```

In C we would write it this way:

```
long scale(int value, int scaler);
```

Here we see two arguments being passed into the function **scale()**. The first is a local value, which we will talk about momentarily. The second, which is of interest to us at the moment, is a constant value, a physical number in this case. If we were to call it in a program somewhere, we would call it like:

```
Vector := scale(Initial_vector, 5);
```

Here we give **scale** the literal value of 5, which would then be stored away on the stack. This also works for data types, such as strings, too. Suppose we had a procedure:

```
PROCEDURE error_handler(number : Integer, message: CONST);
```

We could call it with something like:

```
error_handler(errno, "Disk Drive Door Is Open");
```

Here, we hand off a copy of the variable **errno**, but pass the literal string **"Disk Drive Door Is Open"** on the stack.

This brings up a subtle issue that you may never encounter, but there is that one occasion where it will give you fits trying to figure out what's wrong.

One of the unwritten rules of C, which applies very well here, has to do with passing data on the stack. Each time you pass the entire contents of a variable, record, or a literal value or string on the stack, it takes up space. C encourages the use of pointers for that reason alone, as you can access tremendous amounts of information with pointers that take up very little stack space. Be that as it may, there is a valid place for literals to use the stack.

PASCAL is more reliant on copies of things and literals than C is, and as such consumes more stack space in the process. Stack faulting can occur if you try to place more data on the stack than you have room for. For that reason, if you are going to be shuffling large amounts of data around in your program and you do so in large blocks, then it might be a good idea to increase the size of your stack to allow this to occur without generating problems due to lack of space.

Local Values   Local values are copies of the contents of variables, records, and structures that exist elsewhere. The unique thing about local values is that they share the malleability of changing values, just like referenced variables, but they behave as a

CONST value for all intents and purposes, outside the function or procedure where it is created. In other words, it cannot modify the original variable and its contents from which it got its value.

In a previous example:

```
PROCEDURE error_handler(number : Integer, message: CONST);
```

we saw that two arguments were created. This time we will look at the variable **number**, which is declared as an integer and will assume the value of whatever variable reference is passed to it. Using the previous example of:

```
error_handler(errno, "Disk Drive Door is Open");
```

we see that **number** will take on the value that currently resides in the variable **errno**. Now let's presuppose that **errno** has a value of 17. If we look at **number** on entering the procedure **error_handler()**, we will also find that it now contains the value of 17. However, we can modify **number**, because we declared it to be a variable of type integer, not a constant value. So, if we add 10 to **number**, we end up with **number** equaling 27. Once we return from **error_handler()**, we look at **errno** and discover that **errno** still contains the value 17. This happens because we changed a *local copy* of the value of **errno**, not the value of **errno** itself.

In C this would be equivalent to:

```
error_handler(int errno, char *message)
{

    int local_error = errno;
    local_error += 10;
    display_error(message);

}
```

As you can see, we added 10 to the local copy, but because it was a copy only, we did not change the actual value of **errno**.

Passing by Reference

Passing by reference simply means that instead of creating a local copy of a variable's contents, we hand to the function or the procedure the address of the actual variable, record, structure, and so on, so that we can modify it directly.

In C, for example, we might modify a variable like so:

```
foo( int *value)
{
   *value += 5;
}
```

Now when we call it, instead of handing the value of a variable, we give it the address of the variable, like so:

```
foo( &number);
```

So when the function is called, the contents of **number** are increased by the value of 5.

In Object Pascal this same kind of data manipulation takes place by using the keyword **VAR** to describe an argument in the function or procedure declaration. If we rewrote **foo()** in Object Pascal, we would see it done this way:

```
PROCEDURE foo (VAR value : Integer);
```

In C when we call a function to pass by reference, we explicitly have to tell it to use the address of the variable in question; but in Object Pascal, we would call it the same way as when we only want to play with a copy of it. Thus the code:

```
foo(number);
```

works whether we want to use a copy of **number** or change the actual contents of **number**.

A word of caution. Be careful about this, as not paying attention as to whether you are playing with a copy or the real thing can lead to ambiguity in your code.

Data Declaring Structure

As with PASCAL units, functions and procedures can have **TYPE**, **CONST**, and **VAR** declarations as part of the function. The issue here is visibility or scope. Real quickly, scope has to do with information hiding. If you declare a variable inside a procedure declaration, then global variables outside the function or procedure cannot see it or operate on it. This holds true also for variables declared in other functions and units. They, too, cannot see or modify the variable in question.

So if you want to keep things organized and tidy, you can declare blocks of **TYPE**, **VAR**, and **CONST** within your procedure or function declaration, like so:

```
FUNCTION foo( number : Integer, message : CONST) : Boolean;
TYPE
   group : set of char ('A'..'F');
   coins : Integer;
VAR
   x,y,z : Integer;
   InternalMess : String;
CONST
   MyMess = "This is a constant string";
BEGIN
   number := number +5;
   writeln(MyMess,message);
   Result := True;
END;
```

The constants, data types, and local variable declarations are all unique to function foo() and visible only to code that lies within that function.

Units

Units are the largest organized grouping that makes up a program. A program can be composed of a single unit or several units all at once. These *chapters* of the program *book* let you organize your data and functionality so that you can keep together groups of similar things. As a side note, you will notice in your jaunts through Delphi that the unit structure is built primarily around the Tform object, which is the basis of all user presentations.

Units start with the keyword UNIT followed by an identifier. Delphi usually takes care of this for you, so unless you really need to create your own unit, this is a detail that will never bother you.

A unit is basically composed of three sections: an Interface section, an Implementation section, and an optional Initialization section. A sample unit structure follows:

```
unit <identifier >;
Interface
uses <list of units you need to access>; (this is optional)
<public variable, type, procedure, function and constant declara-
tions go here>
Implementation
uses <list of units you need to access, but keep private>; (this
is optional)
<private variable, type, procedure, function and constant declara-
tions go here>
<procedures and functions go here >
Initialization (optional section)
< any initialization code goes here >
END;
```

Let's take a quick look at each section.

Interface Section

This section begins with the keyword **interface**, and follows the **unit** keyword in the file. This section continues on till the compiler encounters the Implementation section denoted by the keyword **Implementation**.

The interface section is where the issue of scope (visibility) takes place. It is here that you publish to the world those variables, data types, functions, procedures, and units that we want to make accessible to other units within our program. We publish access in this manner:

Uses

This keyword is used to specify not only which units are accessible from this one, but also which units can be accessed through this unit when it is referenced through a USES clause in another unit.

It's really quite simple. Let's say that we have three units—UNIT1, UNIT2, and UNIT3—that make up a program. If I include a reference to UNIT2 in UNIT1, then I can get at the contents of UNIT2, but not UNIT3. If I include a reference to UNIT3 in UNIT2, then we can see the contents of UNIT3 from UNIT2 and UNIT1 by virtue of the fact that UNIT1 has a reference to UNIT2. Conversely, UNIT3 cannot see any of the contents of UNIT2 or UNIT1, as it does not have a reference to either of those, just as UNIT2 cannot see the contents of UNIT1.

We could change that by including references to UNIT1 in UNIT2, and to UNITS 1 and 2 in UNIT3, but the compiler would complain. By doing so, we have just created a circular reference. Essentially, the USES clause in this section behaves very much like a **#include** statement in C.

Type

This keyword starts the subsection that declares data types, records, objects, and structures. Any declarations here are visible throughout the unit, and to any other unit that references this one. The analogous function in C would be the **#typedef** statement. Normally, many projects in C keep data definitions like **#typedef**'s located in one or two spots for ease of maintenance and just **#include** them in the modules that need the references.

Var

This keyword in this section defines global data that can be accessed from outside the unit. In C, data would be declared in the module outside all function code and declarations.

Const

This keyword in this section defines constants that are globally accessible from outside the unit. It tends to mimic the **#define** statement in C.

Procedure and Function Declarations

This is the equivalent of an **extern** prototype in C. Object Pascal is quite strict about this, requiring that all procedures and functions be declared before being used or called. By declaring functions and procedures that are created inside this unit in this section, we are making them accessible for use by units outside this one.

Implementation Section

This is the section that makes things go. Function and procedure code exists in this section, along with other subsections.

Uses

This clause can appear in this section but must do so immediately after the Implementation keyword that starts the section.

This is probably the most important subsection after the code. By creating a USES clause here, we can access data and code outside our unit without fear of creating a circular reference for the compiler. If you remember our UNIT1, UNIT2, and UNIT3 examples, we said that UNIT2 could see only UNIT3, and UNIT3 could not see anybody. Now if we needed to reach back into these other units, we do so here.

To let UNIT3 reference code and data in UNIT1 and UNIT2, we would include a USES clause, like so:

```
USES unit1, unit2;
```

Now UNIT3 has access to everybody, but UNIT2 does not. We create a USES clause in UNIT2 that says:

```
USES unit1;
```

and everybody can see each other.

Type

Creating a TYPE clause in this section allows data type creating, just like in the interface section; except that the data types are visible only to the unit, not to any other unit outside. It is similar to creating a static **#typedef** in C if such a construct existed.

Var

This keyword in this section defines global data that is visible from within the unit itself. In C, data would be declared **static** in the module outside all function code and declarations. Unlike **static** declarations in C, the data is visible everywhere in the unit, while **static** declarations are visible only from the point of declaration downward.

Const

This keyword in this section defines constants that are accessible from inside the unit only.

Initialization Section

This section is optional under Delphi and will rarely be needed, but is covered here for completeness. This section starts with the keyword Initialization and runs down to the final END clause in the file. While it won't appear in most of our unit files, it does provide a unique function. When created, the Initialization section can be used to set up data for that unit. When an application uses a unit, if an Initialization section exists, then it is called first before any application code gets run. This guarantees that any data setup that must take place is done before the data is referenced by any functions or procedures.

Delphi and the Local Database

If you have read the previous chapters on the Object Pascal language, or if you already know your way around Delphi, then we are ready to visit the database section of Delphi, if only briefly to gain an understanding of how things work.

The database support in Delphi is extensive; so much so that to properly explore every facet of it could occupy several books the size of this one. So instead, we will focus on the local database functionality and discuss some of the aspects of how Delphi handles linking your front end with the database.

The Big Picture in Delphi Data Access

When we develop applications in Delphi that use the objects and tools that Delphi provides, we never directly interface with Windows unless we really want to. The same holds true for Delphi and databases. This abstraction that Delphi provides give us several advantages:

Platform Independence

Even though Delphi runs only on Windows 3.x at the moment, the fact that we do not have to write directly to any Windows functions if we don't want to means that our code is portable. By portable, I mean that the application part that calls the libraries responsible for working the graphical interface magic is not dependent upon any specific operating system calls to work. Theoretically, if we had libraries for Windows 95, NT, Motif, X, and OS/2 PM, then all we would have to do is recompile to generate a native application. Realistically, we would still have changes to make, as each environment has its own quirks and requirements that make a perfectly clean port a relative pipe dream. However, if we coded and designed properly, then the changes can be small. While not perfect, it is more livable than rewriting the program from scratch.

Extrapolating this line of reasoning a bit works for databases, although not quite as well. If we know what data fields we want, then Delphi can hide the rest of the details from us in most cases. Sometimes we can even move our database between DBMS packages and still work with the new database. We will get into the reasons why we can do this shortly.

Rapid Development Time

The friendlier the user interface is, the more difficult it is to program for. Does this mean that programming is getting hard? On the contrary, it has never really changed all that much from one intellectual programming fad to the next. What has changed has been the amount of detail that we as programmers are asked to maintain in order to produce the spectacular results that we see on the screen.

In this guise, environments like Delphi help things along by removing much of the detail work that surrounds the presentation of data, and frees the programmer to focus on solving the actual business problem that generated the request in the first place. This is becoming ever more true in database application development.

The sticky wicket with databases has always been that no two database packages ever spoke really well to each other, especially when trying to exchange indexes and data between them. Delphi comes to the rescue here by hiding many of the details of how the index is dealt with, locating the next record, posting results of our edit, and other common database chores. Delphi still requires us to identify to it such things as what the database is and where it is, as mind reading has not become commonplace amongst our computers yet, even though some might beg to differ. However, Borland has made great strides in easing data access worries through the use of such tools as their Borland Database Engine (BDE).

Distributing Applications Built with BDE Support

Normally when we distribute an application built with Delphi, we would provide the user with the main executable, any DLLs needed, help files, any VBX controls we include, and documentation, such as README and UPDATE files. This is pretty standard fare for lots of Windows applications. With Delphi database applications, however, things change.

Because Delphi utilizes the BDE to handle all database interfaces, both local and client/server, it is paramount that the files comprising the BDE be distributed with our application. In light of that, Borland wrote the Delphi licensing agreement to require that we make *all* the files in the redistributable BDE available to people who use your program. This makes it possible for users to update their existing BDE software without interfering with the existing Paradox and dBase applications. Table 10.1 shows the current list of redistributable BDE files.

Table 10.1 Redistributable BDE Files	
File	**Purpose**
IDAPI01.DLL	API for the BDE
IDBAT01.DLL	Batch utilities for the BDE
IDQRY01.DLL	Query for the BDE
IDASCI01.DLL	ASCII driver for the BDE
IDPDX01.DLL	Paradox driver for the BDE
IDDBAS01.DLL	dBase driver for the BDE
IDR10009.DLL	Resources file for the BDE
ILD01.DLL	Language driver for the BDE
ODBC.NEW	MS ODBC Driver Manager 2.00
ODBCINST.NEW	MS ODBC Driver Installation 2.00
TUTILITY.DLL	Tutility file for the BDE
BDECFG.EXE	BDE configuration utility
BDECFG.HLP	BDE configuration help
IDAPI.CFG	BDE configuration file

A quick note about the files. The ODBC.NEW and ODBCINST.NEW files support the ODBC socket. You need to back up your existing ODBC.DLL and ODBCINST.DLL files from your \WINDOWS\SYSTEM directory before installing these. When installing, change the extension of these files to .DLL to reflect their proper file status. Also be aware that the ODBC.DLL Driver Manager in Delphi is not compatible with ODBC 1.x ODBC drivers.

The Borland Data Flow Model

What we will look at for the moment is an example of the Borland data model specifically targeted for the desktop. As you can see from Figure 10.1, the Delphi application has to pass through the Borland Database Engine to get at the local data in whatever format it exists. In reality, Delphi makes a request of the BDE and waits for it to return with the information or some kind of error status telling it why it could not perform the requested action. It is important to remember this one concept:

By abstracting the details of the database away from the application code, Delphi not only allows portable code and fast development, but also makes it possible to easily run Delphi applications in a client/server environment, where the data requested is more

Figure 10.1
The Borland
Database
Engine.

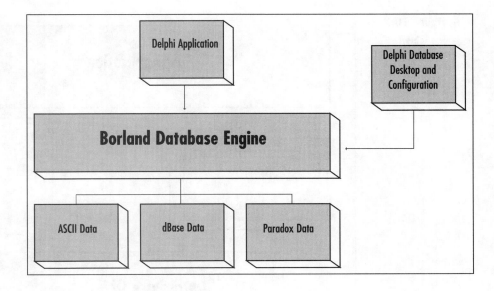

likely to be found on a server somewhere on the network rather than on the local C:.

Let's take a look at data objects that allow for portability in database applications. They are TTable, TDatasource, and TDBEdit.

The Table—A Foundation

In the Borland local data model for Delphi, there are three basic components for dealing with data: the table, the datasource, and edit controls. Query objects can be added as another means of data access and control, but are not required.

In Figure 10.2 we see that the table is the primary interface object between the Borland Database Engine and the application. We will focus on this for a few minutes.

Ttable

A Ttable component, along with the Tquery component in Delphi, comes from the Tdataset class of objects. What this means in lay-

Figure 10.2
The table.

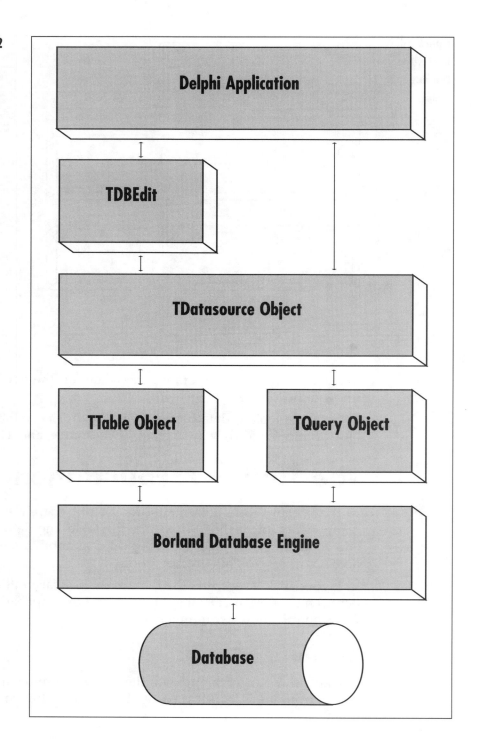

men's terms is that both these objects inherit all the properties and functions that belong to Tdataset, but then add some specific features of their own that make them different. Throughout much of the Borland documentation, these components are referred to together as datasets for brevity. We will interchange the term dataset with table here for purposes of discussion.

Dataset States

Databases, and in Delphi's case, Datasets, exist in some state of operation. When you stop to consider how databases are handled, the concept of states is not so alien after all. For example, if we are updating data, the database can be said to be in an edit state. If we are just looking, we can say the database is in a browse state, and so on.

Delphi allows you to programmatically change the state of the database in question through the use of methods that exist in the Ttable object. This is important, as control over certain functions must be maintained when accessing data in the database. For instance, you would not want to add a blank record, delete a record, or change anything if you are just looking. Table 10.2 shows the states or modes that a Dataset can take on.

Table 10.2 Dataset States or Modes	
Dataset State	**Function**
Browse	This is the default state a Dataset finds itself in when opened. In this state, records can be read only. No changes or insertions are allowed to take place.
CalcFields	This is an automatic state that is entered by Delphi in response to an OnCalcFields event generated by a calculated field on the form.
Edit	This state allows the currently displayed record and associated fields to be edited.
Inactive	This state signifies that the dataset is closed. No access to the database it associates with is permitted.
Insert	This state allows Delphi to insert a new record in the database. By calling the Post method, a new record is created in the database.

Continued

Table 10.2 Dataset States or Modes *Continued*	
Dataset State	**Function**
SetKey	This state is particular to Ttable, and not to Tquery. This state enables the indexing and searching functions associated with Ttable objects. Tquery does not use these, as it relies on SQL to do its searches for it.

Dataset Functions and Properties

To go along with the Dataset states are Dataset functions and properties. These allow us to perform database functionality in a generic fashion. As discussed earlier, by doing database work generically where possible, it makes for a more portable application that is simpler to maintain.

We'll take a look at some of the functions and properties that you will probably use in coding your Delphi application.

Abort Method

This is a bail-out function. By calling this function, it is the same as canceling an operation on the database. The second method to do this is by raising an exception and letting the exception handler catch it. However, it is preferable to control action directly whenever possible.

Where you might find this useful is when you need to test the user's resolve before committing an action, such as inserting a new record, deleting an existing one, or updating the database.

For example, if you wanted to quiz the user just prior to adding a new record, you create a BeforeInsert handler that looks something like:

```
procedure Tform1.TableBeforeInsert (Dateset: Tdataset);
begin

    if MessageDlg('Add a record?'.mtConfirmation,mbYesNoCancel,0)
<> mrYes then Abort;
end;
```

Active Property

The Active property, when True, tells the Dataset object—in this case, the Ttable—to apply data from the current record to the DBEdit objects. In the case where the database has not been opened yet, the Dataset object performs an Open method on the database and then goes about its business.

Where you will find this most useful is in constructing the form with DBEdit objects. When Active is True, the DBEdit objects take on the value of the datafield in the first record in the database. To set it programmatically, you would call it like this:

```
Table1.Active := True;
```

Append Method

The Append method is used to add new records to the end of the database. It is similar to the Insert method in operation, except for one difference. When there is an index involved, Append and Insert behave almost the same. Both attach a new record to the bottom of the database. However, when there is no index involved on the underlying table, then Insert does not move to the bottom of the file to append a blank record. Instead it inserts it at the current point in the database. Append will always put a new record at the bottom of the database. To append a blank record, call the method like so:

```
Table1.Append;
```

This will post any pending data, move the current record pointer to the bottom of the dataset, and set the Dataset state to Insert.

AppendRecord Method

This method is similar to Append, except you can stuff values automatically in the new record you add to the database. For instance, let's say that you have collected a name and want to add it to a database of existing names. You could do this in one of two ways: Implicitly you could say:

```
Table1.AppendRecord(EditFirstName.Text,EditMI.Text,EditLastName.Tex
t);
```

Or explicitly add the data:

```
Table1.AppendRecord('John','Q','Public');
```

BOF Property

The BOF property is a Boolean signaling when you have arrived at the top of the database. This is a useful flag to check to see where you are when walking the database backward. For instance:

```
While NOT Table1.BOF do
begin
  Writeln('Walking backwards…');
  Table1.Prior;
end;
  Writeln('Now I'm at the begining…');
```

BOF will register True only when the record pointer sits at the first record in the database. Thus when you call the Open method, BOF will always return True, as that is where the record pointer is placed every time you open a Dataset.

Cancel Method

The Cancel method is used to cease the current operation and put the Dataset back in a Browse state. This is most helpful when you want to stop and Edit and return the record back to original values. Calling Cancel before Post helps ensure that any changes made for the current record are undone. It is called like this:

```
Table1.Cancel;
```

Delete Method

This method deletes the current record and moves to the next record in the database should there be one. The Dataset is put into Browse state after calling this method. Delete is called this way:

```
Table1.Delete;
```

Edit Method

This method is the most important one for changing data. Before updating any fields within a record, the Dataset must be in Edit mode. The Edit method invokes that mode but does not cause any changes to take place to data in the current record. In order for that to happen, new data must be assigned to a field while in Browse mode, and then a call to Post must take place. For instance, let's say we need to correct the spelling of a current record that has a FirstName field with `**John'** in it. We could write the following to accomplish the task:

```
Table1.Edit;
Table1.FieldByName('FirstName').AsString := 'John';
Table1.Post;
```

Now our record has been changed to reflect the correction.

EOF Property

The EOF property is a Boolean signaling when you have arrived at the bottom of the database. This is a useful flag to check to see where you are when walking the database. For instance:

```
While NOT Table1.EOF do
begin
  Writeln('Walking down the database…');
  Table1.Next;
end;
  Writeln('Now I'm at the begining…');
```

EOF will register True only when the record pointer sits at the last record in the database.

First Method

This method forces the current record pointer to the first record in the database. You call it like this:

```
Table1.First;
```

Insert Method

The Insert method is used to add new records to the end of the database. It is similar to the Append method in operation, except for one difference. When there is an index involved, Append and Insert behave almost the same. Both attach a new record to the bottom of the database. However, when there is no index involved on the underlying table, then Insert does not move to the bottom of the file to append a blank record. Instead it inserts it at the current point in the database. Append will always put a new record at the bottom of the database. To insert a blank record, call the method like so:

```
Table1.Insert;
```

InsertRecord Method

This method is similar to Insert, except you can stuff values automatically in the new record you add to the database. For instance, let's say that you have collected a name and want to add it to a database of existing names. You could do this in one of two ways. Implicitly you could say:

```
Table1.InsertRecord(EditFirstName.Text,EditMI.Text,EditLastName.Tex
t);
```

Or explicitly add the data:

```
Table1.InsertRecord('John','Q','Public');
```

Last Method

This method forces the current record pointer to the last record in the database. You call it like this:

```
Table1.Last;
```

MoveBy Method

The MoveBy method is similar to Next and Prior, with the exception that it can traverse the database by skipping a specified number of records either forward or backward, depending on the value of the integer argument given to it. For instance, if we want to move forward by five records, we say:

```
Table1.MoveBy(5);
```

Or if we want to back up three records, we say:

```
Table1.MoveBy(-3);
```

Next Method

This method forces the current record pointer to move to the next record in the file. If there are no more records, then EOF is set to True. We call it like this:

```
Table1.Next;
```

Open Method

This method opens the database, sets the current record pointer to the first record, sets the BOF and Active properties to True, and puts the Dataset in the Browse mode. We call it like this:

```
Table1.Open;
```

Post Method

This method flushes any changes to the database and forces the current record to be updated. The actions of Post are determined in a large part by what state the Dataset is currently in when it is called. For instance, in the Edit state, the current record is modified; but in the Insert state, Post creates a new record. When the SetKey state is active, Post forces the Dataset back to Browse state. It is called this way:

```
Table1.Post;
```

Prior Method

This method forces the current record pointer to move to the previous record in the file. If it is at the top of the database, then BOF is set to True. We call it like this:

```
Table1.Prior;
```

Tdatasource

A Tdatasource object is like a distribution pipeline. It acts as the go-between for the Ttable object and all the data controls that are TDBEdit objects. When the pipeline is active, the data can flow in both directions. When the pipeline is not active, then nothing happens even though a Table object may be connected to a valid database. Being such a simple object, as compared to a Ttable, there only a few properties and events to be aware of.

Dataset Property

This property determines which table the Tdatasource object will conduct data to and from. This property is modifiable at design and runtime. For example, at runtime we could set the Tdatasource to point to a valid table, like so:

```
Datasource1.Dataset := Form1.Table;
```

Enabled Property

This property controls the data flow to the data control objects attached to the Datasource object. When set to False, all connected data control objects go blank. This is useful if you want to disconnect the Datasource from one Ttable and attach it to another.

Borland recommends, however, that at runtime, we call the DisableControls and EnableControls methods to set this property. By using these methods, we ensure that all attached datasources are dealt with.

AutoEdit Property

This property controls how the attached Dataset will behave when a user starts typing in a data control field that is linked to that dataset via the datasource. If the property is True, then the Dataset will automatically move into Edit mode; otherwise, the application must specifically invoke the Edit mode for anything to happen.

OnDataChange Event

This event gets called every time the current record pointer moves to a new location within the database. In other words, if you call methods, such as Next, MoveBy, Prior, First, Last, and so on, then even this is triggered. You might find this event useful if you want to keep your postings to the database in one location.

OnUpdateData Event

This event is called after the Post method completes, but just before the data is committed to the database. Consider this the court of last resort if you need to control how the data is going to update the database, and whether you want the action to take place.

OnStateChange Event

This event is generated every time the Dataset changes its state. It is useful if you wish to track the current state of the dataset, especially if you want to display that state status to the user on a regular basis.

TDBEdit

TDBEdit objects, or data controls, as they are wont to be called, provide the actual user interface to the database in question. These allow you to see, add, delete, and modify data that is buried within the database. Because of limited space, we will cover these controls only briefly here. If you want an in-depth explanation as to how each one works, please refer to Delphi's Database Application Developer's Guide.

Data Controls

When you open up the Data Control portion of the palette window, you are presented with the control icons shown in Figure 10.3. Each of these represents a different data display and manipulation technique that is almost identical in the standard controls used in non-database functions. The only difference is the requirement to *attach* them to a data field in order to operate.

TDBGrid

This component displays the data from the database in a spreadsheet fashion. By default it picks up all the fields associated with the database and attempts to display as many of them as is reasonable within the form. Those falling outside the visible area are reachable with scroll bars. The grid can also be programmed to dedicate specific columns to data fields.

TDBNavigator

This component provides a ready reference to navigate a database by hand. Each button represents a particular function that acts on the database (see Figure 10.4).

Figure 10.3
Delphi control
icons.

From the Object Inspector (Figure 10.5), you can double-click on the VisibleButtons property and toggle the appearance of each of these buttons on the navigator.

TDBText

This component displays text from a specified column in the current record. It is analogous to a regular Tlabel component. Anything displayed here is strictly read-only.

TDBEdit

This component is similar in form and function to a regular EditBox. By design, the TDBEdit allows the display and subsequent modification of field data within a record. Changes here are not reflected in the database till much later, but you have to start somewhere. One limitation on the TDBEdit component: In order to modify that requested field's data, the Dataset must be in Edit mode, the CanModify of the Dataset is True, and the ReadOnly property of the TDBEdit object is False.

Figure 10.4
The
TDBNavigator
buttons.

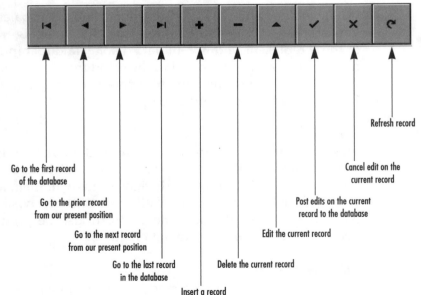

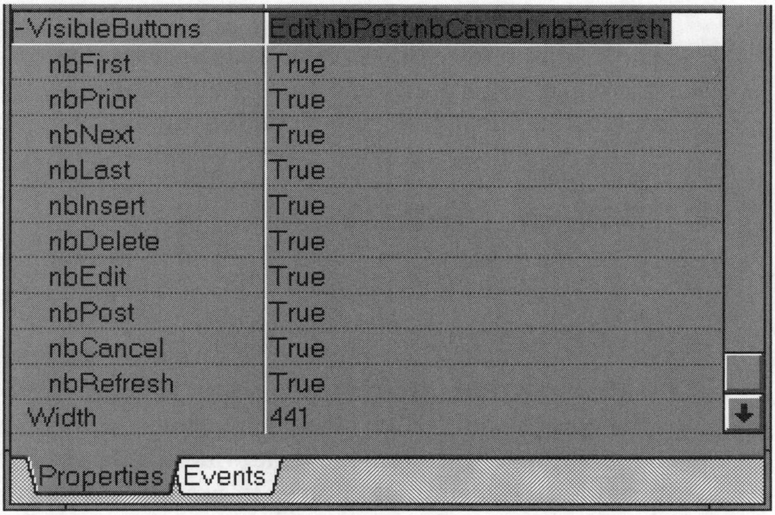

Figure 10.5
The Object
Inspector icon.

-VisibleButtons	[Edit,nbPost,nbCancel,nbRefresh]
nbFirst	True
nbPrior	True
nbNext	True
nbLast	True
nbInsert	True
nbDelete	True
nbEdit	True
nbPost	True
nbCancel	True
nbRefresh	True
Width	441

Properties / Events

TDBMemo

This component parallels a regular memo field. In addition to being able to hold a memo field's worth of data, the TDBMemo can also hold BLOB (Binary Large Object) data.

TDBImage

This component displays BLOB and/or graphic images that may be stored in the database field that it is attached to. This is useful for those database problems where pictures make things more meaningful.

TDBListbox

This component displays a list of items from which the user can modify a particular field within the current data record.

TDBCombobox

This component follows the functionality of it's regular combo box cousin. Here, the user can modify a field by entering that new data in the attached edit control, or select from a list of data items.

TDBCheckBox

This component while similar in appearance to a regular checkbox, sports an interesting feature. It stores a value internally that it matches against the current value in the field it is attached to. When the values match, the box is checked automatically.

TDBRadioGroup

This component works just like a regular radio group. The purpose is to provide a single value to a data field based upon selection. The selection process is mutually exclusive.

TDBLookupList

This component, while similar in nature to the TDBListbox, functions slightly differently. While, like the list box, the LookupList provides a selection of choices to modify a data field, the kicker is that the LookupList gets it's choices from another Dataset. This gives it the ability to tie multiple datasets together on one form.

TDBLookupCombo

This component combines a TDBEdit control with the previously described TDBLookupList. Just like the LookupList, this control gets it's data from another dataset to allow the user to tie two or more databases together on one form. The data from the list is used to update the Edit control that is pointed at our main database, so that we can modify the data field tied to the edit control with data coming from another dataset.

Index

Symbols

<= operator, 243-244
<> operator, 242-243
= operator, 242
>= operator, 244-245

A

Abort method, 324
abstract object, 7-8
accelerator key, 63
accelerator letters, 14
Active property, 325
Add Watch at Cursor... option, 211
Add Watch command, 210
addition (+) operator, 227
Additional Component Page, 16
ALGOL, 3
Aligment property, 150
AlignClick() procedure, 121
Alignment dialog box, 21-24
Alignment Palette, 21-22
AND operator, 229, 273-274
Append method, 325
AppendRecord method, 325-327
applications
    accelerator letters, 14
    building, 44-45

built-in BDE support, 319-320
colors for elements, 19
comments, 45-46
compiling and executing, 36
connecting to databases, 17
constants, 48-49
dead code, 201
debugging, 185-221
designing quality in, 45-51
drop-down submenus, 14
environment-level testing, 53-54
exit points, 46
function reusability, 49-50
function-level testing, 51-52
generating reports, 17
headers, 46-48
Hello World, 34-36
inserting program code, 36
linking Database tables, 17
local pop-up menu, 14
magic numbers, 48-49
main menu bar, 14
portability, 50-51
saving, 36
scrollable window output, 35
shutting down, 111
unit-level testing, 53
units, 311-315
arguments, passing to WIM Editor, 93-94

335